HV
5831
.N7
B73
(1) Brill, Leon
Date Due Authority and Addiction

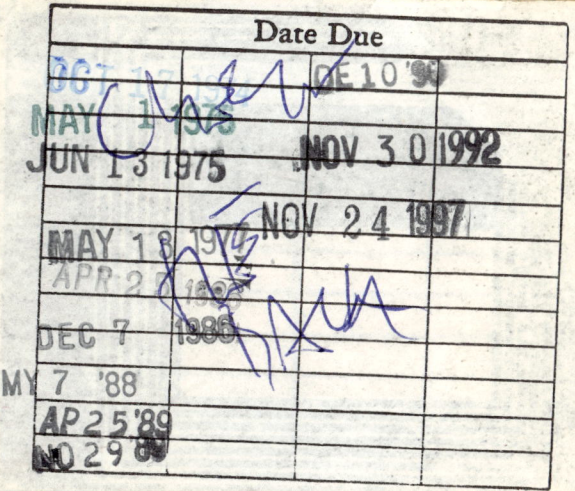

Authority and Addiction

Authority and

Little, Brown and Company, Bos

Leon Brill
Assistant Professor of Psychiatry
Albert Einstein College of Medicine, New York

Louis Lieberman
Assistant Professor of Sociology
State University of New York, Albany

Addiction

With the Assistance of STEPHEN A. GREEN
Graduate Fellow and Lecturer, Queens College of the City University of New York

Foreword by STANLEY F. YOLLES, M.D., Director, National Institute of Mental Health, Chevy Chase

Copyright © 1969 by Leon Brill and Louis Lieberman

All rights reserved. No part of this book may be reproduced in any form or by any electronic or mechanical means, including information storage and retrieval systems, without permission in writing from the publisher, except by a reviewer who may quote brief passages in a review.

Library of Congress catalog card No. 73-82920

First Edition

Published in Great Britain by J. & A. Churchill Ltd., London
British Standard Book No. 7000 0149 2

Printed in the United States of America

To our wives

Foreword

NARCOTIC ADDICTS in the United States are estimated to number 100,000, a figure which appears not to be growing at the same rate as the population in general. This relative decline, however, is of comfort neither to the numbed and tragic captives of drugs, nor to their families, nor to the professionals who attempt to lead them out of addiction and back to normal life. For this "hard core" of addicts is hard indeed, composed as it is of youths and adults who tend to resist treatment, who are difficult to rehabilitate, and who all too frequently achieve abstinence.

We can keep addicts free of drugs while they are confined to a hospital. We can confine them once again if they slip back into drug usage. But we have not yet found out how to treat and rehabilitate addicts with lasting effects. This book deals with a novel approach to our ultimate goal, true rehabilitation.

For five years, the Washington Heights Rehabilitation Center in New York City conducted a narcotics addiction program sponsored by the National Institute of Mental Health, the New York City Department of Health, and the New York City Community Mental Health Board. *Authority and Addiction* reports on the program, and the book's title tersely describes it: Authority was the single most important factor in treatment. It was not, however, authority as a punitive end in itself, but what the authors define as *rational authority*—one which relates the means of authority to the ends of rehabilitation. Furthermore, while the program used coercive techniques (the subjects were probationers under control), it was carried out through reaching-out, or "aggressive" social casework. Thus, in contrast to earlier approaches, which tended to be either punitive or medical-psychiatric, the Center stressed *joint management* by probation officer (coercive) and caseworker (permissive) and demonstrated how a private agency could borrow necessary authority from the court. This joint approach was considered by the project director to be especially appropriate for addicts whose lack of motivation can be overcome only by the use of authority combined with persistent aftercare and rehabilitation.

Unlike traditional programs, the Center project did not insist on immediate and total abstinence as a condition for participation but anticipated some lapses, as the subjects, living within the community and subject to familiar pressures, attempted to regain their places as full and active members. An interesting point of departure was the use of multiple criteria in evaluating a patient's progress. In the past, abstinence alone had been used as the single criterion of success without concern as to whether a patient had worked out his addictive personality and was functioning in a socially productive manner, or whether he had instead gone on to other drug abuse such as alcoholism, or whether he had been acting out in other destructive ways. The authors note that progress became manifest first in such areas as decrease in criminality, increase in work, and improvement in other socially productive behavior *before* progress was seen in terms of decreased drug use.

The report on the Washington Heights program offers promising guidelines for future research and treatment through a multiple approach to the addicts' problems. Within the literature, it represents the first extensive discussion of the systematic use of authority with addicts, and it appears at a particularly opportune moment as increasing emphasis is placed on civil commitment programs such as those carried out under the Narcotic Addict Rehabilitation Act of 1966. It is possible that the techniques explored could be applied to other character disorders and behavioral problems in which acting-out and crisis-ridden behavior represent an almost constant adaptation to the world. Professionals concerned with the treatment management of the homosexual, the juvenile delinquent, the prostitute, the alcoholic, and character disorders in general should find the book of interest. It should also be useful to all treatment personnel who have had limited success with recalcitrant patients and who wish to examine the use of new techniques to bolster traditional ones.

Stanley F. Yolles

Acknowledgments

IT GOES WITHOUT SAYING that no program with the scope of the Washington Heights Rehabilitation Center and sponsored by three Governmental agencies such as the National Institute of Mental Health, the New York City Department of Health (through the Medical and Health Research Association), and New York City Community Mental Health Board could ever be undertaken and carried out successfully without the participation and support of a very large number of individuals.

It is a pleasure to review their names and to acknowledge publicly our indebtedness for their active assistance and cooperation during the life of the program.

We first acknowledge our appreciation to the National Institute of Mental Health for sponsorship and for the major portion of the funding required for the project; next, to the Department of Health for its supplemental contribution for partial financing and staffing; then to the New York City Community Mental Health Board for its participation and support; and finally, to the New York City Office of Probation without whose indispensable cooperation and close involvement the entire program would have been patently impossible.

To select only a few individuals from the National Institute of Mental Health who assisted us, we first mention Dr. Stanley F. Yolles, Director of the National Institute of Mental Health, whose authorization made the entire project possible. In terms of active participation, we would single out Mr. Francis Beck, who at the time of the project was Psychiatric Social Work Consultant for the Regional Office of the then Community Services Branch of the National Institute of Mental Health. Mr. Beck was at our disposal during most of the project and was actively involved in every phase. Dr. William C. Hollister, Chief of the Community Services Branch, was also active in setting up the program and was later succeeded by Dr. James Osberg. Very helpful also were Drs. Harold Skeels and Thomas Gladwin, Social Science Consultants with the Community Services Branch. Dr. Carl Anderson was similarly involved as liaison with the National Institute of Mental Health. Dr. Roger Meyer was most helpful as a member of the Center for Drug Studies of the National Institute of Mental Health.

The beginning liaison with the New York City Department of Mental Health was first established with Dr. Theodore Rosenthal, then Narcotics Coordinator for the New York City Department of Health. Dr. Rosenthal had previously been a member of our National Institute of Mental Health New York Demonstration Center Advisory Committee. Assisting Dr. Rosenthal during the first part of the program was Dr. Robert Osnos; he was followed by Dr. Catherine Hess as Narcotics Coordinator. Dr. Marvin C. Perkins, Director of the New York City Community of Mental Health Board, was the third sponsor. Dr. Samuel B. Oast III served as representative for Dr. Perkins and later as a member of the center's Policy Committee.

The actual contract negotiated by the National Institute of Mental Health was with the Medical and Health Research Association, technically a private organization, but actually closely affiliated with the New York City Department of Health. Dr. Paul Densen, Director of the Medical and Health Research Association and Deputy Commissioner of the Department of Health, was active in relation to the research and administrative aspects of the program. His assistants in the association, Audrey Livingston and Louis Camia, were most cooperative in helping with the frequently entangled finances and budgeting, and we express our special feelings of gratitude to them.

From the New York City Office of Probation, we offer our deepest thanks to Mr. C. Boyd McDivitt, whose excellent thinking helped us in planning and carrying through the cooperative program. Similar thanks are due his excellent staff, which became the lifeline of our program in the day-to-day implementation of our treatment and research goals. We express our gratitude to the three successive supervisors of the Probation Narcotics Unit, Hy Efron, Alan Beckerman, and Herman Joseph, and to the Probation Officers, William Canapery, Paul Coleman, Wendell Gault, Philip Glazer, and Richard Baxt. Our appreciation also goes to the Assistant Borough Director, William Chudd. Our gratitude, also, to Dr. Daniel Sanford, Special Narcotics Counselor for the New York State Division of Vocational Rehabilitation, who was assigned part time to our center and assisted in carrying out our vocational goals.

Pivotal to the functioning of our project was the nursing and social work staff of the Washington Heights Rehabilitation Center. We would especially mention our thanks to Mrs. Yetta B. Deutsch, Supervisor, who helped prepare the public health nursing staff to function in a relatively novel role in treating addicts and their families. This staff was composed of William Sheppard, Bernice Scott, and Marilyn Raymond. Our thanks also to Maria N. Rosenbloom, Supervisor of the social work staff, and to Sally Newmark, Dagmar Ransdorf, Reisa Saunders, and John Loughlin of the social work staff. Our thanks also go to the consulting psychiatrists, Drs. Peritz Levinson and Logan Stanfield.

Appreciation is due to Mrs. Norma Lederman Fox, administrative assistant, who supervised the endless financial matters as well as administrative, clerical, and typing personnel.

Without the diligent and creative efforts of the research staff of the Washington Heights Rehabilitation Center, the vital aspects of evaluation and program feedback would have been missing. We first express our debt of gratitude to Harold Alksne, Social Scientist, who was with us from the beginning and worked with us in all aspects of the research design and evaluation, including the development of the instruments and systems of data processing and retrieval. He was instrumental in helping us to conceptualize the entire program.

A critical member of our research staff was Mr. John Langrod, whose knowledge of the Spanish idiom as part of his multilingual skills enabled us to avoid research problems stemming from work with respondents who were not always English-speaking. A good deal of the interviewing, as well as much of the administrative detail of the research process, was ably handled by Mr. Alfred Kaplan. Mr. Julian Paolucci deserves special mention for his ability to remain on top of the thousands of minute details involved in the coding and data processing in our program. Mrs. Barbara Mitrani, though not involved in the operation of the program, deserves our gratitude for her contribution to the data processing as well as the editing and typing of the manuscript. Her patience and good humor made our task much easier.

Perhaps our greatest indebtedness is to the addicts whom we tried to help. Their cooperation, intelligence, and insight taught us much about the nature and etiology of addiction which we hope will be used to aid others in a similar plight.

We wish to note that parts of several chapters were adapted from the doctoral dissertation by one of the authors (Louis Lieberman) at New York University Center for Human Relations.

L. B.
L. L.

Contents

Foreword by STANLEY F. YOLLES, M.D.   vii

Acknowledgments   xi

1. Survey of Treatment Approaches   1

2. Development of the Center Program   25

3. Rational Authority   49

4. Joint Management   81

5. Reaching-Out	91
6. Evaluation Design and Sample	111
7. Construction of Indices for Evaluation	133
8. Comparison of the Two Groups	161
9. Prospectus for the Future	187
Appendix A Questionnaires and Forms	227
Appendix B Selected Characteristics of Addict Population	291
Index	305

Authority and Addiction

1. Survey of Treatment Approaches*

UNTIL FAIRLY RECENTLY, it was generally accepted that the field of rehabilitation of narcotics addicts was characterized far more by failure than by success. Workers in this area had little hope of achieving successful treatment which would enable the addict to avoid relapse to drug use. The harshness of our laws as they applied to narcotics possession, superimposed upon the complex psychosocial problems of the addict, confronted treatment personnel with the difficult task of keeping the addict totally abstinent. This was considered essential in order to obviate his further criminal involvement, while simultaneously managing the underlying conditions which first precipitated and later helped maintain his drug use.

In examining the variety of treatment methods or modalities currently employed to deal with this problem, we find it possible to cate-

* Portions of this chapter were taken from the following papers, with permission of the National Association of Social Workers: Louis Lieberman, "Current Trends in the Rehabilitation of Narcotics Addicts," *Social Work* 12:53–59, 1967. Leon Brill, "Three Approaches to the Casework Treatment of Narcotics Addicts," *Social Work* 13:25–35, 1968.

gorize them. These different approaches may be classified as follows: punitive, medical-psychiatric, communal, community-based, religious, chemotherapy (cyclazocine and methadone-maintenance), and the use of rational authority.

PUNITIVE APPROACH

There are many laws making it a crime to sell, purchase, or possess, without a legitimate medical prescription, those drugs classified by the World Health Organization as "dangerous drugs," or even to possess a hypodermic syringe unless medically prescribed. An addict who illegally possesses drugs or the implements for drug use may be, and very frequently is, arrested and imprisoned. Since the addict usually needs to seek out illicit sources of drugs, where exorbitant prices are commanded, a criminal pattern of "hustling" for funds is generally soon developed. Under this system, practically all addicts become criminals and are imprisoned for varying periods of time.

It may be argued that the imprisonment of addicts is a form of treatment in that it serves as a deterrent against future criminal acts as well as punishment for the commission of the crime. This "punitive" treatment modality, if we may term it so, has been the most *extensive* "treatment" afforded addicts since the early 1920's and, judging by the severity of the laws, the most *intensive* as well. While some observers have argued the need to change our laws so that drug possession, by definition, would not be considered criminal, thereby eliminating the need for a black market, this is not likely to occur soon. Efforts to rehabilitate addicts have therefore necessarily been geared to the existing framework of the law.

MEDICAL-PSYCHIATRIC APPROACH

Concurrent with this traditional punitive approach (although gaining momentum somewhat later) was the emergence of the medical-psychiatric hospital setting with the recognition that narcotics addiction should be viewed as a sickness, although its nature and etiology were still unclear. In the 1930's, the United States Public Health Service established two Federal hospitals, one at Lexington,

Kentucky, and the other at Fort Worth, Texas. The first was used almost entirely for narcotics addiction treatment and research, the second only partially so. Major treatment emphases developed at these two hospitals have been carried over to facilities such as the former Riverside Hospital and the narcotics wards of the Metropolitan, Manhattan State, and Manhattan General Hospitals, all in New York City.

Essentially, the treatment procedures in these medical-psychiatric settings have consisted predominantly of detoxification, with some rebuilding of physical health, some involvement in a therapeutic relationship (with only selected patients becoming engaged in such a relationship with psychologists, psychiatrists, social workers, vocational counselors, and others in the hospital environment), and minimal emphasis on aftercare help once the patient left the hospital. This approach was predicated on the belief that an addict is sick both physically and emotionally. He is physically sick in the sense that the physiological addiction has led to an altered state of functioning in his body chemistry; and also in the sense that drug use often results in hepatitis, infections from unsterile needles and admixtures to the heroin, malnutrition, and general body neglect. The addict has been deemed emotionally "sick," since it was assumed by most treating personnel that narcotics or other drugs serve various emotional needs which, in their thinking, helped explain his initial experimentation, compulsive craving, and subsequent total involvement. Whether one agrees with this assumption or not is irrelevant to the fact that the medical-psychiatric approach has been one of the two predominant viewpoints in the treatment of narcotics addiction, and will undoubtedly continue to exert an influence for a long time.

These two treatment approaches, the punitive and the medical-psychiatric hospital setting, have been viewed by many as gross failures since they cannot prevent the addict's return to drugs or alter his criminal way of life. Numerous follow-up studies[1-5] have confirmed this.

COMMUNAL APPROACH

Within the last decade, there have emerged a number of new treatment modalities predicated on different assumptions and stressing other themes of rehabilitation. The most highly publicized of these has been the "communal," best illustrated by the work of Synanon and Daytop Village.* While we shall not attempt any elaborate analysis of the structure and functions of these facilities here, we would like to indicate briefly some of the important underlying assumptions of this approach. A more detailed analysis can be found in the literature.[6-9]

The addict who enters either one of these facilities finds himself, in effect, in an entirely new world in which his addict patterns of behavior, values, and expectations are, for the most part, rather vehemently rejected. The rejection does not come from a source totally alien to him. The treatment personnel in these settings are usually not professional persons or representatives of the conventional society from which the addict has retreated, but rather are almost entirely other addicts who have themselves remained abstinent within the communal setting for considerable periods of time. The concept of a communal organization or a community whose members share daily experiences is of vital importance in this setting. In marked contrast to other forms of treatment in which therapeutic contact is maintained for only a very brief time, the communal setting approaches the maximum in sustained contact. The closeness achieved has been described in terms of the "extended family," and banishment from the family group represents a drastic punishment and is used as a means of social control. Also characteristic of the concept of "community" is an achievable status system with leaders as successful role models. The uniqueness of this system is that all status positions are occupied by ex-addicts. The new member is not diagnosed in any traditional psychiatric way, but rather is regarded as an undeveloped personality who needs to "grow up." He can become part of a group that will accept him if he in turn accepts its standards, values, and style of life. The rewards for conformity to the group norms are perceived as valuable and worthwhile, since the other group members, with whom the addict identifies, convey to him the desirability of this normative behavior. This is reinforced by the rewards of status achievement when one conforms to the norms. Violations of norms are treated as if they constitute an attack upon the entire group. In short, the structure of the communal setting may resemble more closely the homogeneity of a folk culture, with strong roots in direct

---

* It should be noted that our illustrations do not necessarily represent "pure" types. Daytop Village, for example, also operates with some techniques of rational authority. A large number of its members are on probation from the Courts of New York, and drug detection tests of thin-layer chromatography (urinalysis) are used. The more recently established "Phoenix Houses" in New York City also fall into this category.

face-to-face interactions of all the role members, rather than the impersonal heterogeneity of our contemporary society.

It had been hoped by the advocates of the communal approach that this type of socialization process would not only affect the addict's adaptation to the internal structure of the organization, but also carry over by enabling the addict to become integrated into the larger society outside. Unfortunately, there is no evidence that this has been achieved. At best, the few "graduates" of these organizations appear to have become professional ex-addicts working within the addiction system.* Although Synanon and Daytop are relatively successful while the addict remains in the cloistered setting, there have been no reports demonstrating that significant numbers of addicts are permitted to dissociate themselves or remain abstinent once they have returned to their old environments.

COMMUNITY-BASED APPROACH

Advocates of this method recognize that the addict's problems developed within the social context of a specific community, and that rehabilitative efforts are therefore best directed to changing him within the same community setting. The physical settings for treatment and rehabilitation therefore tend to be those communities with high rates of drug use. In the community approach, the addict is regarded as a person who has group associations, for better or worse, within the neighborhood to which he will most likely return. Treatment must then be carried out with a view to changing the conditions within the family and community which precipitated the onset of drug use, in terms of primary prevention as described by Bower[10] and Caplan.[11] In brief, treatment of the addict is viewed as a total process involving the interactions of the addict within his community. The community approach also attempts to go beyond the addict himself and into the family, which may have played a primary role in the genesis of his addiction and therefore needs to be involved for both diagnosis and treatment. The family approach is additionally related to preventive work since, as in many illnesses, contagion between family members is possible. While the community-based ap-

* See *A Study of Four Voluntary Treatment and Rehabilitation Programs for New York City's Narcotics Addicts*, by Judith Calof,[12a] and *Synanon*, by G. Endore (New York: Doubleday, 1968).

proach may utilize any number of traditional medical, psychiatric, and casework approaches, it goes further in attempting to alter the community itself as well. It merits particular consideration in the attempts to change stereotyped community attitudes about addiction held by health and welfare agencies, neighborhood groups, "power structures," and employer groups which all too often militate against effective treatment by rejecting the stigmatized addict.

A major weakness of this method is that addicts appear to be unwilling or unable to sustain the therapeutic relationship beyond the periods of crisis which initially brought them to the agency. It would appear that this method would benefit from the use of some strong mechanism or framework for holding the addict in treatment. (Some of these are suggested later in this book.)

RELIGIOUS APPROACH

The "religious" approach can be demonstrated most dramatically in the work of the Damascus Church and Teen Challenge in New York City.[12] Its assumptions are different from the ones already mentioned since addiction as well as alcoholism and homosexuality are viewed not so much as sicknesses, crimes, or even social phenomena as they are sins. The fundamentalist religious perspective of these groups provides a rather intense religious experience for those willing to accept salvation by the acceptance of Christ and religious precepts as a means of being rescued from the life of sin. Converts are expected to act as missionaries in the salvation of other addicts and devote their lives to carrying out the religious theme. In some respects, Alcoholics Anonymous, with its reliance on the "Power greater than I" and its missionary zeal in helping other alcoholics, contains some of these same components. In our discussion with several ex-addicts who became missionaries, we have been impressed by the apparent power of conversion and missionary activities in effecting a profound involvement with a new and more socially acceptable style of life. It is obvious, however, that not all addicts can respond to such missionary zeal or can maintain the deep religious conviction required of them, although a recent evaluation of their results is encouraging.[12a] (They appear to have been especially effective with Puerto Ricans in the Bronx area of New York City.)

CHEMOTHERAPY APPROACH

Cyclazocine

Martin and co-workers[13, 14] at the Public Health Service Hospital at Lexington, Kentucky, have proposed that the regular administration of cyclazocine, a long-acting narcotic antagonist in the benzomorphan series, might be useful in helping highly motivated ambulatory patients to avoid relapse to the compulsive use of narcotics. When given in appropriate doses, cyclazocine reduces the subjective and physiological effects of any morphine-like drug. When given to subjects already physically dependent upon an opiate drug (e.g., morphine), cyclazocine, like nalorphine, can also precipitate a severe withdrawal syndrome. The regular use of cyclazocine reduces or prevents the development of physical dependency upon morphine-like drugs. Once present, cyclazocine presumably prevents morphine from reaching the usual receptor sites in the nervous system. As a result, patients pretreated with cyclazocine in appropriate doses will not feel the effects of ordinary doses of morphine-like drugs and will not become physically dependent even with their regular use.

The use of cyclazocine was based on the hypothesis first proposed in detail by Wikler[15] that, in addition to any characterological disorders which may have led to narcotics use, the narcotics-dependent individual has acquired a complex set of classically and instrumentally conditioned responses. According to the hypothesis, this conditioning contributes to the tendency to relapse to narcotics use when the individual returns to the environment in which drugs were previously used.

Within the framework of this hypothesis, we can think of the initial injections of a narcotic drug as emitted responses that bring relief of basic anxieties; this relief then reinforces the tendency to repeat the emitted drug-using response. However, with repeated use there is not only repeated reinforcement, but also the development of a certain degree of physical dependence. This gives rise to a new inner distress that is dramatically and specifically alleviated each time an opiate drug is used. The repeated relief of withdrawal distress thus provides a new and powerful mechanism for further reinforcement of drug-seeking behavior. If in the process of becoming dependent upon narcotics an individual experiences withdrawal symptoms, we may speculate that these withdrawal symptoms can become conditioned, in the Pavlovian or classic sense, to the stimuli present in the individual's internal and external environments. As a result, at some later time, when the individual is no longer physically dependent, the sight of old friends preparing drugs or of the buildings where he once sought to buy drugs, or perhaps feelings of anger or depression may trigger the conditioned withdrawal phenomena.

A case in point is the observation that addicts who have been away from New York in a hospital or prison for years will experience "withdrawal symptoms" when they again see the George Washington Bridge, for example, or return to their old haunts, though they clearly could have no physical dependency upon opiates after so long a period of abstinence. When experiencing withdrawal symptoms it is not surprising that an individual may interpret the symptoms to mean that a narcotic drug is required. If he uses a drug, the distress may be relieved, but the cycle will be reinitiated. Some addicts seem to become conditioned to the needle and welcome it often even if they are reasonably sure that it does not contain enough drugs to produce an effect. More recently it has been suggested that sustained drug use brings about physiological changes which persist long after actual use ceases and which may push the addict back to drugs when he returns to the community.[15a]

The use of cyclazocine may eventually offer a technique for determining the importance of these conditioning factors in the perpetuation of compulsive narcotics use. The drug-seeking behavior of a patient maintained on cyclazocine who uses narcotics and gets no relief should eventually be extinguished.

There are now at least two major studies on the use of cyclazocine under way in New York City. Both have been in progress for approximately three years,* but the number of patients under treatment is still too small to draw more than tentative conclusions. In a study conducted by one of the authors at the Albert Einstein College of Medicine, twenty-two patients have been treated thus far. All of them have been ambulatory for periods up to eighteen months. Even with the limitations of a drug that must be taken daily, the cyclazocine study has demonstrated that some compulsive narcotics users do have considerable motivation to become abstinent and can do this

---

* Other studies were subsequently begun in New York City—at the Manhattan State Hospital and at the Civic Center Clinic in Brooklyn—and have also appeared in other parts of the country and abroad.

without prolonged hospitalization in some cases. Cyclazocine served as a valuable lever for therapy since, by stabilizing patients and blocking the effects of their opiate drug use, the process of rehabilitation became more rapid and effective. Conceivably, cyclazocine could eventually find wide application in reinforcing the goals of probation. At present, it does seem to fill a very important gap in the therapeutic armamentarium and appears to be of value for individuals who are not ready to concede their need for long-term inpatient treatment or for ambulatory maintenance on synthetic narcotics such as methadone.

A number of the patients in the program were "hidden" drug abusers who had never been through the usual round of jails and prisons and had never been detected. When stabilized on cyclazocine a majority of these patients did extremely well or else reduced their use from full addiction to occasional "chipping." Others found interesting ways to use the cyclazocine, such as permitting themselves to take occasional shots without worrying about getting "strung out." The patients accomplished this by intermittently discontinuing cyclazocine to permit themselves to feel the effects of the opiate drugs. A few were failures or else could not tolerate the side effects of cyclazocine and asked to be switched to methadone. There were no shifts to other drugs such as barbiturates, amphetamines, or alcohol, which would have been considered undesirable.

Cyclazocine was most recently tried with some confirmed addicts, the "street junkie" type, who were failing on probation and came into the program as a last resort. These patients did far better on cyclazocine than prior to using it, but also developed ingenious ways to avoid using the drug as prescribed. To cope with the temptation of avoiding the daily ingestion of the medication, a longer-acting form covering seven to ten days is being developed. As in other programs, one of the big problems here was maintaining patients in the program on a continuous basis and helping them accept a drug that was unpleasant in comparison with the "beautiful" feeling of heroin. We found that when patients came in under probation or parole, the means for holding them in treatment were reinforced.

Methadone Maintenance

In our opinion, among the most important narcotics-research projects underway in this country at present is the study of the use of methadone in the social rehabilitation of chronic, compulsive heroin-users. Several investigators have worked with methadone, but by far the largest and most thorough study is that begun in 1963 by Dole and Nyswander at Manhattan General Hospital and Rockefeller University[16] which is now being replicated in various parts of New York City, some even assaying innovative "variations on the theme."

Doctors Dole and Nyswander set out to answer one question: "Is there a drug that will permit chronic, compulsive heroin-users to become law-abiding, productive members of society by substituting a legal narcotic for heroin, thereby eliminating the need to steal large sums of money to support an illicit habit?" Ideally, such a medication would have the following characteristics: it should be orally effective, nontoxic, and safe to give over prolonged periods; relieve the chronic preoccupation with the use of heroin; and make it possible to arrive at a stabilization dose not requiring frequent readjustments. Since, as is the case with many other drugs, there is an abuse potential which could create a problem for the community in terms of illicit redistribution of the drug to nonaddicts, it is important that sufficient controls be built into each program. This can be done if the duration of action of the drug is long enough to permit an individual to ingest the medication under direct observation at reasonably spaced time intervals. Methadone is now administered at one-day intervals, but attempts are being made to develop a longer-acting form. More important, such a drug must be acceptable to patients.

On the basis of clinical experience to date, it is clear that methadone, used appropriately, has all the previously mentioned characteristics. Furthermore, when patients are given extremely large doses, a tolerance is induced to methadone itself and all other opiate-like drugs. The regular prescription of methadone is not tantamount to a daily prescription for euphoria. As a general rule, the tolerance to methadone is so marked that stabilized patients feel little or no subjective change when they take their daily dose. What is more salient is the improvement in social functioning and the tolerance induced to other intravenous narcotics. Our experience at the Albert Einstein College of Medicine supports the conclusions of Dole and Nyswander. They found that because far larger quantities of heroin are required to produce the same subjective effects as before in patients stabilized on methadone, there is an effective deterrent to the repeated use of illicit narcotics.[17] It is worth noting that, in this respect, the effect of methadone is somewhat similar to that of cyclazocine. It is anticipated that with methadone the repeated ineffectual use of heroin should result in a gradual extinction of the heroin-seeking behavior in much the same manner as occurred with cyclazocine.

In the Dole-Nyswander program, more than 1000 patients have been treated with methadone. Many have shown dramatic changes in their lives. According to an earlier report of Dole and Nyswander, nine out of ten patients in the program for more than a year are working and self-supporting.[18] The longer patients have been in the program, the better their social adjustment. While methadone makes the patient accessible to rehabilitative efforts, it cannot of itself constitute the rehabilitation. Our experience at the Albert Einstein College of Medicine seems to indicate that various forms of rehabilitation, including individual and group psychotherapy, counseling assistance with daily problems of living, and vocational rehabilitation need to be built into any chemotherapy program.

Treatment with methadone has been subjected to much criticism on varying grounds, some coming from individuals who have had very limited direct experience in attempting to rehabilitate compulsive drug-users in the community, but who nevertheless maintain a rather moralistic attitude toward drug use. Another main source of criticism has stemmed from ex-addicts, who believe that anything short of total abstinence is self-deception, and that the use of drugs in therapy is contraindicated. The latter has been called "the substitution of one addiction for another," and has been inappropriately compared to the practices of some English physicians who prescribed heroin and cocaine. It is worth emphasizing, however, that the methadone technique incorporates several aspects that make it distinct from the practice in England.[19] Unlike heroin, methadone is long-acting and orally effective so that the entire dose can be given under direct observation and there is thus no opportunity for illicit redistribution. This is in contrast to the British practice of prescribing drugs for self-administration. There are also other differences, such as the regular monitoring of urine to detect the possible use of illicit narcotics, barbiturates, or amphetamines by thin-layer chromatography (TLC) urinalysis techniques.

Since methadone is taken orally, one of its main advantages is that it helps pull addicts away from their use of the needle, the ritual usually followed in the use of drugs. Hopefully, also, the related life style of the addict will be altered. This is reinforced by the fact that medication is dispensed in a legitimate agency. This draws addicts away from the underworld culture and brings them into contact with our own "square" culture, its values and goals. However, from our point of view there is still some danger to patients in using a specialized narcotics facility in that it perpetuates the stigma and reinforces their self-image as, and close association with, drug addicts. It would be preferable if the use of methadone or, for that matter, other treatment methods were carried out in a nonspecialized facility in order to avoid the reinforcement of the addict self-image.

In methadone programs, there is an assumption that social productivity and curtailment of the antisocial career will be facilitated if the patient is stabilized on methadone. This orientation seems far more rational than the previous insistence on total immediate abstinence at all costs. We are not advocating the wholesale prescription of methadone for patients, which would be irresponsible. Rather, all methadone programs must have research and evaluation built into them to learn whether, how, and for whom they are effective. In New York City, provision has been made for replication of the program in different parts of the city. Eventually, we should be able to say concretely whether or not it is effective and, if it is, for whom. It is likely that it will be effective for many, but not all, addicts. It is also conceivable that a number of patients will be rehabilitated and will be able to give up the prop of methadone maintenance as well. Experience shows that methadone can serve as a remarkable lever in treatment since, where other methods have failed, it rapidly stabilizes the patient and alleviates his depression and anxiety so that he is free to look at himself more closely and move rapidly toward productive social functioning.

Ideological debates between those who advocate chemotherapy solutions and those who support total abstention programs tend to obscure the real issue: the necessity for the rehabilitation of lives wasted in the pursuit of heroin and the concomitant criminal way of life. Such debates preclude realistic large-scale planning, which should involve a multifaceted approach to permit any and all treatment techniques to be applied to save lives. There are certainly sufficient addicts in this country to permit all methods to be employed in whatever numbers addicts wish to enter these programs. Many addicts would not want to go into a chemotherapy program, but would prefer not to be dependent on any drug. There should be available programs for their rehabilitation stressing abstention from all drugs. Since many addicts have not been able to abstain in the past and have failed in such treatment encounters, they should be permitted to be maintained in some chemotherapy program. The goal is rehabilitation and research to replace the futile argumentation rampant through the 1950's and late 1960's.

RATIONAL AUTHORITY APPROACH

Background and Definition

The last approach is the prime focus of this book and is the one which the Washington Heights Rehabilitation Center used as the base for its program for a period of five years. Rational authority relies upon the addict's status of probationer or parolee to hold him in a treatment setting long enough to permit desired changes to be effected. Prior experience had led us to the understanding that most addicts are either unwilling or unable to sustain treatment for long periods of time on a voluntary basis. The use of rational authority could help overcome the patient's resistances to involving himself meaningfully in treatment, build the relationship, and brake his acting-out behavior by holding him in a treatment milieu and imposing a series of coercions and controls as required.

Legislation recently enacted in New York, New Jersey, and California, and also by the Federal government, for the civil commitment of addicts has increasingly forced our attention on one of the components of all such legislation; namely, the use of "compulsion," "coercion," "constructive coercion," [20] or "rational authority" in the treatment of narcotics addicts. Whatever one may term this element, in its simplest form it involves the rehabilitation of addicts on an involuntary rather voluntary basis. We prefer the term "rational authority" * because these programs derive their legitimate coercive powers through the *authority* of the courts, and these are *rational* in the sense of utilizing it in a humane, constructive manner by relating the *means* of authority to the *ends* of rehabilitation. Although other forms of authority, both personal and professional, have been utilized by public health nurses, social workers, and other helping professions in hospitals, courts, and health and welfare agencies, this is not the type of authority dealt with in this book, which emphasizes the derived use of court authority by the helping professions.

Our use of authority in the rehabilitation of offenders is not in

---

* This term has been used in a similar sense, though in a different context, by Erich Fromm in *Escape from Freedom, Religion and Psychoanalysis*, and other writings.

itself an entirely new technique. For many years, persons have been placed on probation as an alternative to imprisonment, while others have been released from prison on parole before completion of their sentences. There have been recent changes from the emphasis on use of authority as a punitive *end in itself* within the large case loads of probation and parole officers to the use of authority as a *means* for implementing intensive casework within smaller case loads for rehabilitation purposes. As a consequence, probation and parole officers are increasingly able to use the authority of their office as a lever to structure their relationships and firm up the probationer's or parolee's constructive strivings in order to effect desired behavioral changes. The officers may accomplish this through their greater involvement in the addict's day-to-day activities because of the smaller case loads now being established in some programs and the opportunity for more intensive help. Evaluations of such programs for narcotics addicts in the states of New York, California, Pennsylvania and elsewhere indicate that when addicts are thus supervised, there appears to be less likelihood of their return to full addictive behavior and criminality.[21-23]

Reaching-out

As noted previously, one of the problems in the treatment of drug addicts was the observed inability of addicts to sustain prolonged relationships with a therapist or caseworker on a voluntary basis and to involve themselves meaningfully in treatment on a regular basis. In order to overcome this problem, a solution was proposed, based on the possibility of using probationary supervision of drug addicts as the *central* holding and treatment technique. The program of the Washington Heights Rehabilitation Center was designed to demonstrate and test the value of combining the use of authority by a probation officer with the more intensive techniques of social casework, including *reaching-out* to addicts and their families. By *reaching-out* we mean the following: most narcotic addicts have been found to be "not motivated." They often come from multiproblem, lower-class families too apathetic to seek help. (Middle-class addicts may more often be found in the ranks of the "hidden addicts," we believe, because of their greater ease in passing themselves as "squares.") This so-called lack of motivation may actually be the different way of life of lower-class groups, focused upon their immediate impulsive needs rather than long-term goals. They do not come to agencies of their own accord (nor are agencies always ready to receive them) or on a sustained basis, but rather at times of crisis. It was therefore assumed that we would need to reach out to them, follow them into their homes and into hospitals and jails, wherever they were to be found, in order to maintain the treatment relationship and involve them more consistently in the rehabilitation process.

This aggressive casework was viewed as an ancillary form of the use of *rational authority,* the fulcrum and primary variable in the program. It was felt that reaching-out efforts coupled with the use of rational authority might help workers cope successfully with the addict's "lack of motivation," apathy, and resistances to changing his deviant way of life. In the sense of providing a firm structuring of the treatment relationship, setting limits, and providing controls through the use of a graduated series of sanctions, it was conjectured that *rational authority* might minimize the addict's acting-out behavior, help him grow within this structure and internalize the controls he lacks, and, hopefully, help him give up his destructive way of life.

Components in the Use of Rational Authority

In considering further what components were involved in our use of rational authority, we noted the following elements:

The concept of authority as a *holding device,* i.e., a means of holding the patient in a therapeutic setting. This was accomplished for us by the fact that our patients, approximately 95 (with an additional control group of 95 patients carried by probation alone), were male addicts who had been convicted by the court of a criminal or drug-related act, and had subsequently been placed on probation. As part of the conditions of probation, the probationer was required to come to the Washington Heights Rehabilitation Center and cooperate with a Center worker and probation officer in their "joint-management" decisions. The holding function of rational authority is of great importance since we know that addicts are often caught up in a life of frequent crises, where the impulse to run from the therapeutic setting and act out is often overpowering as soon as their anxiety or depression is mobilized. Consequently, by holding the addict to the treatment setting through his perennial crises, we provided the basis for building a sustained relationship between the addict and worker.

Rational authority was also employed as a *structuring device.* Immediately after the addict was placed on probation, a joint conference was held with the probationer, probation officer, Center worker, and, if possible, members of the probationer's family. At this meeting, the probationer was reminded of the conditions of probation to which he had agreed before being placed on probation and the consequences of violation of these conditions. He was further informed that all decisions made in his behalf (and also, hopefully, with him) would be made jointly between the worker and the probation officer. As indicated, this decision-making process was termed "joint-management." The addict was informed that, contrary to the relationships he might have experienced in the past with other agencies, there would prevail a full sharing of information between the worker and probation officer at the Washington Heights Rehabilitation Center, and that the usual notion of confidentiality of data would thus not be maintained here. The rationale for this kind of sharing was derived from previous experience with drug addicts; namely, their tendency to manipulate the probation officer and worker and play them off against each other ("wedging") in the service of the addicts' impulsive needs, as they had formerly played one parent against the other.

By rational authority, we also meant *communication* to the addict that the worker represents an extension of the authority of society. The addict was expected to conform to certain behaviors, such as abstinence from drug use; to refrain from criminal as well as other antisocial behaviors; and to understand that deviations from certain standards could not be tolerated.

Role of Rehabilitation Worker

The central focus of the use of authority was to devise a series of graded sanctions or coercions which would help the addict internalize controls and be rehabilitated even, and often, in spite of himself. In practice, the rehabilitation worker, either a social worker or public health nurse, attempted to utilize the authority derived from her association with probation in any number of ways at a point in the relationship prior to the addict's slipping back into his old behavior patterns. Workers thus employed varying degrees of personal and professional authority, ranging from mild disapproval, through acts indicating disbelief in the addict's statements, to the ultimate of returning him to prison if this was therapeutically and practically indicated by virtue of the seriousness of his deviant behavior.

To cite some illustrations, when the worker felt that the addict was beginning to use drugs again, she might tell him that he must submit to a thin-layer chromatography urinalysis test. The addict did not take this test voluntarily, but was compelled to do so as one of the conditions of probation. He was not given prior warning and thus had no opportunity to prepare himself for the test by abstaining from drug use for a few days. If the test results showed up "questionable" or "positive," the worker would then attempt to determine the extent of drug use. If results approached the level of heavy or continuous use or if the probationer appeared readdicted, the worker could then compel him to be hospitalized. Refusal to go into a hospital could constitute a violation of the conditions of probation. The worker might also, when indicated, insist that the addict seek employment, avoid association with other addicts, or refrain from any other behavior she believed detrimental to the probationer's recovery at this point.

It should be reemphasized that the addict was told at the initial structuring conference that he must cooperate with the worker and probation officer in any decisions made in his behalf. This was reinforced in his subsequent contacts with the Center when, from time to time, he tested limits by refusing to cooperate or come to the Center. At such times, the worker employed various devices, depending upon her own creativity and professional skill, in utilizing authority to meet the challenge of the patient's testing-out and resistance or weakness. The worker could take a very firm stand, when necessary, by making it clear to the addict that he was losing control and that his behavior, unless checked immediately, would lead ultimately to violation of probation and remand to jail. The worker could further force him to take certain actions she felt were indicated, such as hospitalization, by using her derived authority as a lever.

While it may be argued that what we have presented here thus far is not very different from the customary practices of probation or parole officers, it should be reiterated that these methods were for the first time being employed by the Center workers *themselves*, who derived the authority from their association with a probation officer and the courts. *It was an important function of this project to demonstrate how a private agency, by working in joint-management with probation officers, could utilize this borrowed authority in the case management of offenders, work conjointly with probation officers to help reinforce the goals of supervision and rehabilitation, and devise a series of sanctions which could reinforce the treatment process.*

Results of Program

As a result of our experience at the Washington Heights Rehabilitation Center, we believe that the firm structuring of the relationship which was developed, the setting of limits and the direct confrontation with the realities and legitimate requirements of society, as represented in the therapeutic context we offered, have relevance for all offenders and "character disorders" and can be of specific benefit in the rehabilitation of narcotics addicts. We know from past experience that all the addicts we encountered had problems in relating to authority and authority figures. All too often, however, their initial confrontations with authority figures and institutions followed upon earlier traumatizing experiences with either punishing and rejecting or weak, overindulgent, and inconsistent parents; or, upon later experiences with what seemed to them to be the depersonalized abstract laws of society, which reflected the distance from their own parents. These laws might be crystallized in the person of the policeman, who, in carrying out the dictates of society, was seen by the addict as punitive, irrational, dishonest, corruptible, impersonal, and uncaring. For many of our patients, then, it became possible for perhaps the first time, in spite of their initial fear of closeness, to relate to another human being who cared for them, yet did not use them as their parents had, and could be rational, helpful, nondestructive, and consistent.

One's "success" is, of course, a question of the highest interest when operating a demonstration program; yet, it is a difficult one to answer specifically. As indicated previously, the primary purpose of the Center was to test the effectiveness of the two treatment variables —*reaching-out* and *rational authority*—in working with addicts. While we cannot now by any means claim that rational authority is the answer to the treatment of all narcotics addicts, we do know that this approach works for some. We have been primarily interested in learning for whom this particular kind of program works and, conversely, what types of addicts do not respond to the use of rational authority. There is a great need to learn how to match addict types with treatment types and to develop a typology for the differential diagnosis of addicts. We were also interested in elaborating techniques for the use of authority, and hoped that treatment tools could be developed to enhance the effectiveness of our services.

As mentioned, it was necessary to modify our traditional insistence on total immediate abstinence for addicts as the single criterion of success. Our program was predicated on the belief that it is better for a person *not* to be using drugs. We have no quarrel with other programs which attempt to stabilize the addict on a methadone-maintenance basis. One of the authors, in fact, helped conduct such a program at the Albert Einstein College of Medicine.[24] We believe these should be tried and properly evaluated as to their usefulness for certain kinds of addicts. We were more immediately concerned with enabling addicts to function in the community *without* the support of narcotics. At the same time, we realized that it is unreasonable to expect the addict to surrender, totally and immediately, a vital defense mechanism which has helped him function for years. A considerable period of time was required before he became fully involved in the "addiction system," during which time a tolerance was built not only for the *physiological* effects of drug use, but also for the negative self-image of the "junkie" and the associated way of life, the "hustling syndrome." We believe that, in the same fashion, an undetermined period of time must elapse before the addict can free himself of his chronic illness, and its associated activities and behaviors, and function in the community without leaning on drugs. We have elsewhere described this period as the interval during which the addict must build up his tolerance for abstinence.[25] We believed it was through the holding function of rational authority that we could engage an addict long enough to develop his *tolerance for abstinence*.

As part of this process, we need to understand that addicts will experiment with the condition of being abstinent without always being successful. Addiction is generally viewed as a chronic illness, and it is apparent that it takes time to grow out of the addiction system. Thus, when we discovered that the addict was beginning to use drugs again or was involved in criminal activity, we neither rejected him nor automatically dropped him from the program. Instead, we anticipated these slips as occurrences to be expected and, further, as warnings to the *worker* that the addict must be brought closer into the relationship. It was necessary that the use of authority be made even more explicit to prevent the addict from slipping back into his old patterns, since he was unable to check his antisocial behavior without the aid of strong external supports and controls.

What has been presented thus far is the briefest survey of the leading themes and techniques of rehabilitation which are carried on today, ranging from the traditional imprisonment of the addict as offender to the current techniques being developed. The field of narcotics rehabilitation offers many kinds of treatment, all apparently having some validity and success while acknowledging some failure. The fact that one type of treatment is valid does not mean that all others are not; nor do the newer trends in rehabilitation exclude the more traditional approaches. If the addict violates the law by stealing, he will still be viewed by the court as a criminal and will be punished. The traditional medical-psychiatric approach may still be needed regardless of the other treatment settings being utilized. There is thus still a rationale for medical detoxification and for treating the physical symptoms of drug abuse as a first step. The withdrawal process, particularly for barbituate addicts, poses special problems that are not sufficiently stressed in the literature.

To judge these traditional approaches as failures because they have not had a notable impact on reducing recidivist rates and to overlook their value and function in the total rehabilitation scheme would not only be premature, but a distortion of perspective. Although we may find that the recidivist rate for any one type of treatment is alarmingly high, it is also true that some success is achieved. If we view drug addiction as a vastly complex phenomenon, involving an intricate interaction of emotional, social, psychological, and pharmacological factors, then it is not surprising that *no one method* can cure all addicts. We know very little about the impact of different treatment techniques upon addicts or about the addict population itself, nor have we measured the long-term effects of treatment that may appear to have failed at the time it was offered. We may go further and state that it is a gross misrepresentation of the facts to talk about *the* addict as if all addicts were cast from the same die. As long as we in the various treatment agencies do not know how to screen and discriminate among the many different kinds of personalities, life styles, and conditions of readiness for treatment of persons *labeled* as addicts, then we are just as guilty of stereotyping, although on a more "professional" level, as those who see the addict in terms of the "dope fiend."

For example, let us consider two fairly common types: (1) the youngster who began to smoke pot at age twelve and graduated to mainlining heroin by age seventeen, for whom narcotics is not only a way of life but the whole of life, cannot be classified from the point of view of rehabilitation needs in the same manner as (2) the addict who began using drugs at the age of twenty-six, is still living with his wife and three children, and makes a comfortable living at his job as he has done for the past ten years, and for whom narcotics use is certainly not the sum of his gratifications and activities.

To isolate the first youth in a treatment setting away from his community that serves to support and reinforce his drug life would seem warranted, but it may not be wise to isolate the addict who has a job and family with whom he lives and whom he cares for, and who has so far avoided detection in his community. Youths who have been raised in a Pentecostal religion may feel comfortable in a setting such as Teen Challenge, but would the middle-class Jewish youth or the intellectually oriented musician be equally comfortable? We would question the wisdom of placing a neophyte drug user, whose involvement with the addiction system has been only marginal and transitory, and who has not fully accepted an addict self-image, with a group of long-term addicts who will teach him the tricks of the trade.

These are obvious cases; others may not be so clearly defined. In consideration of this problem, a typology of addicts was developed by Meyer et al. which elaborated the need for a more realistic description of addict life styles, in terms of wide differences in degree of conventionality and criminality in the addict population.[26] In our rush to develop programs which will be panaceas for addiction, we have been notably careless in our thinking and planning. What is strikingly absent from the network of rehabilitation agencies and interested persons is the kind of cooperation and evaluation of programs which would enable us to determine what kinds of addicts succeed in which programs. We have a multitude of programs, but no one can say who needs what kind of treatment. Can we imagine calling a medical doctor competent if he used his favorite drug on each and every patient coming into his office regardless of their needs and differences? What would we think of a psychotherapist who institutionalizes all patients who come to him for help without evaluating the degree of their illness? In effect, when we in any agency apply our treatment to all who come for help, this is precisely what we do. And even for those agencies which do select treatments, we have still to see any validation of their criteria. We might justify this present irrational behavior in rehabilitation if our agencies were to view our efforts as one of *learning* instead of *applying*. To do so would require that careful evaluation be built into all programs and that we start with the assumption that some addicts and only *some* can be helped by any one method. As long as the proponents of any treatment approach believe that it is the *only* correct one for addicts, then they are doing a gross injustice not only to the addicts whom all agencies are trying to help, but to the agencies and foundations who have put up the money for programs that are finally evaluated as failures. If only 10 percent of the patients treated in any particular setting appear to have been helped noticeably by that agency, we should learn enough about their social and psychological characteristics (as well as the treatment variables employed) to determine whether or not there is any consistency of type of patient who can benefit from that kind of treatment.

At present, whether by design or accident, the area of rehabilitation is characterized by very limited sharing of information and no coordination of research and evaluation efforts to learn how to match an addict with the appropriate treatment approach. While it may be a natural outgrowth of organizational structure to protect one's program from the scrutiny of external evaluators, there is no justification at this stage of development of our rehabilitation knowledge to maintain this position. Until we can learn what kinds of addicts are helped by what kinds of treatments, then our treatment programs, as dramatic and exciting as they may sound, will prove of only slight value.

REFERENCES

1. Alksne, H., Trussell, R. E., Elinson, J., and Patrick, S. *A Follow-up Study of Treated Adolescent Narcotic Users.* Unpublished report of the Columbia University School of Public Health and Administrative Medicine, 1959.
2. Duvall, H. J., Locke, B. Z., and Brill, L. Follow-up study of narcotic drug addicts five years after hospitalization. *Public Health Reports* 78:185–193, 1963.
3. O'Donnell, J. A. A follow-up of narcotics addicts: Mortality, relapse, and abstinence. *Journal of Orthopsychiatry* 34:948–954, 1964.
4. Lambert, A. et al. Report of the Mayor's Committee on Drug Addiction to the Honorable Richard C. Patterson, Jr., Commissioner of Correction, New York City. *American Journal of Psychiatry* 10:433–538, 1930.
5. Pescor, M. J. Follow-up study of treated narcotic drug addicts. *Public Health Reports* Suppl. 170, 1–18, 1943.
6. Casriel, D. *So Fair a House: The Story of Synanon.* Englewood Cliffs, N.J.: Prentice-Hall, 1963.
7. Markoff, E. L. *The Dynamics of Synanon.* Neuropsychiatric Institute,

UCLA Center for the Health Sciences, Los Angeles, Calif., 1964. (Prepublication copy)

8. Yablonsky, L. *The Tunnel Back: Synanon.* New York: Macmillan, 1965.
9. Shelly, J. A., and Bassin, A. Daytop Lodge: Halfway house for drug addicts. *Federal Probation* 28:46–54, 1964.
10. Bower, E. M. Primary prevention of mental and emotional disorders: A conceptual framework and action possibilities. *American Journal of Orthopsychiatry* 33:832–848, 1963.
11. Caplan, G. *Principles of Preventive Psychiatry.* New York: Basic Books, 1964.
12. Wilkerson, D. *The Cross and the Switchblade.* New York: Bernard Geis Associates, 1963.
12a. Calof, J. *A Study of Four Voluntary Treatment and Rehabilitation Programs for New York City's Narcotics Addicts.* New York: Community Service Society of New York, 1967. (Mimeo)
13. Martin, W. R., Fraser, H. F., Gorodetzky, C. W., and Rosenberg, D. E. Studies of the dependence producing potential of the narcotic antagonist 2-cyclopropylmethyl-2'-hydroxy-5, 9-dimethyl-6, 7-benzomorphan (cyclazocine Win. 20, 740, ARC 11-C-3). *Journal of Pharmacology* 150:426–436, 1965.
14. Martin, W. R., Gorodetzky, C. W., and McClare, T. K. A Proposed Method for Ambulatory Treatment of Narcotics Addicts Using a Long-Active Orally Effective Narcotic Antagonist, Cyclazocine—An Experimental Study. Committee on Problems of Drug Dependence; Minutes of the 27th Meeting, February, 1965, Houston, Texas. National Academy of Sciences, National Research Council (1965b).
15. Wikler, A. Conditioning Factors in Opiate Addiction and Relapse. In D. M. Wilner and G. G. Kassebaum (Eds.), *Narcotics.* New York: McGraw-Hill, 1965.
15a. Dole, V. P., and Nyswander, M. E. Heroin addiction: A metabolic disease. *Archives of Internal Medicine* 120:19–24, 1967.
16. Dole, V. P., and Nyswander, M. A medical treatment for diacetyl-morphine (heroin) addiction. *Journal of the American Medical Association* 193:646–650, 1965.
17. *Ibid.,* p. 649.
18. *Ibid.,* p. 646.
19. Brill, L., and Jaffe, J. H. The relevancy of some newer American treatment approaches for England. *British Journal of Addiction* 62:375–386, 1967.
20. Soden, E. W. Constructive coercion and group counselling in the rehabilitation of alcoholics. *Federal Probation* 30:56–60, 1966.
21. Diskind, M. H., and Klonsky, G. *Recent Developments in the Treatment of Paroled Offenders Addicted to Narcotic Drugs.* Albany: New York State Division of Parole, 1964.
22. Burkhart, W. R., and Sathmany, A. *Narcotic Treatment Control Project,* Research Report No. 19, Phases I and II, Research Division, Department of Corrections, State of California, Sacramento, 1963.
23. Konietzko, K. *Interim Report of the Philadelphia Parole Narcotic Project,*

Commonwealth of Pennsylvania, Board of Parole. Presented at the 25th Meeting of the Committee on Drug Addiction and Narcotics of the National Research Council, February, 1963.
24. Brill, L., Jaffe, J. H., and Laskowitz, D. Pharmacological Approaches to the Treatment of Narcotics Addiction: Patterns of Response. In National Academy of Sciences, National Research Council, *Committee on Problems of Drug Dependence,* 1967, pp. 5145–5151.
25. Alksne, H., Lieberman, L., and Brill, L. A conceptual model of the life cycle of addiction. *International Journal of the Addictions* 2:221–238, 1967.
26. Brotman, R., Meyer, A. S., Freedman, A., and Lieberman, L. A Preliminary Report on Social Types of Addicts. Presented at the Meeting of the National Research Council, Ann Arbor, Mich., February, 1963.

2. Development of the Center Program

HISTORICALLY, the Washington Heights Rehabilitation Center program evolved out of two earlier studies sponsored by the United States Public Health Service. The first of these, the Lexington Follow-Up Study (1952–1961), had as its subjects approximately two thousand dischargees from the Public Health Service Hospital at Lexington, Kentucky.[1] The primary goal was to learn the addiction status and rates of abstinence of these dischargees once they returned to New York City and, incidentally, their adjustment in other areas of living. A further goal was to learn whether discharged addicts could be located at all, and to establish a continuing relationship with them with an eye toward setting up future treatment programs. To the surprise of all participants, it proved possible in more than 97 percent of the cases to locate these patients and to establish continuing contacts with them. This was sufficient to ensure a sustained and reliable source of information. The high rate of relapse found among them confirmed the growing conviction that hospitalization alone, unless followed up by aftercare in the community, was ineffective.

The *New York Demonstration Center* (1956–1961), the second study, represented a community organization project whose goal it was to refer selected patients to a wide range of community agencies and, at the same time, help these agencies open their doors and extend their services to addicts.[2] This project resulted in the opening of a number of hospitals and social agencies and the modification of restrictive agency policies toward addicts in New York City. A number of specific treatment techniques for the rehabilitation of narcotics addicts in the community was also suggested.

One of the problems emerging from this Center's experience was how to hold addicts in a voluntary treatment program through their perennial crises. The need for some kind of structure to maintain them presented itself.

In planning how to proceed beyond the New York Demonstration Center program, our experience suggested that a number of questions would need to be considered in developing any new program to serve addicts:

1. How can we hold the addict in treatment for extended periods of time?
2. How can we involve in treatment patients who are essentially apathetic, "unmotivated," and resistant?
3. How can we deal with the community forces which contribute to, and reinforce, the patient's addiction, and utilize them in rehabilitating the addict?
4. How can the addict's family be brought into the rehabilitation process?
5. How can we deal with the addict's recurrent crises?
6. Is total, immediate abstinence a realistic goal and should it be used as our only criterion of success?
7. How do we evaluate a new treatment program?

It was felt that the design of any new approach for rehabilitating addicts should include the means for dealing with these questions. By 1962, some of the new rehabilitation themes discussed in Chapter 1 were either already existent or in the process of being developed. One could, for example, find the *communal* Synanon in Santa Monica, California, which was receiving increased publicity; the East Harlem Protestant Parish Narcotics Center, under the Reverend

Norman Eddy, a *community-based* approach in a religious context which had been established in New York; and Teen Challenge, a *religiously* oriented program for addicts and other youthful deviants underway in Brooklyn. The New York State Parole Division had already developed small case loads wherein parole officers worked with addicts in an intensive service-demonstration project.

In 1962, however, the dominant themes and approaches in terms of number of addicts treated were still the *punitive* and the *medical-psychiatric* hospital models. The best known of the hospital settings was the Public Health Service Hospital at Lexington, Kentucky, which had been the main or only public treatment facility for the eastern half of the United States for over thirty years. In New York City, although the Riverside Hospital for adolescent narcotic users was in process of closing down after ten years of service, narcotics wards were available in general hospitals such as Metropolitan, Manhattan State, and Manhattan General. Other facilities and agencies were available, although on a very limited basis. In spite of misgivings, a number of social agencies in New York City were slowly opening their doors to selected addicts. All these facilities utilized at least one of the themes discussed in Chapter 1, with the exception of chemotherapy.

In terms of the prevailing experience of community agencies and of the New York Demonstration Center in treating narcotics addicts, two points essential as part of the treatment process had become increasingly clear: (1) that we focus on the local community in order to intervene in the contributing familial and social components; and (2) that some method be developed for maintaining addicts in long-term treatment in the community.

In planning how to proceed beyond the New York Demonstration Center program, cues were derived from our own experience with voluntary patients, as well as the parole experiences in California and New York City. It was believed that we would need to go beyond these parole experiences to deal with the questions posed previously. The primary variable to be utilized in the new program was *rational authority*. Related to this was the necessity for *reaching-out* to an apathetic and resistant population. Both these variables have been discussed in Chapter 1 and will be elaborated further in subsequent sections. In a sense, they provided the answer to the first two questions posed previously, namely, how to hold patients continuously in treatment and how to break through their inertia and resistance. Various other treatment concepts were also thought through in response to these questions and became a comprehensive rationale for the program that was to be developed at the Washington Heights Rehabilitation Center.

COMMUNITY-BASED ORIENTATION

Since it is generally recognized that the majority of known addicts come from the most deprived areas of the city where a variety of social problems intermesh, a *community-based* program would appear to offer a number of distinct advantages. Although it would be premature to attempt to delineate the intricate interrelationships between community forces and individual pathology, the elements inherent in the individual's prior familial and social relationships would seem to offer good potential for intervening in the cyclical pattern of addiction, detoxification, and relapse. In other words, those forces which served to perpetuate the addiction could be brought into play in the rehabilitation of addicts, providing that treatment personnel operated in the community which originally fostered the addiction. While we did not as yet understand what could be accomplished in the local neighborhood, we believed that the stereotyped idea of treatment exclusively in an institutional, drug-free environment had not worked because the addict, upon discharge, invariably returned to his local community, where the factors which initiated and helped maintain his addiction again became operative. These factors might include relationships between the addict and his peers, employers, police, teachers, family, and others. Although many of these prior relationships had been destructive, they would still need to be used and converted to the service of rehabilitation, especially so in the case of the nuclear family.

These considerations, leading to the community-based approach, (as subsequently embodied in the Presidential Commission's Report on Mental Illness and Health and the concept of the "comprehensive community mental health center"[3]) required that a wide spectrum of services be offered. This helped ensure such essentials as greater accessibility, improved coordination and continuity of services, as well as a community psychiatry and public health approach. Greater effectiveness was also provided through emphasis on education, consultation, training, prevention, and research.

FAMILY-CENTERED APPROACH

This approach was in line with the increasing consensus in the field of mental health that work with the entire family is needed in order to understand and treat a sick member of that family.

Although Freud contributed greatly to our understanding of the intrapsychic functioning of individuals, his view of individuals as closed systems and his reluctance to involve other family members in the treatment process established the dyadic therapeutic relationship as the exclusive form of treatment. Evolutionary thinking since then has progressed from viewing the illness as solely within the patient to tracing it to the relationship between the patient and other family members, and to understanding that these family members are also involved in a shared psychopathology, with the patient serving not only as "scapegoat" but also as the family agent who helped maintain the family balance.[4] The most recent emphasis has been on the study of the "transactional dynamics," or processes, in which the family, apart from being the pathological entity, is also viewed as containing the potential for beneficial change and individuation of its members.

According to Boszormenyi-Nagy,[5] involvement of the whole family affords therapists the opportunity to study directly the secret, warded-off feelings which were hitherto either projected, expressed symbolically, or acted out. Families studied were found to have their own internal communications network where hidden "games" were played, family myths established, and shifting alliances formed with secret rules, taboos, attachments, and displaced hatreds. In this matrix, the most esoteric maladaptive symptoms of the "scapegoated" patient could be comprehended as a logical and coherent expression of the family maladaptation. Pathological behavior was thus not limited to the patient alone, but could be observed in all members; and the roles of "sick" and "well" members could readily be shifted as the family homeostasis required. In the transactional approach, the motivational structure was widened from individual to familial: the behavior of any one member could be influenced by the "important others" in the family who were in a position to gratify or frustrate. What had started out as a study of these transactional processes in schizophrenic families was eventually discovered to be valid for families of addicts, neurotics, alcoholics, delinquents, and acting-out "character disorders" in general.

Apart from the Freudian contribution to intrapsychic processes, Boszormenyi-Nagy[5] cites three other approaches which have enlarged our understanding of family process: (1) communication theorists' interest in the levels of expression of verbal and nonverbal behavior, (2) role theorists' concern with the effect of role development and assignment on identity formation, and (3) "game" or strategy theorists involved in defining the networks of relationships and reciprocal behavioral patterns in which individuals find themselves.[6]

In all these concepts, we find the core idea of a family-centered approach; namely, that the illness of one member is a symptom of a larger, shared family pathology. The development of this approach has been from the pathogenic patient to the pathogenic parent to the pathogenic family. The concepts outlined previously indicate that, at various points, the tensions generated within the pathologic family are projected in a variety of ways onto a particular family member who is "sacrificed" to maintain the family balance. It is no longer the individual, therefore, but the family as a biosocial unit which must become the primary object of investigation. By observing the family interacting together, aspects which never came to light before can begin to be observed.[7]

CRISIS-INTERVENTION

Since addicts live in a series of crises, we needed to learn how to intervene effectively in their crises in the hope of engaging and holding them in treatment. The use of authority becomes a powerful instrument for sustaining contact with the patient through all his vicissitudes.

Crisis-handling, as such, is by no means new to the field of treatment and rehabilitation. Although crisis-intervention has been utilized for several decades now, it was not understood as a distinct treatment approach until recently. During the 1940's, a series of events emanating from the war situation helped focus on crisis-intervention as a device through which patients could be helped to mobilize their strengths and cope with emergencies. Hopefully, this might function as a learning situation for enhancing their problem-solving abilities and managing future emergencies more effectively.

During World War II, army personnel observed that when a soldier suffered a traumatic episode and was removed from the combat area, this experience and associated immobilizing symptom-patterns became increasingly fixated and difficult to treat the farther the soldier was removed from the scene of the occurrence and the support of his unit. The opportunity for immediate "ventilation" and discharge of his accumulated anxiety through a drug such as sodium pentothal, accompanied by brief rest and early return to duty while remaining close to the scene of occurrence, resulted in remarkable recoveries and the arrest of more serious debilitation.[8] In relation to civilian treatment, the prevailing shortage of treatment personnel and the results of the war experience began to have an impact on the way services were provided to the psychiatrically ill at home. The concept of "brief service" in the local community appeared gradually, to contrast with long-term hospitalization in a distant institution. Emergency clinics operating twenty-four hours a day were prepared to deal with acute psychiatric crises. This led to a community-focused approach and to day-and-night hospitals where the patient could retain his associations with job, friends, family, and community. These trends have coalesced in the last few years to form our idea of "community psychiatry" and a public health approach, culminating in the concept of the comprehensive community mental health center.

Earlier in this evolution Eric Lindemann had turned his attention to the bereavement phenomenon, to death and mourning and patterns of reconciliation through effective "grief work."[9] He generalized this to viewing crisis-intervention as a unique approach to the immobilizing problems confronting individuals in our society; and he helped to formulate a theoretical framework that recognized the importance of psychosocial events in fixing the individual at various "points of regression." Like Caplan,[10] his orientation was to see crises as opportunities for environmental manipulation which could enhance therapuetic goals, whereby not only could the detrimental effects of crises be vitiated but the individual could be afforded an opportunity for growth. Individuals in crisis were noted to be more amenable to help from outside sources. As Parad and Caplan[11] suggest, in studying crisis, "Adaptive responses often produce mentally healthy solutions to hitherto unresolved problems."

It should be explained that "crisis," in the sense used by Caplan, does not exist in the same way for addicts, and therefore does not provide the same opportunity Caplan described for constructive problem-solving. The addict's crises are inherent in his way of life, which is impulsive, with constant turmoil and little stability. Their crises occur in the manner of Bonime's depressives; i.e., they stem from a pathologic need for narcissistic supplies and not from maturer human needs. The addict's crises and anxiety are engendered by the danger of failure of his outside "narcissistic" supplies; no matter what the fulfillment, his needs are only intensified and remain unsatisfied. The constant need for pharmacological replenishments constitutes a continuous potential source of crisis apart from the underlying characterological factors. Our social definition of "addiction" as criminal behavior further reinforces the addict's crisis-ridden existence.

The concept of using and deliberately introducing "graded" crises for crisis-resolution in a structured setting, as developed by Cummings and Cummings, has great relevance for our discussion of rational authority, although they were thinking of a therapeutic milieu within an institutional setting.[12] According to Cummings and Cummings, a number of theories of ego formation rest upon the assumption that periodic disequilibriums between a developing child and his environment are followed by resolution and reequilibriums at a higher level of ego organization. Their extension of this concept is one of ego growth through crisis-resolution; i.e., at each of these periods of openness and vulnerability, a successful resolution of the crisis enhances the ego, that is, strengthens the individual's ability to confront future crisis successfully. In a recent article, Bettelheim[13] wrote along similar levels, stressing the importance, even as early as the first six months, of permitting infants to face certain ego crises and learn to resolve them, thus adapting to frustration rather than having all frustration and crisis resolved for them by the parent.

Ego growth may thus be viewed as a series of disequilibriums and subsequent equilibriums between the person and his environment. It therefore seems reasonable that growth could be induced by presenting the individual with a series of graded crises under structured circumstances that maximize his chances of resolving them. In other words, crisis-resolution may become a therapeutic tool that can be controlled. Growth is accomplished by increasing the repertoire of ego-crisis situations, thereby sharpening ego boundaries, improving the perception and ability to cope with reality. In this discussion, we would like to underline the importance of providing a structure which compels the individual to face crises rather than avoid confrontation. We believe this can be accomplished through the use of rational authority.

Crisis-intervention with addicts has a different quality from the mode described by Caplan. The addict's pull is generally toward further involvement in the addiction system; i.e., relapse to drugs, acting-out behavior, and the illicit way of life associated with it. Treatment intervention is therefore focused, first and foremost, on the need to hold the addict in treatment during his periods of crisis, since he has learned to resolve his anxiety and depression by running, avoiding confrontation with himself and close relationships with other persons, as in treatment. The effort to hold the addict in treatment through all his vicissitudes, to help him stabilize his life and achieve success, must often occur in spite of himself and entails a battle of wills in which the therapist needs all the weapons in his armamentarium that he can muster. The external structure imposed by using rational authority is an attempted substitute for the absence of internal controls. The Cummings' discussion of use of graded crises in a structural setting appears to have great relevance for our use of rational authority with addicts.

TOLERANCE OF ABSTINENCE

When the program for the Washington Heights Rehabilitation Center was being formulated, the prevailing view in the narcotics field, which reflected the traditional orientation of the Federal Bureau of Narcotics, was that total and immediate abstinence constituted an indispensable element in the rehabilitation of narcotics addicts. Therefore, in any program treating addicts, the starting point invariably needed to be detoxification, either in a hospital setting, involving the use of methadone for a substitution withdrawal to alleviate discomfort, or without the use of any medication, such as at Synanon. The condition of abstinence was, for the most part, the primary goal of treatment. If an addict returned to drugs, he was usually terminated abruptly from the treatment program. This was frequently felt justified by the therapist since the exigencies of having to "hustle" for money for drugs made it difficult for the addict to prolong the treatment relationship. It was logically difficult to set up a treatment program with the primary goal of abstinence, while knowing in advance that the likelihood of its being achieved was very slight. Consequently, the Washington Heights Center workers, although believing it more desirable to be abstinent than to continue using heroin, nevertheless had to take into consideration the likelihood that the patient would relapse.

In considering the nature of drug-use and the factors involved in most addicts' inability to avoid relapse to drug-use, as well as why treatment programs seemed unable to prevent the addict's relapse, we developed a theoretical framework describing the evolution of an individual from nonuse through the early stages of addiction to a theoretical cure. (See Chapter 9.) This model, reported elsewhere,[14] was termed the "Life Cycle of Addiction." In brief, it describes the various stages an addict goes through before becoming fully addicted. He passes through a period of experimentation with drugs, then regular use, and on to addiction. At each step, he learns to tolerate a behavior pattern which is new to him and, therefore, not normative for the background from which he came.

A process of socialization must take place before the neophyte drug user can become an adequately functioning member of the addict's world. This socialization entails not only learning techniques and customs which enable him to function, but also developing a tolerance for a negative self-image with which he must feel comfortable. His responses become the responses of an addict to other roles within the addiction social system. When he has become fully socialized as an addict, his most immediate and natural responses are those of an addict. If he is then detoxified, his identity and response habits are not extinguished. Just as he goes through a number of stages before becoming a successfully functioning member of the "addiction system," so we believed he must go through a similar series of stages in which he again experiments with a conventional way of life no longer normative, and learns to tolerate it if he wishes to remain within it. When he wants to stop being an addict, conventional society is no longer normative and he needs to learn to deal with this. We expected that the addict, in developing this tolerance, would experiment with being abstinent; but we anticipated that he would probably fail because he had not yet learned to build up his tolerance for being abstinent. Before building up this tolerance, it could be predicted he would go through a series of repeated abstinences and relapses.

In the Washington Heights Rehabilitation Center program, we were nevertheless trying to engage the addict in a long-term relationship while he remained in the community. This meant that we would have to maintain the relationship even while the addict relapsed to drugs. Early in the project, we made it clear to the addict that we expected him to work toward abstinence. By this, we meant that we would not terminate him from the program if he used drugs, but that we would expect him to give them up or, if he found this impossible on his own, to enter a hospital and a drug-free environment for a brief period to recover his balance. While the addict needed to learn to tolerate abstinence, the workers, in a parallel sense, had to learn to tolerate relapse without terminating the relationship.

NEED FOR RESEARCH

It was recognized early by the Director of the Washington Heights Rehabilitation Center that treatment would have to be evaluated. There would be no point in demonstrating, for example, that 40 percent of the patients were abstinent after one year since we would have very little with which to compare this figure in order to determine whether it represented success or failure. Furthermore, since we accepted the fact that addiction is a chronic illness, and it was likely that most patients would go back to some form of drug use, more extensive criteria for the determination of success and failure had to be developed. While it was expected that in any program there would be some success as well as failure, the most important consideration from the research perspective in this program was the determination of whether the present methods of selecting defendants for probation brought us the kinds of patients for whom this program represented a likely treatment modality. Since the key variable in the study design was to be rational authority, i.e., the use of probationary controls plus authoritative techniques, the primary task of the research unit was to be the evaluation of whether probation plus intensive social casework (Washington Heights Rehabilitation Program) was better than probation alone. A second function of research was to learn whether probation controls were more effective than voluntary treatment, voluntary out-patient treatment, or traditional hospital settings. However, as it later turned out, the scarcity and weakness of statistical data from other programs made it all but impossible to compare our results with most of these programs. A third function of the research team was to learn a good deal more about how one could effectively do evaluative research in the area of addiction, since there were no previous thorough evaluative studies of addicts in treatment beyond the usual recidivist studies.

WASHINGTON HEIGHTS REHABILITATION CENTER: EARLY PLANNING

Physical Setting

In planning the physical setting, it was decided to locate the Center in a store-front type of facility in the addiction area (Washington Heights) in order to reach out more effectively to the addict and his family. This was located on a street highly accessible to subways and buses. It had formerly been an auto warehouse, which was later converted into the Center through partitioning and installing the required facilities. The Center thus created served a number of purposes: it was located in, and identified with, the addiction area itself; it was accessible to the addict and his family; and, since it was visible and open in every way, enhanced the possibility of acceptance by the community. It was thus able to relate to the community and to reach out with a minimum of barriers. Another aspect of this openness was to increase our effectiveness in organizing the many resources of the community by using the Center as a visible fulcrum to maximize our management of a local addiction problem. Apart from the approaches to the community through treatment, all members of the staff moved out to the neighborhood by speaking frequently to a wide variety of neighborhood groups and by becoming members of neighborhood councils and church groups interested in narcotics addiction and related problems.

Sponsorship of Program

In planning the direction our further investigation should take, the Director met with a number of leaders at various community levels to learn their thinking about the needs of city and state; and to determine how a new program, sponsored by the National Institute of Mental Health, could meet this need. Most of the suggestions were general rather than specific; and, therefore, the Director had to fall back upon his own experiences and understanding as to the kind of service-research program which would be most helpful to the city at this time. The New York Demonstration Center had pointed up the difficulties of working with patients on a voluntary basis, and one of the prime variables indicated was the use of authority. After a number of preliminary contacts with various courts, an agreement was reached with the New York State Parole Division for referral of patients.

The Department of Health was, at this time, becoming more involved in the narcotics addiction problem through the appointment of a narcotics coordinator strongly interested in cooperating with the Federal government in a joint program. The New York City Community Mental Health Board also indicated its interest in this problem, and there was preliminary agreement regarding triple sponsorship of a program including the National Institute of Mental Health.

Nursing Services

In view of the association with the New York City Department of Health, it was agreed that nurses would participate in a manner similar to social workers to learn how they could work with addicts and their families. In considering the kinds of nurses to be employed, we needed to choose between "specialized" and "generalized" nursing services. By "specialized" we meant full-time nurses specially trained by us to work with addicts and their families. By "generalized," we meant part-time public health nurses already operating in local District Health Centers, who would incorporate this additional responsibility within their existing functions.

Although the use of generalized nurses was more along the traditional lines of the Department of Health, our overall thinking favored the use of specialized services as part of a new research program. It was hoped that the techniques these nurses learned could, in time, be passed on to the generalized nurses. It was agreed that, in contradistinction to the New York Demonstration Center where the emphasis had been on referral to outside agencies, the social work and nursing staffs would themselves assume responsibility for treating the addict and his family, while enlisting all possible ancillary community resources to provide a wider spectrum of services.

Defining Nature of Program

A number of questions emerged early in planning this program and remained to plague the sponsors and treatment staff through most of the project. One of these concerned definition of the nature of the program, whether it was to be demonstration and service, or research. The initial thinking on the part of the NIMH was that the funds had been appropriated in terms of service and demonstration rather than research, and what was required was a descriptive evaluation of a service program rather than a tight experimental design. The proposal elaborated at this point required that the population be divided into two comparable groups, one compulsory and the other voluntary. Provision was also made for evaluation of the progress of patients in both groups by using a number of criteria apart from abstinence, including employment, improved social functioning, and interpersonal relationships both inside and outside the family. The kind of evaluation visualized at this time was on a descriptive level. Social workers and nurses were instructed as to the kinds of information required to elicit the significant characteristics of the patients being served and descriptive indices of their progress within the treatment program. At this point, no provision was made for a controlled objective research evaluation by researchers independent of treatment in order to minimize bias.

Publicizing Program and Obtaining Patients

In line with our original decision to have our population equally divided between voluntary and compulsory patients, publicity releases were issued to some of the professional publications, such as newsletters of New York City community agencies. A number of agencies and neighborhood groups were also contacted and they began to refer patients.

While it proved easy to fill our quota of voluntary patients, it was far more difficult to obtain compulsory patients from the New York State Division of Parole because there were few residing in the Washington Heights area. It will be recalled that the New York State Division of Parole had had its own experience with smaller case loads, although this was the first time they were cooperating with a community agency in the manner visualized for the program.

Goals for Cooperation

In this trial phase, the goals set up for our cooperation with the New York State Division of Parole were outlined as follows:

1. *To explore the potential role of a local health department in working with some portions of the narcotics-addict population and their families.* A variety of services, performed primarily by social workers and public health nurses working out of a local health department, will be used in reaching and helping narcotics addicts in order to improve the chances of their remaining abstinent or decreasing the use of narcotics.

2. *To develop and test some selected techniques for their effectiveness in work with narcotics addicts.* Particular attention will be given to *use of authority* and to *reaching-out,* as well as to their implications for the functions of the social worker and public health nurse.

3. *To develop methods for ongoing evaluation of the program and its components.* A basis for continued improvement of the program should become available. The effectiveness of techniques used can be assessed. The degree of success with patients in the program might be evaluated by criteria such as abstinence or decreased drug use, employment, and improvement in social functioning and interpersonal relations both within and outside the family.

4. *To lay the basis for more rigorous or definitive research and evaluation in the community management of the narcotics addict and his or her family.* One clinical social worker or public health nurse for every twenty-five patients registered was suggested as a trial quota. Center hours would be established on the basis of client needs and administrative considerations. Ongoing services would entail home and office visits spaced at intervals deemed advisable for individual patients. Aggressive efforts were to be made to establish and maintain direct communication with suspected or known addicts and their families for as long as some kind of "beneficial impact" could be effected to reduce or eliminate these addicts' use of drugs and improve their social functioning by offering appropriate rehabilitative services.

Use of Authority

Social workers and nurses were to attempt to develop effective ways to use authority in working with cases referred by the courts and other correctional agencies. The project staff would attempt to apply its basic generic skills not in a conventional manner, but in new and creative ways to help the individual addict discontinue drug use. The staff would explicitly convey to patients referred by the courts and other correctional agencies the fact that the community does not allow the unauthorized use of narcotic drugs; and that, if the patient did not seriously attempt an improved adjustment, recommendations for further action or other disposition would be made to the court or other correctional agency. (This was in contrast to our later formulations, which provided for a series of sanctions or coercions, with allowance made for inevitable relapse.) The staff would make every effort to communicate concern for the individual, and would exhaust their ingenuity in attempting to effect an improvement. With these patients, a differential use of authority would be made to produce changes for the better.

Admission to Program

Admission to the project services would be without fee and limited to residents of the Washington Heights Health District, in which the project was located, up to the point of maximum load level as determined by the project staff. Every effort was to be made to maintain an approximately equal case load of voluntary and compulsory cases in accordance with the aim of determining whether a constructive use of authority could assist the addict. At that time, no age or sex limitations were to be stipulated unless these were felt necessary or desirable. Intake was to be through referral from a community agency (from courts, city, state or Federal parole, hospitals, or public health nurses) or directly by client application.

Center Staff

Social workers at the Center were required to operate by applying their traditional generic skills to the two new variables, use of *authority* and *reaching-out,* in order to learn imaginative ways for using these variables to hold addicts in treatment, build the relationship, and offer a variety of services within the framework created. Although social workers had had some experience with both variables, they had not been used in this way before with addicts in a family-centered approach; nor had their use of authority (as with patients committed to mental hospitals) been the same as at the Center, where the use of authority became a prime focus of attention and needed to be taken on directly by the social worker and applied in a graded series of coercions.

It was anticipated this use of authority would be difficult because of the social workers' (and the helping fields, generally) "trained incapacity" to use authority in treatment. Also new was the use of joint-management techniques. While this contained elements of a team approach, such sharing of traditionally confidential patient material and the joint decision-making with a legal agency were unique in the practice of both probation departments and social agencies.

It was hoped this authority could provide the framework in which the traditional generic services to addicts could be maximized. Within this context, social workers thus rendered all the usual help, based on an initial psychosocial assessment of problems of the addict and his family and the interactions between them. Other forms of help included counseling and supportive help, referral to a wide variety of community facilities such as welfare, vocational rehabilitation, training, employment, and housing. Because of the difficulty in making referrals, workers usually needed to exercise great precaution in preparing patients and new agencies for referrals, actually accompanying the patient to the new agency to ensure follow-through (on both sides). Where a number of agencies were involved, the worker needed to assume leadership for coordinating their various services to ensure that they were being integrated into an effective helping service. Workers also participated in the research aspects by helping plan the various instruments and later completing the various research forms.

The public health nurses at the Center found themselves in a role unique for them, since they were assuming full responsibility for the addict and his family in a manner similar to the social worker's, although with a very different background in training and experience. Nurses were greatly troubled at the outset by the need to understand the very involved drug-addiction mechanisms and family interactions without the requisite training in psychodynamics. At first they tended to condemn the addict and overidentify with the mothers and family without understanding the symbiosis and "two-way street" interactions. They learned that their interviews, home visits, referrals, relationships with social agencies, and case recording, while seemingly resembling those of social workers, were, in fact, qualitatively very different. Although the nurses had always focused on the health aspects of a family's problems (and continued to do so), they now needed to deal with very serious emotional problems and involvements, and destructive acting-out behavior.

In terms of the new variables, the nurses found it easier to relate to the use of authority since they had always worked under some control, usually in the form of medical direction, and could carry out the authority and structure firmly. They needed to understand that working with addicts was a lengthy process which could not be resolved through brief contacts and numerous referrals as they had done with patients in the past. When their referrals were not followed through by patients or did not work out, they felt lost since they had used all the weapons in their armamentarium and felt defenseless in dealing further with the addicts. There eventually developed a better understanding of the addict and his family's problems —the mutual interactions and the means for coping with them. Although the nurses found it simpler to relate to the two variables, their work was in many ways more complicated because of their lesser preparation for this assignment. They were left free, nevertheless, with only as much supervision as they felt was indicated, to develop their own techniques on the basis of their previous experience and training.

Additional Staff

The *psychiatrist* was used primarily as a consultant for both the treatment and research aspects of the Center program. He participated in the initial psychosocial assessment of all patients and the differential diagnosis of troublesome cases. He was also a participant in the research through the use of his initial and terminal evaluations of patients to measure progress. The psychiatrist also served as a teacher, lecturing staff on different aspects of addiction, schizophrenia, character disorders, or whatever the staff required in the way of learning at a particular time. He also helped to evaluate psychiatric reports from other agencies.

The *medical doctor*, too, was part of the intake process. It was believed that a thorough physical examination was indicated for all patients in view of their erratic way of living, which entailed gross bodily neglect and danger of infection through the use of unsterile drugs and needles. Where a more thorough workup was required, referral was made to the Department of Health's Adult Maintenance Clinic, an excellent, comprehensive, free service for city residents.

A *research staff,* consisting of two sociologists, a research analyst, an interviewer, and coders was responsible for carrying out the evaluation of the treatment program as well as the control group.

Initial Progress

In June, 1963, after a year of operation, a survey was made of how the program had progressed up to that time. The first experience in using authority with the state parole had proved unsatisfactory. When parole officers referred parolees, they did so from the traditional standpoint of the Center's serving as an ancillary community resource to offer services or counseling and advise Parole periodically of the patients' progress or regression. Although this relief from their massive case loads was welcomed by the parole officers, the absence of a firm structure served to provide the addict with an opportunity to manipulate his environment; in this case, the Center worker against the probation officer, as well as the reverse. It became apparent that the Center's program would need to be reformulated along lines which used authority far more firmly in order to structure the treatment situation and implement the treatment goals of the Center. Further, the prior institutionalization of Parole patients made it difficult to evaluate the specific helping role of the Center program.

Needed Reform

In surveying the program in June, 1963, it was apparent that many aspects required revision. The Advisory Committee was changed, therefore, to an enlarged Policy Committee, in the hope that a new design and better measurement of patient progress through the establishment of a control group could improve the basic service-action program. We had also been unable to obtain our quota of patients from Parole. There was also a question, in terms of a public health approach, whether it might not be better to work out an arrangement with the Office of Probation since probationers would not have been in jail, as had parolees. There would then be a better opportunity to test directly the effects of our use of authority and reaching-out without a period of incarceration and with the addicts' delinquency more recent and "alive."

It became increasingly clear that the introduction of a research staff was essential to help clarify and implement the evaluation of the new program. In subsequent meetings with the NIMH and the Policy Committee, it was decided that the voluntary group would be dropped for a variety of reasons. The primary reason was that the sponsoring agencies felt the new study should rely exclusively on the use of rational authority since voluntary programs appeared ineffective and therefore little was to be gained by such comparisons. It was agreed that there would be a phasing-out of these voluntary cases. Also, the approximately one and one-half years of the Center's operation would be considered in the nature of a "dry run," which had helped us study the parameters of the program and set up a firmer research design.

The cooperation of the courts of the City of New York and its Office of Probation was obtained to write into the conditions of probation the special criteria required by the Center for the new probationary group. These criteria stipulated (1) that prospective probationers accept the services of the Washington Heights Rehabilitation Center for an indeterminate period and "to the extent necessary to effect their rehabilitation"; (2) that they come regularly to the Center and use whatever medical and hospital services were indicated; and (3) that they submit to periodic thin-layer chromatography urinalysis tests. In addition, the probationer had to agree to the usual conditions of probation as follows:

1. Report to your probation officer as directed.
2. Follow the advice and the directions of the court and probation officer.
3. Do not leave the jurisdiction of the court without permission.
4. Notify your probation officer promptly of any expected change in address.
5. Attend school or work regularly.
6. Do not indulge in any unlawful, disorderly, injurious, immoral, or vicious habits or conduct.
7. Avoid undesirable persons and places.

By this time, we had recruited two sociologists and a research analyst, who were able to complete a revised draft proposal incorporating these new conditions. The research unit also developed a variety of instruments to assist in the evaluation of patients at intake, including a questionnaire for initial screening. Before preparing this research proposal, the research unit, in conjunction with the treatment staff, had conducted a survey during the summer months of the treatment activities and had clarified what was understood thus far of reaching-out and the use of authority. It was clear that tremendous ambiguity and resistance prevailed among the treatment staff regarding the use of authority.

The need for a much firmer arrangement with an agency such as the New York Office of Probation had become apparent during the first one and one-half years and made clear the need for Probation to spell out their participation in the Center program more specifically. As a fortunate contingency, the Office of Probation had just set up its own Special Narcotics Unit, which indicated its willingness to cooperate with us.

As visualized under the new research proposal, there were to be three groups of 100 patients each. Group I was the "joint-management" or "experimental" group in which the Narcotics Unit would be working very closely with the Center staff, but the Center staff would have primary responsibility for treatment. Group II was the "specialized probation" case load, served entirely by the Narcotics Unit in small case loads. Group III, the so-called traditional, large case-load approach generally prevailed in Probation. It should be mentioned that there were never enough patients to fill Group III, and this group, in time, had to be dropped. What emerged, interestingly, was that we could barely obtain enough cases to meet the needs of the program, and therefore had to revise our area boundaries to include parts of the East Bronx and large portions of Manhattan.* It was evident that only a very small number of addicts was being placed on probation in the city.

A series of meetings was held with the Center staff as well as the Office of Probation to alert them to the goals of the program and their own participation in it; and this continued throughout the life of the Washington Heights program. A number of the questions cited earlier continued to require clarification throughout 1963 and, in fact, throughout the life of the project. The confusion regarding

* The problem of obtaining an adequate sample and the need to modify the original criteria in order to obtain such a sample are not unique, as can be noted from the very interesting recent study of community work with schizophrenics by Pasamanick et al., as described in their book *Schizophrenics in the Community*. The authors describe the many problems encountered in obtaining a suitable sample and the need to modify their original design in order to accomplish this.

"service" or "research" continued until the two groups described previously were formed. There was continuing variation of attitude in both agency staffs regarding the nature of the authority to be used, some seeing it still in terms of the old punitive approach. It was necessary that the Center staff explain continually that the authority contemplated was a "rational authority," to be used as a holding and structuring device to brake the acting-out behavior of patients by devising a series of graduated deterrents and sanctions.

To obviate the barriers between court and community agency which had prevailed hitherto, provision for full sharing of information, continuous communication, and joint decision-making between the two agencies was made. Arrangements were further worked out with a variety of community agencies to provide such services as detoxification, medical care, vocational counseling, job referral, housing, and welfare help. In the event of relapse, hospitalization was not to be sought first, but beginning sanctions were to be imposed. In the event of more serious transgressions of continuous drug use, the addict would then have to be hospitalized. Caseworkers and public health nurses were to work intensively with small case loads of fifteen addicts and their families. They were also to assume responsibility for drawing in other community agencies and coordinating their common efforts into an integrated helping service.

From a research standpoint, careful attempts were made to incorporate the evaluation and research believed essential for all narcotic addiction programs. Instruments were devised to evaluate the effectiveness of the program in terms of bringing about desired behavioral changes in the areas of drug abuse, work, interpersonal relationships, leisure-time activities, and criminality; and to conduct a process evaluation of the impact of the special rehabilitation efforts carried on by the public health nurses, social workers, and probation officers, as they appeared to the narcotics addict.

REFERENCES

1. Duvall, H. J., Locke, B. Z., and Brill, L. Follow-up study of narcotic addicts five years after hospitalization. *Public Health Reports* 78:185–193, 1963.
2. Brill, L. *Rehabilitation in Drug Addiction—A Report on a Five-Year Community Experiment of the New York Demonstration Center,* Mental

Health Monograph No. 3, Public Health Service Publication No. 1013, Revised, 1964.
3. *Action for Mental Health—Final Report of the Presidential Joint-Commission on Mental Illness and Health.* New York: Behavioral Sciences Book Club, 1964.
4. Ackerman, N. W. *Psychodynamics of Family Life.* New York: Basic Books, 1958.
5. Boszormenyi-Nagy, I., and Framo, J. L. (Eds.). *Intensive Family Therapy.* New York: Hoeber Medical Division, Harper & Row, 1965.
6. *Ibid.,* pp. xvi ff.
7. Bowen, M. A Family Concept of Schizophrenia. In D. O. Jackson (Ed.), *Etiology of Schizophrenia.* New York: Basic Books, 1960.
8. Grinker, R. R., and Spiegel, J. P. *Men Under Stress.* Philadelphia: Blakiston, 1945.
9. Lindemann, E. Symptomatology and management of acute grief. *American Journal of Psychiatry* 2:101–104, 1944.
10. Caplan, G. *Principles of Preventive Psychiatry.* New York: Basic Books, 1964.
11. Parad, H. J., and Caplan, G. A framework for the study of families in crisis. *Social Work* 5:46, 1960.
12. Cummings, J., and Cummings, E. *Ego and Milieu.* New York: Atherton Press, 1962.
13. Bettelheim, B. Where Life Begins. *New York Times,* February 11, 1967.
14. Alksne, H., Lieberman, L., and Brill, L. A conceptual model of the life cycle of addiction. *International Journal of the Addictions* 2:221–238, 1967.

3. Rational Authority

THE CONCEPT OF AUTHORITY has drawn considerable attention from sociologists and social philosophers, primarily in the context of society's position vis-à-vis the individual. Sociologists have pointed out that, in traditional society, society and authority are hardly distinguishable because moral discipline, which is essential for the collective interests of society, frees man by "constraining" him. This idea was considered by Durkheim,[1] who stressed the importance of full acceptance by all members of society of those moral constraints which exist within the "collective consciousness" as one of the means necessary for the reduction of such antisocial behavior as crime.[2] It is through this "collective consciousness" that that authority is derived by which traditional society has maintained control over the individual. Weber, too, lists this traditional authority among the types of authority he discusses.[3] He defines it as power legitimized by the sanctity of ancient custom, which, through the culture, becomes accepted almost without question by the individual.

With the complexity and heterogeneity of modern society, traditional relationships between man and society have undergone considerable revision. Traditional types of authority have far less hold on the individual than before. As Durkheim noted, traditional authority no longer tightly controls the individual. Instead, much to society's detriment, man emerges in many ways independent of society's traditional morality. Weber, too, sees traditional authority as a transitory phenomenon, which is supplanted over time by both charismatic and legal types of authority. Charismatic authority is based on devotion to a specific and exceptional individual, such as a great political leader or religious prophet; while legal authority has led to the modern bureaucratic system and codification of law.

For the many individuals who are socialized into this society, we can only speculate why some accept the major authority mandates of the society while others reject authority on many levels, ranging from mild rejection of parental values to serious antisocial or criminal activities. For the population of narcotics addicts, we have persons who clearly reject various forms of authority. We have much clinical evidence confirming the male addict's difficulties in accepting the authority of the parents, or perhaps being deprived of a father who could act as an authority figure.

We also note in the majority of narcotics addicts the rejection of traditional precepts, which state that one should live a productive life rather than a frivolous one for "kicks." This is usually accompanied by the rejection of legal authority through the use of illegal drugs itself, and the later criminality to obtain money for drugs. It is the violation of the latter authority which brings the narcotics addict, as a criminal, to the attention of the public. When he is apprehended for some crime, society demands that he be punished. In certain instances, either upon conviction or after the criminal has spent some time in jail, it may be decided that, instead of incarceration, he be permitted to remain in the community under probationary or parole supervision. In these instances he is placed in a relationship with an official who represents the legal authority of the courts. It is this use of authority which was employed at the Washington Heights Rehabilitation Center. The origins of our use of authority with offenders thus go back a considerable length of time; in fact, to the origins of the concept of parole.

CONCEPT OF PAROLE

Parole, which may be defined as "the conditional release of an offender who has already served a portion of his sentence in a correctional institution,"[4] may be found in the long-standing military practice of releasing captive soldiers on their promise not to take up arms again.[5] Although the differences between military prisoners on the one hand, and "regular" criminals on the other are relatively great, the concept of a promise of good behavior is explicit in the "paroling" of each.

The English system of indenture, which was in practice by the late eighteenth century, also contained some aspects which can be found in the modern parole system.[6] Here a prisoner could be released by promising to bind himself to a colonist as a laborer for a period of up to seven years. At the end of this period of labor, the individual would be granted his freedom. By the late eighteenth and early nineteenth centuries, private philanthropic organizations devoted to the aftercare of released prisoners began to be formed.[7] These organizations existed predominantly in the United States and indicated, by their very existence, a growing sense of societal obligation to those criminals released from prison and without the wherewithal to adapt themselves successfully to a functional existence in society.

Alexander Maconochie, an Englishman, formulated a system of prisoner release in 1838, but had to wait until 1854 before his system was put to a meaningful test. Known then as the "Irish System" (it was in Ireland where its first real test took place) and the "Progressive Stage System," it stimulated a great deal of controversy. The system involved a series of stages through which the prisoner progressed, starting from solitary confinement, moving through a variety of work stages, each of which employed a decreasing amount of supervision, and ending eventually with the conditional release of the offender. Generally, Maconochie's system was successful; it was his system which provided the basis for reform agitation in the United States.[8]

The first establishment of a parole system in the United States was at the Elmira Reformatory in New York in 1869. In 1884, Ohio became the first state to extend parole to all prisons within its borders. In 1910, the Federal prisons in the United States began to use parole, and by 1944 all states had a parole system.[9]

Parole incorporates two major steps: selection of the parolees and, following this, their supervision in the community. The selection process itself is based on two separate considerations: first, the eligibility of the individual for parole; and second, his suitability for parole. The eligibility of an individual for parole is determined solely by statute and may differ from one parole system to another. The suitability of an offender also varies among different parole boards, but is based on the board's disposition toward a given individual or a certain "type" of criminal rather than on any kind of law. Prediction tables have been used in an attempt to reach as high a point of success as possible, and represent an attempt to inject some type of valid testing into the selection of prospective parolees.

The supervision of the paroled offender continues the state's legal control over him. Like the determination of the offender's suitability for parole, methods of supervision vary from one system to another and, indeed, from one individual within a given system to another. Basically, the intention is that the parole officer insure the compliance of each offender, as well as his general movement in the direction of "normal" functioning in all aspects of social existence, with a set of regulations (these regulations will vary from one jurisdiction to another). This is no easy task for the parole officer, and the gap between the control which he is expected to maintain and that which he is able to maintain is usually wide. Large case loads and "impossible" parole regulations contribute to the problem.

The final step in the parole system is the offender's termination from it. This may be accomplished in three different ways: the original sentence may expire, a decision to release the parolee from further custody at an earlier than originally expected date may be made, or the offender may be returned to prison for committing a new offense or by violating some portion of his parole regulations.

PROBATION

Probation, like parole, is a system which is based upon the concept of legal authority and which attempts to maintain a measure of legal control over those offenders who have been placed within its structure. Unlike parole, probation affects individuals prior to, and in lieu of, their commitment. Probation may be ordered by a judge prior to a trial and conviction, if the offender has pleaded guilty; or after conviction in conjunction with a suspension of sentence. Probation, therefore, provides an alternative to imprisonment and does not remove the individual from the community.

There are two main elements involved in the structure of a probation system: the suspension of sentence (which has its roots in early criminal law) and the supervision of the individual by a probation officer. Eligibility for probation, as for parole, is usually a matter of statute. A felon, for instance, is usually not eligible for probation in most jurisdictions. Suitability for probation is based upon the results of a presentence investigation, usually conducted by a probation officer attached to the court, in conjunction with the attitudes of the judge toward the particular offender. The supervision component of probation is a major one and probably originated in the work done by John Augustus, a Boston shoemaker of the 1840's. Augustus took an interest in such persons as convicted prostitutes, alcoholics, and petty thieves, and put up their bail. They were released in his custody, and he then took responsibility for finding suitable homes and jobs for them. (It has been noted by Korn and McCorkle that his success rate was probably a good deal better than that of many official agencies since.) The example set by Augustus was not emulated quickly, and the spread of probation was slow. Massachusetts passed the first statewide probation law in 1878.[10]

A wide range of benefits deriving from the system of probation has been cited. Among them are:

1. Probation offers the individual another chance in that he is not committed to prison, but instead maintains his status in the community and averts the stigma of a prison sentence.
2. By remaining in the community, the individual is afforded a chance to continue a way of life approved by society.
3. The community has a definite interest in the liberty of any individual who is carrying on a constructive and functional existence.
4. The supervisor in charge of a given case has the full use of all community resources available to him in his attempts at rehabilitation.
5. Financially, probation is much less expensive than institutional treatment.

Not all probation departments are structured or operate in the same manner. Some of the differences among various probation agencies are:

1. The quantity and quality of the personnel attached to the department.
2. The investigating practices of the departments.
3. The offenders considered eligible for probation.
4. The conditions to which the probationer is expected to adhere.
5. The conditions for the eventual release of the individual from his probationary status.

One may raise question as to the need to build into any rehabilitation program an authority beyond that found in typical probation or parole programs. As we shall discuss later in this chapter, two additional forms of authority were used at the Washington Heights Rehabilitation Center, personal and professional.

CONTROL AND PERMISSIVENESS

A tendency toward permissiveness with clients seems evident in the training of many of the kinds of personnel expected to be involved in the types of programs we are about to consider. It has been questioned whether the establishment of some forms of authority would be useful in such programs. Jacob Chwast notes that, while he "fully appreciates the value of the case worker's or therapist's democratic acceptance of the right to self-determination of the client, some adaptation of this principle which emphasizes the helpful role of control and authority with antisocial clients or patients requires consideration."[11] The consideration of the use of authority which Chwast suggests may not be an easily accomplished aim. Chwast himself pointed out that there seems to be a rather profound distaste for the use of controls by the helping professions in our society. He mentions three factors which may constitute the basis for this:

1. The ideology of a free society has been often equated with complete freedom from restriction and steadfast resistance to

authority. In other words, the fact of our free society lies at least partially in a desire to be as little restricted in our existence as possible.
2. There has been a movement toward almost unrestricted permissiveness in our child-centered approach in education and child-rearing. This is possibly due to an overly mechanical usage of the contributions made by John Dewey in this area.
3. Certain psychoanalytic and psychotherapeutic practices support noninvolvement with the patient by the therapist beyond the therapeutic hour. This almost total lack of relationship with the patient outside the therapy session has helped reinforce the apparent distaste for the use of any controls.[12]

It would seem that a reconciliation between control and permissiveness should be attempted with the understanding that this could be of great importance in the treatment of the offender. As Chwast notes,[13] "Just as the individual's control in the population at large ranges along a continuum, the control which our agencies (casework, psychiatric, protective, and correctional) offer can also be charted on a continuum. The ideal conditions for treatment occur at the point at which a given agency's control capability intersects with the precise control needs of each individual served.

The difficulty in moving agencies in the direction of incorporating controls is hard to predict. It can be assumed that the overall aim in the treatment of offenders would be a shifting away from the need for external controls as the development of the individual's internal controls takes place. The function of the institutionalized agency controls would be the replacement of those which the individual has as yet failed to develop.

CONCEPT OF AUTHORITY AT THE
WASHINGTON HEIGHTS REHABILITATION CENTER

The program of the Washington Heights Rehabilitation Center was geared to the concept of what we termed "rational authority" in the treatment of problems of drug addicts. Such an approach seemed indicated on a number of different levels.

Psychological Level

One of the pivotal questions in the treatment of drug addiction is whether the addict's psychopathology predates his use of drugs and is causally related. Individuals who work with addicts have recognized the addict's problems in all topological areas, i.e., ego, superego, and id (if we use Freud's schema). Workers have commented on the addict's weak ego, which is often poorly related to reality and capable of gross distortions (although it is in many respects admirably attuned to his impulsive needs and way of life); on the powerful drives under very weak control; and on the "lacerating" or punishing superego and "superego lacunae." All these combine to contribute toward the development of the acting-out personality or so-called character disorder, which has been the diagnosis most commonly attributed to the majority of addicts. The essential characteristic of such "character disorders" is the tendency to act out, often antisocially, whenever tension is engendered.

Addicts are reputed to have a low frustration tolerance for anxiety and, if given the opportunity, will attempt to escape the sources of their anxiety, whether internal or external. Consequently, when anxiety is mobilized in the therapeutic relationship, we find that they will disengage themselves from treatment entirely or else appear only at times of crisis. This inability of addicts to sustain treatment over a period of time has constituted one of the key reasons for our past failure to help them. The use of authority in the Washington Heights Rehabilitation Center program became a device for holding addicts in a treatment situation, usually against their will, until they could learn to tolerate tension, face themselves in the context of the realistic demands of society, and begin to assume responsibility for their lives.

Sociological Level

It is generally recognized that the majority of identified addicts derive from urban, lower-class, and minority group populations, and that they usually live in deprived areas characterized by a series of interlocking social problems. They most often come from broken homes with a matriarchal family structure where serial mating occurs and the young males lean heavily on the social supports and identifications obtained from peer group associations in order to achieve their masculine identification.

A number of treatment problems also emanate from the fact of class differences between patient and therapist so that it frequently becomes difficult or impossible for middle-class treatment personnel to communicate with lower-class individuals and create a common consensual framework. The reluctance of addicts to become involved in treatment has been described in such terms as their being "not motivated," having a "different life-style," being "apathetic," or coming from "multi-problem" families poorly equipped to cope with the numerous stresses of life. Regardless of these therapeutic rationalizations regarding the inability of the worker to establish a meaningful relationship, we have found that opportunities for successful social adaptation are in reality markedly limited for the lower classes. Hence, to paraphrase a sociological inquiry, *Knowledge for What,* we may ask "Therapy for What?" From the addict's point of view, he properly perceives that the therapist is, in fact, trying to engage him in a conventional life, which will often mean low pay and prestige, continued insecurity, and poor access to the goals of our affluent society. This conformity, which society demands of the addict, is neither respected nor valued when it is achieved.

Addicts also properly perceive that the "things" of success can be purchased through the overriding symbol—money—which suggests an alternative potential for affluent living through a criminal way of life. This partial reality-perception of addicts places the middle-class therapist in the awkward position of compelling addicts to remain in an underprivileged position, which the therapist would never condone for himself. The problem of developing techniques to break through this misnamed "inertia" and "lack of motivation" which seeks other than middle-class goals and which is based on "impulse-ridden gratifications" has constituted one of the crucial problems in working with addicts, i.e., holding them in treatment long enough to restructure their attitudes and relationships to the socially sanctioned system of often limited opportunity.

Physiological Level

The facts of physical dependency and tolerance have been amply described in the literature. It is known that, as opiate users get caught up in drug use, they will in time become physiologically addicted. In the course of their addiction they will at some point be unable to procure drugs and will experience withdrawal distress. The fear of withdrawal, according to Lindesmith, then becomes one more factor for maintaining their addiction.[14] To understand the physiological aspects of addiction, we also need to think in terms of conditioning theories, especially as elaborated by Wikler.[15] Wikler's emphasis has been on instrumental and classic conditioning as primary factors in the development of addiction. His theories shed light on why recidivism is so common.*

There are still many unanswered questions about the mechanisms involved in dependency and tolerance and the effects of possible bodily change in reinforcing the likelihood of relapse to drugs. There is no doubt, however, that if changes are to occur and the conditioning processes of addiction are to be reversed, the addict must be held in a continuous treatment program. We have used rational authority as one of the means for accomplishing this goal.

FORMS OF AUTHORITY

The main forms of authority used at the Washington Heights Rehabilitation Center may be categorized as (1) structural, (2) personal, and (3) professional.

Structural Authority

The fact of an addict's probationer status structured his relationship with the Office of Probation and with the Center. This relationship required that his behavior conform to the conditions of probation lest he be considered in violation of its conditions and in danger of remand to the courts. In some ways, this was the simplest use of authority. It was ever present and could be invoked with the simple reminder to the addict, "You must do this because you are on probation." The addict responded in his status as a probationer and was constantly aware of the requirements adhering to this role. This reminder of his probationer status was reinforced each time he came to the Center when he might well have preferred to go elsewhere. Every act by which he conformed to the instructions of either a Cen-

---
* See pp. 9 ff. in Wikler's article.

ter worker or probation officer served to reinforce his status. Coercion was most easily activated within this authority structure since the worker and probation officer shared the power of invoking the ultimate powerful sanction of imprisonment should the addict not conform to the requirements of the program.

Personal Authority

Somewhat more difficult to deal with, but in many ways equally important, was the use of personal authority. This was more dynamic in the sense that it was not, as in the case of structural authority, merely a role relationship in which mutual expectations were defined by the norms attached to each status. It was, rather, a psychodynamic relationship in which the worker took on symbolically, in the eyes of the addict, the authority of an individual in a position to exert authority. As such, the worker often represented the parent who could be stern and speak harshly when displeased, but also could be warm and laudatory when the addict "behaved" and was obviously making an effort to conform to the reality demands of society as reflected by the worker.

In using personal authority, the kind of rapport established and the degree of therapeutic involvement developed were vitally important. Once a patient had learned to value the opinion of the treating person, its possible withdrawal became a powerful lever to help him curtail his acting-out behavior. The relationship established through the holding function of structural authority thus became a central dynamic permitting personal as well as professional authority to be employed effectively. A frown, a disapproving expression, or an angry tone assumed added power, for it represented the potential withdrawal of support on which the patient had learned to depend.

It is obviously difficult to measure such use of authority. The researcher would have to sound-photograph each therapy session to determine the degree of personal authority exercised in such session for each case. Since the impact of a gesture such as a frown varies greatly with the import placed upon it each time by the recipient, this would prove an almost insoluble methodological problem.

For this reason, although personal authority was employed, it was not considered a variable in the evaluation. In our staff meetings a good deal of training time was spent discussing the nature of personal authority and explaining to the workers how personal authority could reinforce structural and professional authority, so that some uniformity of treatment approach might be achieved. This, of course, applied to the other forms of authority as well.

Professional Authority

Perhaps the most familiar use of authority occurred when the worker invoked his professional competence as a basis for influencing the addict along desired lines. Here the addict related as a patient or client to the role of therapist or caseworker. We considered this use of authority the most natural and spontaneous for our staff because it permitted the caseworker to draw upon his professional training and professional self-image in guiding or directing the addict's actions. When the worker presented a strong professional image, the patient was aided in overcoming his fears of closeness and dependency and thus was helped to lean on this strong and knowledgeable authority. The caseworker was then, by his professional training and competence, in a favorable position to offer suggestions, criticism, and support and to serve as a conventional role model to help the addict recreate his life style along more favorable lines.

It should be clear that these three types of authority were not mutually exclusive and could often be used simultaneously in specific instances, without the worker's awareness of the type of authority actually being employed at the moment.

STAGES AND DYNAMICS IN THE USE OF AUTHORITY

In the various uses of authority, different procedures and developments emerged in the handling of each case. In all cases a *preliminary social assessment conference* and an *initial structuring conference* helped pave the way for the later use of authority.

Preliminary Social Assessment Conference

Immediately after the addict was placed on probation, a meeting of the probation officer, the Center worker, and in the early stages of the program, the respective supervisors was held to plan the initial meeting (Initial Structuring Conference) with the probationer and his family. In preparation for this meeting, any recorded information available about the probationer was reviewed and preliminary impressions of the probation officer were shared with the Center worker. At this meeting a beginning assessment was made of the patient's situation, his feelings about being placed on probation and his having to report to the Center as well, his state of readiness to accept help, and any areas in which the caseworker might help the addict.

Initial Structuring Conference

The initial conference with the probationer, Center worker, probation officer, and if possible, the family was visualized as constituting the cornerstone of our use of rational authority and the orientation point for all future contacts. The primary focus of this meeting was to help the probationer and his family adequately absorb the fact that the Center worker and probation officer were sharing the authority and management as an undivided team. This situation differed from traditional ones in which Center workers lacked a coercive role and responsibility for use of authority in the management of the case, simply relegating this function to the probation officer. This new role relationship avoided the traditional dilemma of a divided team, with the worker appearing as the "good" or protecting mother and the probation officer as the "bad" or disciplining father.

It was at this first initial structuring conference that the conditions of probation were carefully read and explained. They included the requirement that the probationer come to the Center regularly, usually at least once weekly. Questions raised by the probationer and his family were discussed, and the feelings which surrounded such questions dealt with. The framework of authority and the consequences of violation of the required conditions were made clear. At the same time, an effort was made to demonstrate to the probationer and his family the fact that the agency worker and probation officer were interested in helping them and were united in their determination to exercise their skills and authority toward the goal of the probationer's rehabilitation. The belief was also conveyed that this combination of authority and the traditional helping services constituted the best means of assisting him.

The conference thus represented the first visible evidence of the authority of the new program and the conditions the probationer had accepted, with all the responsibilities and consequences it entailed. It was explained to the probationer and his family that, within this framework, a wide variety of services would be offered both to him and to his family. Every effort was made to reinforce the positive aspects of this new relationship and to deal with resistances and negative feelings toward the program and the dual involvement with Probation and the Center.

This cornerstone conference may be visualized as a form of the "psychiatric contract" described by Menninger; that is, the agreement a therapist and patient reach upon beginning treatment, with the specification of the roles and responsibilities of both participants.[16] The specifics of this contractual relationship—such as the fact that the treating person, whether social worker or nurse, would share authority with the probation officer, and that information given by the probationer to one would be freely communicated to the other—were carefully defined. This was to insure that the probationer would not have a chance to "wedge" between the worker and probation officer, i.e., manipulate one against the other in the service of his own impulsive needs, as had happened so often in the past in the case of community agencies working with probation or parole departments. It was deemed important that all these conditions be spelled out carefully, not only for the sake of the probationer and family, but also for the Center staff themselves. Center personnel could then feel more comfortable in carrying out these conditions, as in communicating with the probation officer when a patient was not coming in, or was "slipping," or was not adhering to the agreement made by the probationer. The cornerstone conference was also useful as a reference point in the event of future acting out on the part of the probationer since he could not say he had been unaware of these conditions. He could also be reminded of the conditions and held to them.

Thus, an essential point in developing the relationship with the addict was to spell out clearly the expectations which the joint-management team had of him and, perhaps equally important, the expectations members of the joint-management team had of each other. In order to build this understanding and give the addict and his family additional support, efforts were made at this initial conference to help the addict express his real feelings about the new relationships and to elicit his problems so that beginning connections could be made to demonstrate our interest and ability to help him. Very often this Initial Structuring Conference was used to establish rapport with the family which the Center worker would be visiting later. Excerpts from some Initial Structuring Conferences are offered here to illustrate these points.

CASE DISCUSSION

Initial Structuring Conference—Paul

In the preliminary Social Assessment Conference held with the probation officer, supervising public health nurse and public health nurse, Paul's past history, current situation, and plans were discussed. The probation officer had previously reviewed the probation requirements with Paul. In addition to the previously agreed-upon requirements of probation, i.e., attendance at the Center and acceptance of TLC (thin-layer chromatography urinalysis) tests on request, he was to accept residence at the HARYOU (Harlem Youth Opportunities Unlimited) residential center when this became available. This requirement was made in view of Paul's expressed resentment over his mother's pregnancy by a man not his father, the first since his birth 19 years ago; and also because his brother Ted, also a drug addict, now on Riker's Island, would soon be released. The probation officer had spoken with HARYOU, which indicated it would provide Paul with reading and writing instruction, areas in which he was deficient.

Paul and his mother were admitted to the interviewing room. Each sat in the chairs offered them. Paul sat with his back to his mother, facing me and in clear view of the probation officer. The mother held her head down most of the time unless spoken to directly.

The interview began when the probation officer introduced me to the mother and to Paul. He reminded Paul that I was the worker from the Center of whom he had already spoken earlier at the Remand Center. The probation officer likewise reminded Paul that he had made the choice of this probation program in preference to jail, and he thought that this was a good choice.

The probation officer emphasized that Paul would be held to all the additional conditions of probation they had discussed in regard to drug use: submitting to thin-layer chromatography (TLC) tests, hospitalization if indicated for the full period of time, and living at HARYOU as soon as such facilities became available. At this point, I stated that although the probation officer would take some of the tests, I too would be responsible for requesting spot-checks at the Center, should I think this necessary. I suggested that it was possible that Paul would be seeing me more often than the probation officer, but he should know that, although he was speaking with me, it was as if he were talking to the probation officer since we would remain in close contact and report frequently to each other. Paul said he understood this. He also said that he agreed to everything the probation officer outlined.

The probation officer told Paul and his mother that we wanted to help him, but that Paul would have to learn how to use this help. He reminded Paul that we could always find out if he was using drugs through the urine tests and that it would be better if he himself reported any slips to us. I explained that it might seem confusing that we first say he was not to use drugs and then that in the event he should do so, we would use urine tests or insist on hospitalization. By this, I explained, we meant to recognize the difficulty presented by the ever-persistent temptation of drugs and didn't want him to be sent to jail for a single shot. He was reminded that he would be under strict supervision and that any slips could be readily detected. His sharing the information about his occasional drug use would be an indication of his cooperation, concern about what was happening to him, and interest in enlisting our help to cope with it. He would find out that we were expecting a lot from him, but we thought this was the only way to really help him. We would uphold our promises as well as our demands and expected him to keep his side of the contract.

I told Paul that, at first, he would be seeing many people at one time and might become confused, but that he would soon "get into the routine." I made an appointment to see him again at 9:30 A.M. at the Washington Heights Rehabilitation Center, at which time he would also be introduced to the research worker. The research aspect of the program had not been explained before and was clarified at this time. It was stressed that information given the research worker would be absolutely confidential and shared with no one else.

The probation officer then contacted HARYOU regarding reading and writing lessons; Paul was scheduled for an appointment. The probation officer then wrote out the probation requirements on the probation card. In addition to the previously stated requirements, Paul was asked to choose the curfew hours he considered reasonable. He settled for 11 P.M. on weekdays and 12 midnight on Fridays and Saturdays.

While the probation officer took Paul aside to administer the TLC test, I spoke with his mother. She said that she was pleased that Paul had been selected for this program. When questioned about her pregnancy, she said the doctor suspected twins; she had gained an excessive amount of weight. She had an appointment the next day for an examination to determine the possibility of multiple pregnancy. Plans for the baby (babies) were sketchy. The possibility of adoption was broached. The mother had not considered this because she felt that adoption was impossible; she had thought about leaving the child somewhere, but realized this was illegal and dangerous. She felt inadequate to rear this child and believed her present two children were an example of this inadequacy. As a consequence, she could not tolerate such failure again. Since she had believed that she could no longer become pregnant, this pregnancy came as a shock to her. We planned to discuss this further during my first home visit.

At the end of this initial conference, definite appointments were arranged with the probationer and the family as a means of implementing the structure being established and making visible the outlines of our future cooperative relationship.

Appointments scheduled with Paul were:

1. With me at Washington Heights Rehabilitation Center, December 18, 9:30 A.M.
2. With Mr. G. at Washington Heights Rehabilitation Center, December 18, 10:00 A.M. (questionnaire).
3. At HARYOU with Mr. D., December 21, 11:00 A.M.
4. At probation office with probation officer, December 28.

Initial Structuring Conference—Tony

Before the Initial Structuring Conference, a brief preliminary conference was held with the assigned probation officer, who gave us a copy of the investigation summary prepared by his Department about Tony and the family. Together, we outlined our approaches in the initial interview, agreeing that the probation officer would lead the discussion, explaining the principles and conditions of probation. Later, he would introduce me and I would discuss our Center program, stressing throughout the concept of joint-management.

Tony was referred to the Center in a telephone call by the supervising probation officer to the supervising public health nurse early this afternoon. At the time of the call, Tony and his mother were waiting at the Probation Office for assignment to his workers in the joint-management Group 1 program. I, as intake worker for the day, arrived at the Probation Office within an hour, accompanied by the supervising nurse. There we found Tony and his mother still sitting in the reception area. Tony was sitting a seat apart from his mother, who was slouched over asleep.

The probation officer, the supervising nurse, and I then saw Tony and his mother together. When called, they entered the probation officer's office, acknowledged our introductions, and sat side-by-side facing the three of us, who were seated on opposite sides of the desk. The mother, a plainly dressed, rather good-looking young woman, sat upright and was at first quietly attentive to the probation officer. Tony seemed much less comfortable and tended to change his position often and shift his hat from hand to hand. Both kept their coats on throughout the session, and Tony shed his only when called to submit urine for the TLC test.

The probation officer began by explaining to them what probation is and what it meant in Tony's case. To outline the conditions of probation, he handed Tony a blank copy of the Order of Probation and asked him to read it aloud. The probation officer had earlier indicated he would do this to get an idea of Tony's reading level and skill, with a view toward possible referral to JOIN. Tony read the paper fairly well, but stumbled over some words. To cover his obvious embarrassment, he volunteered that he used to read well, but in the year he had been out of school had "lost it," and grown more accustomed to using "street language." He insisted on trying again and again to pronounce the words, repeating that he could read, but was just not used to "those legal terms." It was here that the mother entered actively into the session, insisting that Tony could read and used to read better when he was in parochial school. From here on, through the rest of the session, she dominated the conversation, speaking loudly and at times rapidly and with much emotion about Tony, herself, her husband, and the other children. She openly blamed Tony's "downfall" on his having "slipped away from the church," and on Tony's father, who removed him from parochial school and entered him in public school against her wishes. She apologized again and again for the fact that she was too weak from "having too many babies" to be able to keep a proper eye on what was happening to her children.

During all of this, Tony registered embarrassment, annoyance, and disgust, and several times when the probation officer and I interjected a question which his mother answered in similes and metaphors, he would say to her with a pained expression, "That's not what they asked you," or "That has nothing to do with this." Finally, by mutual agreement, the probation officer and I decided to interrupt the mother's interventions by administering the TLC test to Tony. As the probation officer was explaining the test to him, and when the mother asked, "Do they give him shots for this?", I had the feeling that she really did not understand his drug use.

While Tony and the probation officer were out of the room, I took the opportunity to explain to the mother the program at our Center and our agency's participation in the joint-management of Tony's probation. I am not sure she heard all of what I said, or understood what she heard, but she did agree to have me visit her at home, adding that she preferred that I speak to her and her husband separately, and cautioning me not to reveal to him anything she had said about him today. We made an appointment for a morning visit to her home. She said she was sure her husband would be home because he is out of work and ailing with pains in his side.

When Tony returned to the room, his mother was relaxed enough to allow the probation officer to continue to review the conditions of probation. I added to the seven conditions, an eighth one, that he also "report" to the Center whenever and as often as I directed. We both stressed that noncompliance with any of the eight conditions constituted violation which, at the discretion of the two of us, could result in remand to legal custody. The probation officer explained that flexibility would operate in the conditions and decisions, and I emphasized to Tony his responsibility for contacting either or both of us whenever he found himself in a predicament that might be interpreted as an unwitting violation. Should he, for example, need to cancel an appointment for a legitimate reason, he was obliged to telephone in advance of the appointment hour. I believe he understood this, although I sensed his displeasure with the whole arrangement (though he could not then express this openly). The probation officer gave Tony his first return appointment, writing this data on his "report card." I also gave Tony an appointment to see me at the Center, writing my name and the appointment data on our Center stationery, and instructed him in our use of this means of recording appointments, in which the last date would always be his next appointment. To the mother I also gave a note with my name written on it, and encouraged her to feel free to contact me at any time.

DEVELOPMENT OF TECHNIQUES

In the course of the Center staff's discussions on how to implement the use of authority, a number of questions were posed. At the beginning there was a question as to how the roles of probation officers, social workers, and nurses would differ from each other.

The Center program stipulated that a representative from the Center, whether social worker or nurse, would work with a probation officer and constitute a "team" in the joint-management of each case. A social worker and nurse would not share the same case but, rather, each would assume full individual responsibility for helping a particular patient and his family. The specific ways in which each discipline applied its traditional techniques in using the two variables, rational authority and reaching-out, were left to the discretion and initiative of the individual workers. Nurses, therefore, found themselves operating in a relatively new capacity when they assumed this responsibility for the case management of addicts and their families. The reasons for this were both theoretical and practical; among other factors was the consideration that the Department of Health, one of the sponsoring agencies, relied more heavily on nurses than on social workers for the bulk of its functional activities (social workers served as consultants). It was hoped the techniques developed by these "specialized nurses" might be carried over to their "generalized nurses" and to other programs in the community.

In establishing the joint relationship, it was first proposed that the probation officer constitute the primary source of authority while the Center worker assumed greater responsibility for the offering of services. This initial arrangement was supported by the fact that the probation officer was already an officer of the court and responsible for executing its directions. In practice, this distinction became less precise as the Center worker herself exercised her derived authority as she found necessary. Her use of authority was facilitated by the fact that the probation officer was continuously drawn into the case management through the sharing of information about all contacts with the patient and his family, through participation in joint decision-making, and by such combined activities as visiting the home jointly with the Center worker when the authority needed to be made more visible. This series of joint activities provided the worker with an opportunity to use legal and professional authority effectively, even in the absence of the probation officer. The extent to which this authority was activated was determined by the specific case issues.

It was suggested that social workers and nurses give greater recognition to the probationer's ambivalence and resistance to treatment, attempt to deal with these feelings, and interpret the authority used since the ultimate effect would lead in the same direction; namely, that the probationer needed to adhere to the conditions of probation and come in on a regular basis. Because of variations in prior training, role image, experience, and understanding of emotional factors, basic differences in how probation officers, caseworkers, and nurses worked with probationers were expected. Idiosyncratic differences from worker to worker within each discipline were also anticipated, but the determination of techniques and approaches was left to individual initiative.

At a later date, some of the staff commented that using authority had been a revolutionary experience for them in that they had never before forced individuals to come in for treatment. The staff had initially expressed feelings of guilt and resistance to informing probation officers if probationers were not reporting for appointments, or if they were relapsing to drugs. There was some feeling, at first, that the use of "compulsion" or "coercion" represented an extreme approach, and that resorting to threats somehow seemed inconsistent with social work or nursing goals. There was also some questioning by the newer workers as to whether "threats" were really needed to help addicts come in for treatment. At staff meetings, the Center reviewed the historic use of authority by the different professions, as in relation to the mentally ill in state hospitals, in child welfare programs, and by public health nurses for tuberculosis and venereal disease control in the Department of Health's Epidemiological and Public Health Service Programs, as well as the more familiar usage of probation and parole. In addition, they were reminded of our prior experience with voluntary patients—the overall problems and difficulties in holding addicts in therapy.

In spite of these discussions and all training efforts, nurses and social workers continued to experience great difficulty in applying authority and implementing its use in the Center program. This resistance to using authority continued for some workers throughout the life of the program. The total extent of this problem was never fully clarified, although some portion was undoubtedly due to idiosyncratic problems with authority, "trained incapacities" inherent in the original professional training, the structure of the program itself, personality clashes, and fear of the patients. Other aspects derived from the nature of the addiction problem itself; namely, the workers' recognition of the difficulties related to insisting on total, immediate abstinence in a very seriously disturbed population and the futility of hospitalization and other measures, as well as the long-term nature of the illness.

To help clarify the use of authority for the worker, we initially drew distinctions between the terms *compulsion* and *coercion*:

coercion represented a form of authority which applied the *threat alone* of using force to influence individuals to undergo change; compulsion, on the other hand, was the condition of forcing a person to do something against his will, with threats which were actually followed through by completed acts. More briefly compulsion was the completed act of forcing a person against his will, while coercion was the use of threat alone to enable a person to do what we believed he should do (so that compulsion would not *need* to be employed). It was clear that since drug addicts had failed to make the "proper" choices in life, it was necessary to help them change their destructive way of living. The Center program was thus built around the use of coercion which could lead to compulsion. It was agreed that the central variable in the program would be this use of authority, and that the actual methods and conditions for implementing it would constitute one of our main foci of study. Appropriate attention would be devoted to individualizing treatment in terms of specific client needs and client readiness for help and change.

As indicated, there were sharp variations in approach on the part of individual staff workers. A few were able to accept the responsibility of using authority personally without reservation while others preferred to have the probation officer assume this role. These latter workers appeared to concur with the traditional belief that the use of coercion should be restricted largely to the probation officer in order not to endanger the therapeutic relationship. It was clear that some redefinition would be required before coercion could be viewed more positively and more effectively by the staff.

It was evident that authority could not be used in a mechanical and stereotyped way, but would need to be applied on the basis of a careful psychosocial assessment of the patient's needs. Because of the wide variations in patients and families, in the kinds of problems presented and states of readiness for help, the timing and degree of most of the use of authority and reaching-out became most important. It was conceivable, for example, that in some cases a temporary use of drugs should not be seriously censured if the patient were struggling to function on a higher level in other areas of adaptation such as work, or if he were experiencing severe stress or crisis. The program goal guiding the workers' interaction with patients was the gradual achievement of abstinence, i.e., movement in the direction of abstinence and improved social functioning.

Later in the program, as workers took stock of their experience, they noted that they had found interesting ways to implement the use of authority. They felt they had slowly learned to assume greater responsibility for using the authority derived from the cooperative arrangement with the Probation Department. Probationers were firmly informed from the outset that the workers were both ready and willing to make decisions and recommendations which would be honored by the probation officer. As a result, the probationer would have to face the consequences of his choices. By establishing a very firm structure and offering him a wide range of services and a supportive relationship, we hoped to maximize his ability to make the "correct choices."

In contrast to past practice, where workers used the concept that "It is the system that is punishing you, not I," and projected responsibility upon the probation officer, workers now took on this responsibility and adapted a new image for themselves. The image was that of a firm but benign authority allied to the constructive elements in the addict's strivings, an authority not very tolerant of behavior detrimental to the client and one prepared to coerce him in a variety of ways to give up his destructive behavior. Some of the workers viewed this new role as comparable to that of a firm and consistent parent. With the probation officer, they represented a united front utilizing rational authority to assert the values of our society, and their right and responsibility to influence the addict's behavior. As with the growing child, a system of rewards and punishments was activated in which increasing leeway and freedom could be tolerated as the probationer matured and made more constructive choices. This could be expressed concretely in terms of the probationers' needing to come in less frequently or being subjected to less scrutiny and control as they improved. On the other hand, if probationers appeared to be losing control, authority could be made more visible and forceful and increasingly coercive acts could be applied to help them regain their balance. At one point, some of the techniques used were detailed by workers as follows:

1. Discussing the problem with the probationer and conveying authority by the tone of voice, general bearing, and demeanor.
2. Drawing in of the probation officer to reinforce the Center program and joint efforts, i.e., interviewing the probationer with the probation officer and supervisor in attendance to present, in essence, a reinforced system rather than relying upon one individual to enforce the goals of the program.
3. Reinforcement of authority through family involvement.

4. Frequent careful review and reminder of the conditions of probation with the patient.
5. Use of letters and telephone calls to maintain contact with the patient and reinforce our structuring efforts.
6. Thin-layer chromatography tests to determine the validity of the patient's assertions that he is drug-free.
7. Visits to home by both worker and probation officer.
8. Threat by workers of forced hospitalization of patient.
9. Meetings with patient and family in probation office.
10. Threat by workers of remand to jail.
11. Remands by judge arranged by staff.
12. Citing patient for violation of probation.
13. Brief remand to jail.
14. Prolonged remand to jail or reformatory.

USE OF AUTHORITY WITH INVOLVEMENT OF PROBATION OFFICER TO HOLD PATIENT IN TREATMENT—PHIL

In some cases, the involvement of patients in rehabilitation proved not so easy. Unreconciled anger over any restrictions in their ability to act out and to involve themselves in deviant activities was often shown early in the treatment process and in efforts made by these individuals to terminate their involvement with the Center. In such cases the probation officer was quickly called on the scene to help hold the patient in treatment. The addict's presence at the Center was not voluntary and the posture of the agency had to be that such terminations were not acceptable under any conditions. The following excerpt from a case record demonstrates the early use of authority as a holding function through joint activity with the probation officer.

Phil, a twenty-three-year-old patient and high school graduate, lived with his parents in a crowded three-room apartment. His father, a baker by trade, supported the family on a salary of $95 per week. While periodic upheavals, usually related to the patient's demands for money, occurred in the family, neither parent was prepared to act firmly to change the status quo except by leaning heavily on the nurse or probation officer. For fourteen months, the probationer managed to coast along on probation, keeping appointments fairly well, using drugs sporadically, and making token efforts at job-hunting. By this time, it had become apparent that the probationer was satisfied to continue this pattern unless the nurse and probation officer intervened more forcefully.

Although the probation officer conceded that the probationer was making a marginal adjustment, he was not convinced, as was the nurse, that a court review would be effective and was not prepared to intervene to change the situation. Since the nurse and the probation officer appeared to be reaching an impasse in their joint-decision-making, the case was referred to their respective supervisors, who both supported the nurse's recommendation that the probationer be given an "ultimatum"; unless he found a job within two weeks, he would be remanded to court for review of his status. Within a week, Phil got a job which he held for seven weeks, quite confident that he could get another immediately if required. The use of direct confrontation by the probation officer and nurse made visible to him the shakiness of his current behavior and the need to continue working toward better goals of achievement.

DRAWING-IN OF PROBATION OFFICER TO REINFORCE AUTHORITY WITH PSYCHOTIC PATIENT—MIGUEL

During the summer, Miguel had discovered an organization known as Scientology, part of a system known as *dianetics* founded by L. Ron Hubbard. Both Miguel and Maria, his common-law wife, became increasingly engrossed in this organization and felt it to be the answer to their problems. It is not surprising that this organization appealed to Miguel since it offered simple answers to his problems and offered a strong structure and feeling of belonging which he found helped in maintaining a stricter discipline over his emotions and behavior. Miguel had found the use of structure similarly helpful in relation to employment. He felt that he no longer needed to see me; and, indeed, his involvement with Scientology precluded his seeing me since he worked for the organization seven evenings a week after work. He did not know how he could see either the probation officer or myself and became quite upset when I suggested that he would need to find time to include us, although I would not be rigid about it. I did nothing to undermine his involvement with Scientology, since it seemed to serve excellently to hold Miguel's psychosis in check, involving him in a nonthreatening, socially acceptable situation and offering him a variety of outlets for his problems. I therefore attempted to use Scientology as an adjunctive service though still needing to maintain contact for our own treatment and research purposes.

When Miguel's contacts with the Center appeared to be petering out entirely, I met with the probation officer to discuss with him the need for reinforcement to keep Miguel coming in, even if less regularly, as a condition of probation and means of helping himself. A visit was subsequently made to his house and another visit scheduled at the probation office. At a subsequent joint meeting with the probation officer and nurse, the need to maintain his contact with us was again outlined as previously detailed at the Initial Structuring Conference. I indicated that it would be acceptable for him to come in less often, perhaps every two or three weeks instead. He told me that Maria was no longer interested in seeing me, since she did not consider herself our client. We left it at that. This was, of course, her prerogative, though it would have been useful to include her in our planning. At the joint conference, Miguel agreed to see me every other week and the probation officer agreed to close his case at the end of the year if his very good adjustment was maintained.

Miguel responded very well to this structure, and, in fact, began to come in voluntarily on a weekly basis and then every other week. He interpreted our recent conferences as evidence of our real concern about helping him. The point that emerged was that Miguel could not respond to the use of authority if the reins were too tight or the lines too rigidly drawn. Rather, he needed to feel that he was sharing in it and that our use of authority emanated from our real concern about him.

At this point, he was well adjusted in his job, had received several promotions, and was due to become a trained engraver. He was earning more than $100 a week; and, at the end of his apprenticeship and journeymanship, would be making close to $200 a week. Miguel was able to separate from his common-law wife, who he realized was not helping him in any way. He moved into a hotel and subsequently moved in with another girl in December. He proudly brought in his girl to meet me later.

On the whole, therefore, Miguel has made a very good adjustment, responding well to our use of authority. He has not used heroin since he has been on probation, has worked steadily from the beginning, was able to end a poor relationship, and has kept his appointments both here and at the probation office.

REINFORCEMENT OF CENTER AUTHORITY THROUGH INVOLVEMENT OF FAMILY—CARL

Carl told me quite firmly, following his release from Riker's Island, that he wanted no help from us and intended to stay on drugs, which was his only way of enjoying life. He was aware that this would probably mean being in and out of prisons for a good part of his life, but at the moment he was not prepared to manifest concern about this. In keeping with his views, Carl soon relapsed. After a series of crises in the home, he was admitted to the Metropolitan Hospital. When I visited him there, he had already been there three or four days, and whether or not he stayed for the full month's treatment remained to be seen. His past behavior made it appear most unlikely.

In my previous attempts to work with the family, I found it a major undertaking to bring order into this chaotic household. It was also risky, since I did not know whether the mother could function if there were no crisis on which she could project her inner discomforts. Carl's need for constant crises and turmoil contributed to the mother's need and constituted a closed circuit in which it was difficult to intervene. His use of drugs and also of alcohol served to keep the pot boiling. I had hoped that the use of Librium would give him something to lean on and reduce his anxiety to a point where he would not need other drugs. His mother, however, sabotaged this because she was suspicious of all drugs, including those prescribed by our Center. She proved strongly resistant to any discussions attempting to make such differentiations.

I arranged a home visit when the family was together, jointly with the probation officer. We asked them when they had last sat down for a family discussion. The father replied that, as far as he could remember, it had never happened before. I asked him if he understood why Carl had been placed on probation. He replied that he knew Carl had not been "doing right" and I persisted in requesting that he tell me more precisely what Carl had done that was "wrong." Mr. G. thought it was because he had not been working and had been associating with the wrong people, to which I replied that this in itself would not entail his needing to be on probation. It was clear that Mr. G. knew that Carl had been involved in something illegal, but could not bring himself to mention the word "drugs." At this point, Mrs. G. became very tense and anxious and walked over to me and whispered that I was not to mention that Carl had been using heroin and that she wished to talk to me alone later about this. I wondered about this use of "secrets" and playing games and felt the father most certainly did know. I told the family that I was there because, first, Carl had been doing something that might endanger his life and, second, because I thought the family should be involved, as they were in fact, in whatever was going to happen. I referred to Mr. G.'s earlier explanation that he used barbiturates and alcohol, which could be a lethal combination. Mr. G seemed unimpressed by this, and I realized that he did not really at this point relate his problem to Carl's and that he was not concerned about what was happening to Carl since he was really too preoccupied with his own problems.

The probation officer arrived about this time, and I explained the conditions of probation and how we expected Carl to conduct himself in the future. He outlined the need to come regularly to the Office of Probation and the Center, as well as the need to get a job and to abstain. I thought he did this very well, and Mrs. G. especially seemed impressed and pleased. We also described the need to work closely with the family if we were to help Carl. This set the stage for a closer involvement with them in which they could be helped with their problems and could also lean on the worker and probation officer for support and strength when they needed to act jointly and firmly in relation to Carl. We also helped them when it was clear that their own problems were intervening and impelling them to push Carl into self-destructive behavior, including relapse to drugs. The family later assisted the probation officer and worker and, additionally, could for the first time exercise a freer parental authority and control to which Carl was gradually able to respond.

In some cases, we were in a position to extend the concept of joint-management or cooperation with other agencies in the community with a feedback of information and more effective cooperation, which helped us maintain better control of the patient and work more effectively with him. In some instances, it was possible to establish communication with employers for whom our probationers worked and who were already acquainted with their history. The following indicates a situation in which this communication proved important.

USE OF EMPLOYER CONTACT TO REINFORCE PATIENT'S RELATIONSHIP TO CENTER—MR. B.

Mr. B. regularly failed to keep his appointments with the Center in the first months. This prompted me to schedule a joint-conference with the probation officer and patient. Mr. B.'s irregularity in appointments, in addition to the increased evidence of what he claimed was "prescribed medication" began to indicate that he was relapsing to drug use. His employer, who knew of Mr. B.'s addiction history and court involvement, had called us earlier to complain that Mr. B. was taking too much time off from work to "keep appointments" with us. He became concerned about Mr. B.'s evident use of drugs and said he wished to reinforce our efforts to help in any way he could.

In the ensuing joint-management conference, an outline was made for Mr. B.'s expected attendance at the Probation Office and at the Center twice a month. Mr. B. claimed that it was because of a second job that he had been leaving his employer early. The employer subsequently played the role of the good father, talking more often with Mr. B., maintaining contact with us, and encouraging Mr. B. to come regularly and to follow through on the treatment efforts. Mr. B. was also able to involve his employer in further planning for his vocational rehabilitation. The employer was also most understanding in allowing Mr. B. time to visit our office "as long as it was for a good purpose," and even allowed him time for hospitalization to recover from his earlier relapse.

USE OF AUTHORITY IN FORCED HOSPITALIZATION—ROGER C.

The central elements in our reinforcement of the use of rational authority became confrontations with reality and reality testing to correct distortion; and setting limits and offering strong support for movement, including firm and direct guidance when indicated as well as coercion when patients appeared to be losing control.

In the case of Roger C., a joint conference was held at the Office of Probation with the probation officer, Mrs. C., Roger, and myself, at which time the probation officer and I confronted Roger with evidence of his drug use. When we pressed on him the need for hospitalization, he was resistant, denied that he was addicted or indeed was using drugs at all, and attempted to explain his obviously debilitated condition by saying that he had been working late at night, getting little sleep, and eating poorly. Neither the probation officer nor I accepted this story and told Roger this point-blank, to which he reacted in a disappointed manner. Mrs. C., on the other hand, expressed her satisfaction with the stand we had taken, but seemed pessimistic that Roger could ever really abstain from drugs.

Roger professed to be worried about his job and felt he could make it without hospitalization. We agreed to allow him time to improve his condition: he would need to report daily to me at the Center for the next three weeks in lieu of hospitalization and submit urine specimens each day for TLC (urinalysis) testing. If at the end of this time all the tests were found to be negative, he could forego hospitalization and begin the plans for readjustment and training we had earlier outlined with him. If we found even one positive TLC test, we would insist upon immediate hospitalization. This was very carefully spelled out to Roger; and, when he indicated that he understood the proposal, I gave him a definite appointment at the Center for the next day.

Because Mrs. C. had complained several times that she did not feel well and because Roger was in an obviously debilitated condition, I suggested they could both go to the Department of Health's Diagnostic Clinic for a complete medical workup. While they were present in the office, I telephoned the Diagnostic Service Center and made appointments for them to be seen at the Clinic. I told Mrs. C. that I would be in touch with her with further instructions before her appointment day.

Roger did not keep his subsequent appointment, but came in on the following day and was not able to deliver a urine specimen. He finally had to confess to continued use of heroin and then himself requested immediate hospitalization. Mrs. C. had called meantime to tell me she was sure he was using heroin and that he had told her that he now was ready to enter the hospital. Manhattan General Hospital was contacted and a request for emergency admission made. I telephoned Mrs. C., told her what was happening, and suggested she come to the Center to accompany Roger to the hospital. Mrs. C. responded within a half-hour and I accompanied Roger and his mother to the hospital, where I left them in the waiting room. A telephone check later in the day confirmed that Roger had been admitted that afternoon. Mrs. C. telephoned the Center still later that afternoon to report to me that Roger had been admitted.

Authority was used later when Roger threatened to leave before the three weeks' required stay. He completed his stay and was then followed very closely after his discharge to obviate any further relapse to drugs.

WORK WITH TWO PROBATIONERS RESISTIVE TO TREATMENT AND TO AUTHORITY—JESUS N.

Mr. J., the probation officer, introduced me to Mr. N. and then proceeded to read the conditions of probation. He prefaced the reading with the statement that, although Mr. N. knew the probation conditions, he was reading them for the three of us so that we would all hear them together as a basis for our working together. As Mr. J. read the conditions of probation, he remarked a number of times that Mr. N. had actually been following these conditions to date; and then pointed to the positive things he was doing. There was very little reaction from Mr. N. until the provisions of probation concerning visits to the Washington Heights Rehabilitation Center were listed. At this point, he expressed particular concern with the term "frequency" of contacts, thinking that by "frequent" I meant daily. (Perspiration began to flow freely about the base of his neck.) After the conditions of probation had been completely read, I clarified the fact that we would probably be seeing each other on a weekly, but not daily basis.

We agreed on the next appointment date and then began to discuss the possibility of home visits. Mr. N. listened silently for a few minutes and then stated that he had to "say his piece" because that was how he felt; and he felt that he was not interested in the program if his whole family was going to be involved in it. It was bad enough that he had caused his family so much trouble, and wouldn't I feel terrible in their place if strangers kept coming in asking all kinds of questions? I agreed that I would have real objection to having people ask me questions about myself and other family members if I did not understand the purpose of these questions. Jesus said that his mother was especially excitable and always thought that when anyone came to the door it was for the worst. I attempted to enlist his support and understanding in involving his mother, especially since I was already aware the family had numerous problems which must also be troublesome to Jesus, with which I would like to help. I attempted to discuss the problems deriving from the fact that two of his relatives from Puerto Rico had just arrived and were staying in his home. However, this had little effect upon his acceptance. Because of time limitations at this meeting, I agreed to discuss this question further with Jesus when we saw each other again and to leave to Jesus the decision of when and how his family could be visited. Jesus said he would discuss this with his mother and asked that he be present when I did see his family, to which I, of course, had no objection. At our next meeting, Jesus said his mother would be interested in talking to us. The home visit made then laid the basis for continuing visits to the family and involvement of them in the treatment process.

SITUATION OF PROBATIONER RESPONSIVE TO USE OF AUTHORITY—MURRAY L.

Murray was referred to the Center by the New York City Probation Department, for participation in our joint-management program. From the beginning and then throughout his probationary period, Murray was able to relate readily to the structure set up and to conduct himself in an exemplary manner. He found employment quickly with a municipal hospital and continued to work on municipal jobs from the time of his acceptance into the program until the termination date. During the Christmas holidays in 1965 and afterward, he took on additional part-time jobs. He took tests for the New York State Employment Training Program, but later learned that the rolls were overfilled. He was not interested in any of the other programs available at that time. Although he was disappointed with this, he did not let it discourage or deter him, but returned to his regular job and planned to await the next training period. In retrospect, there has been a noticeable growth in his self-confidence since he was first accepted into the program. He has been able to assert himself more and more, and was recently able to question the union regarding back pay and overtime due him. He also consulted the union and enlisted their support when the hospital asked if he would do a job he felt was not required by his job description.

With few exceptions, Murray has maintained regular appointments both at the New York City Probation Office and the Center. He initially saw both workers once weekly, but recently was given alternating weekly visits in view of his good adjustment. Murray was able to establish new friendships among nonusers, which has helped him move further out of his family life and change his self-image. He felt he was doing well, as he was indeed, and was reluctant to delve deeply into emotional areas. It appears that there are only loose emotional ties with the family, who seem to be detached individuals. With the exception of his brother Don, who died in 1962, he speaks very little about the other family members. He has nevertheless remained in the parental home because he feels he still needs its structure and safety. He recognizes that his ability to move out on his own will be an indication of his growth, but he is not yet prepared to do so. He has accepted the Center and the additional visits entailed as a necessary part of his probationary sentence. Thin-layer chromatography tests taken both by the probation officer and myself have been consistently negative. Because this patient is a full-time employee and has done so well, his probationary sentence will be terminated by the court without the need for his personal appearance.

REFERENCES

1. Durkheim, E. *The Elementary Forms of the Religious Life.* Glencoe, Ill.: Free Press, 1965, pp. 237–241.
2. Durkheim, E. *Rules of Sociological Method* (8th ed.). Translated by S. A. Solvay and John H. Mueller and edited by G. E. G. Catlin. Glencoe, Ill.: Free Press, 1950, pp. 65–73.
3. Weber, M. *The Theory of Social and Economic Organization.* Glencoe, Ill.: Free Press, 1947, pp. 341–358.
4. Korn, R. R., and McCorkle, L. W. *Criminology and Penology.* New York: Holt, Rinehart and Winston, 1959, p. 606.
5. *Ibid.,* pp. 607, 608.
6. *Ibid.,* p. 608.
7. *Ibid.,* p. 609.
8. *Ibid.,* pp. 609, 610.

9. *Ibid.*, p. 610.
10. *Ibid.*, p. 448.
11. Chwast, J.   The significance of control in the treatment of the antisocial person. *Archives of Criminal Psychodynamics* 2:817, 1957.
12. Chwast, J.   Control: The key to offender treatment. *American Journal of Psychotherapy* 19:116–117, 1965.
13. Chwast, J.   The significance of control in the treatment of the antisocial person. *Op. cit.*, p. 824.
14. Lindesmith, A. R.   *Opiate Addiction*. Bloomington: Indiana University Press, 1947.
15. Wikler, A.   Conditioning Factors in Opiate Addiction. In D. M. Wilner and G. G. Kassebaum (Eds.), *Narcotics*. New York: McGraw-Hill, 1965.
16. Menninger, C.   *The Theory of Psychoanalytic Technique*. New York: Basic Books, 1958.

4. Joint Management

ONE OF THE GOALS of the Washington Heights Rehabilitation Center program, as described in an early formulation, was to "learn how the New York City Department of Health can cooperate with a court agency to manage the narcotics addiction problem in a circumscribed area of the city, that is, Washington Heights." The center was to work exclusively with male probationers of all ages referred by the Office of Probation through the Courts of the City of New York to observe how the two agencies could cooperate to help addicts change their way of living and avoid relapse to drugs.

What was unique about the program and distinguished it from earlier studies was the kind of cooperation envisioned, a joint management between the Office of Probation and a community-based agency, which would offer intensive services involving the sharing of information and joint planning and decision-making. It was hoped that the vistas of case planning would be enlarged when responsibilities were shared, and that a wider diversity of community resources could be brought into the cases, allowing a greater chance of success. In addition, we felt that the material collated for diagnostic thinking would be increased and impressions of the client would have the benefit of viewpoints from different disciplines. Because of these factors, conclusions and subsequent plans would be profoundly influenced as data and impressions were drawn from a more diversified analysis of the dynamics involved in the case.

CONDITIONS OF PROBATION

Toward this end, the Center worked out a proposal which was, to our knowledge, unprecedented in that it had written into the conditions of probation the stipulations that addicts (1) come to the Center regularly for one or more years, to the extent necessary to effect their rehabilitation; (2) submit to periodic spot checks of their abstinence through use of thin-layer chromatography (urinalysis) tests; and (3) undergo all medical and other treatment indicated. To avoid the barriers which had existed hitherto between court and community agency, provision was made for continuous communication and joint planning between the two agencies. Arrangements were further elaborated with a variety of community agencies to provide such additional services as detoxification, medical care, vocational counseling and training, job referral, housing, and welfare help. In the event of relapse, hospitalization was to be sought first; but more stringent sanctions would be invoked if needed. Caseworkers and public health nurses were to work intensively with small case loads of some fifteen addicts and their families, and assume responsibility for drawing in other community agencies and coordinating their common efforts into an effective helping service. The use of authority was to serve as the cornerstone structuring device.

While it may be argued that the program we have presented thus far is not very different from the customary practice of probation and parole officers, it must be reiterated that community agency workers were using these methods for the first time. It was an important function of this project to demonstrate how private agency workers could utilize borrowed authority in the case management of offenders and thus help reinforce the goals of supervision and rehabilitation.

HISTORICAL PERSPECTIVE

From a historical perspective, the use of authority in relation to the treatment of addicts had been conducted most recently in California in its Department of Youth and Correction, in New York State under the New York State Division of Parole, and in the Pennsylvania Division of Parole. As far as we knew, however, there had never been any joint cooperative projects focusing on the use of authority between a state agency and an agency such as ours. We believed it important to learn whether a social agency could work together with probation and parole, somehow utilizing the legal authority of these agencies to hold recalcitrant patients in treatment. The need for this approach had become increasingly apparent in recent years and had gained impetus from the enactment of New York State legislation creating a state narcotic addiction control commission, as well as from the new Federal civil-commitment legislation. It was clear that a wide spectrum of community agencies would be required to implement the controls established under this legislation.

BARRIERS BETWEEN COMMUNITY AGENCY AND PROBATION DEPARTMENT

In thinking back to the ways community agencies had hitherto worked with probation and parole, it was evident that there had long been cleavages and barriers between them. In the light of findings (such as those of Stanton and Schwartz) from psychiatric hospitals, we could now see these more clearly as destructive. This problem was especially focal in the case of addicts who had perpetually manipulated one parent against the other ("wedging") to achieve their own ends; it was noted that disagreements among staff were quickly followed by deterioration in the patient's behavior.

Our past experience suggested that community agencies often saw themselves as the "good mother" protecting the patient-child from the "bad father," the probation officer, and projected all blame upon him. This was even rationalized as constituting a good approach, since the parental image could be split in terms of a bad parent and a good parent, and the relationship with the good parent could thus be reinforced. Apart from rendering a disservice to the patient who already had problems with (male) authority, this tactic was resented by probation officers who had gone through much effort to refer a probationer to a community agency, but received little or no feedback regarding his progress. Probation officers often found a wall placed between them and their clients, especially if the addict was acting out and not progressing in treatment.

We desired to obviate such a contingency in the program established at the Washington Heights Rehabilitation Center by having the staff work very closely with the probation officer to overcome the danger of wedging. It was hoped the workers would not evade using authority directly even though the extent to which they actually possessed it was not always clear. Workers were encouraged to use their derived authority as fully as possible, relying on the probation officer to back them up in their decision-making and direction of the probationer.

To vitiate any possibility of disagreement and misunderstanding and to permit full sharing and joint planning in behalf of (and with the) probationer, full exchanges of information between the Center worker and probation officer were encouraged. In practice, therefore, a social worker or nurse could recommend that certain indicated actions be taken by the probationer, and could discuss them with the probation officer in advance to learn whether these steps were, in fact, feasible within the framework of the Probation Department. When a joint decision was reached, it was communicated to the probationer, and firm provision was made to ensure his adherence to it. It was assumed that the treatment staff would have problems in the area of confidentiality and "giving away" of information discussed privately with the patient. Efforts were therefore made to anticipate this problem by communicating to the patient from the outset, in the initial structuring conference, that there would be no withholding of information between the two agencies. The Center staff might then have less feeling about having "misrepresented" themselves to probationers and then having shared their information with Probation.

CASE PLANNING

Another difficulty encountered in joint management was involved in case planning whereby differences of opinion occurred in the diagnosis of the observed dynamics and subsequent planning. At times, this situation created tensions which resulted in conferences between supervisors and workers. Sometimes differences could not be resolved. However, the instances when sharp differences occurred were rare, and usually concordance between the conflicting viewpoints could be reached after a time.

To recapitulate, the addict was told at the initial structuring conference that he must cooperate with the worker and probation officer in any decisions made in his behalf; this discipline was reinforced in his subsequent contacts with the Center when, from time to time, he tested limits, acted out, or refused to keep appointments. At such times, the workers employed various devices, together with the probation officer.

STRUCTURING THE RELATIONSHIP

In terms of structuring the joint-management relationship, we proceeded in a graduated series of steps from the time of the probationer's arrest. The utmost effort was made to take advantage of the fact that the probationer had narrowly escaped going to jail and had "voluntarily agreed to accept probation and come into our program." This basic fact established the framework on which the whole structure was founded, and provided the means for shaping the subsequent treatment and joint-management relationship, which included the probationer and his family, caseworker or nurse, and at times, supervisors. At the first confrontation or encounter, the conditions of probation were carefully outlined to the probationer and his family, and the fact that he was expected to adhere very closely to them was emphasized. The joint relationship between the caseworker and probation officer, the probationer's need to come in regularly to the Center as well as to the Probation Department, and the need for the family to become involved were also carefully conveyed, as was the use of TLC spot-checks by either worker or probation officer to confirm abstinence. It was stressed at this first meeting that the probationer would be expected to move toward employment or training as quickly as possible, while avoiding relapse to drugs.

Although it was obviously difficult at such a comprehensive first meeting, the probationer was also given the opportunity to ventilate and articulate his negative or ambivalent feelings about the new arrangement. Definite appointment schedules were then set up; and from the very beginning a framework was established within which the probationer could be sustained and carried along. If he missed the first meeting, stringent efforts were made to ensure that he was adhering to the defined regimen, with a series of coercions being brought into play if he did not respond.

JOINT INTERVIEW

One of the most effective tools derived from the joint-management program was the joint interview which occurred between the client, probation officer, and caseworker. Joint interviews occurred periodically on the cases on an as-needed basis.

These arrangements for joint cooperation were complicated from at least two standpoints: the first involved training of the Center staff, which had no prior experience with the new variables. Our program required that they modify their traditional techniques and find ways to reach and hold these probationers. It should be noted that the schooling and experience of social workers and nurses had conditioned them against the use of this kind of authority in interagency cooperation. We found, however, that with the nurses the problems were somewhat less than with social workers. This could be explained by the fact that nurses had worked more consistently than social workers under the direction of doctors and therefore seemed to relate better to using authority and direction as part of a team. In addition, public health nurses had a concrete service to offer by attending to the health needs not only of the probationer, but of the entire family. This was found to be a very meaningful focus for help.

MEETINGS BETWEEN PROBATION AND CENTER STAFFS

A series of joint meetings between the Probation and Center staffs was planned so that they could regularly share their experiences and air their difficulties in implementing the initial agreements as outlined in the project proposal. In the course of these meetings, both staffs evidenced great diversity of approach in the ways in which they viewed the program and interpreted the variables. Continuous effort was required to clarify the actual program as devised by the Director and sponsoring agencies. The probation officers, for example, who were already burdened with their own case loads of twenty-five patients each—"Group II" (the control group)—concluded that their involvement with the "Group I" (joint-management Center patients) should be minimized. It was explained that even though the Center staff had primary responsibility for offering the treatment services, their involvement with regard to information-sharing, joint planning, and decision-making was indispensable at all times.

Sometimes it seemed difficult to implement joint management, as when probation officers succumbed to the wedging tactics of the probationer and agreed that he did not need to come to the Center after all, so long as he was reporting to them. Just as it proved difficult for the Center staff to implement the use of a firm authority and to test it out in all its ramifications, so probation officers appeared to have similar reservations about using an authority which they had practiced for so many years. They seemed to be moving toward a far greater permissiveness in line with the older social work image, an image enhanced by the social work training being encouraged in the New York Probation and Parole Departments. In many cases, however, a great deal of effort was expended by the probation officer in trying to enforce compliance with the probation regulations with regard to attendance at the Washington Heights Rehabilitation Center. Sometimes this led to the creation of situations which necessitated court actions and violations of probation. If joint-action management is to be reconsidered, casework treatment should be more selective.

USE OF AUTHORITY

As stated, the question of the Center workers' use of authority in the joint-management relationship and the degree to which they might actually exercise this derived authority continued to be a matter of concern until the very end of the program. This was exacerbated by probationers, who tended to confuse the probation officer and Center worker, or to view both as probation officers without any clear delineation of roles. The Center staff was better able to see its own role later as rather different from that of probation officers, in terms of helping the probationer voice his negative feelings, ambivalence, and hostility. As one caseworker expressed it early in the program:

> We need to establish for the probationer an image of ourselves as both identical with the probation officer and yet different. The goals of probation and those of our Center in relation to the probationer's rehabilitation are the same. However, our *method* of helping him may be different. One of the differences—and we must be conscious to convey this at the very beginning—is our recognition of the probationer's resentment over having come to our Center. We must remember that it is natural for him to feel angry to be forced to give up his way of life. While we support probation's conditions and help the probationer see that his way of life has led him into trouble, we must at the same time express empathy with the difficulty inherent in having to change. Let us remember that the probationer really doesn't want to be here; that behind his conformity there is suspicion and antagonism and anger and a desire to escape scrutiny.

A number of details needed to be defined as we went along, as, for example, who was to assume leadership for outlining the probation conditions in the initial conference (whether it could best be done by the probation officer as the actual authority, or by the Center worker, in order to underline her direct assumption of responsibility for this authority); and how one involves families not legally bound by this authority, though still very much concerned with the addict's problem. For a long time, there was considerable apprehension on the part of all staff members with regard to the use of authority and the joint-management relationship. One worker formulated the problems as follows:

> Probation officers and staff need to work out the details of joint-management very carefully. At what points should probation be made more visible or less

visible? Should we always insist mechanically on a patient's coming in regularly to the Center, or could this be varied? Should the supervision of the probation officer be relaxed if the probationer is doing well? What is to be done in the event he is deteriorating? What sort of procedures should be instituted for probationers who do not keep appointments? What is the basis for probation officers' home visits? Should they visit alone and without consulting the social worker as they have in the past, or must everything be planned with the Center worker? Should all information confided by the probationer be shared with the probation officer? Should the two workers make joint visits to the home? On what occasions? How could the probation officer and Center worker cooperate once a probationer has been referred to an outside agency such as a vocational training center or a hospital, in order to hold him there?

RELEVANCE FOR OTHER PROGRAMS

As has been mentioned, the findings of the joint-management procedures studied at the Center should have relevance for new programs being instituted under the New York State Narcotics Control Commission and the Federal Narcotic Addiction Rehabilitation Administration (NARA) Civil Commitment Program, for these programs will also use local aftercare and voluntary community agencies. The techniques worked out at the Center may be transferrable to other agencies working with legal authority not only in relation to addiction, but also to other problems. It has been noted that alcoholism programs are developing in the direction of using coercion, and authority is increasingly being considered for such problems as sexual deviancy. In the future, family agencies, mental hygiene clinics, and vocational and other kinds of community agencies may be able to use such a borrowed authority to help them cope with the very considerable problems posed by resistive or acting-out patients.

5. Reaching-Out

THE REACHING-OUT APPROACH USED was not a new concept, but was thoroughly grounded in the philosophy and practice of public health nursing and social work. Two main dimensions have generally been pointed up in reaching-out: behavioral and attitudinal. By *behavioral* we mean concrete acts on the part of the worker in moving beyond the confines of the agency walls to the patient, whether at home, at work, on the street, in prison and hospital, or wherever the therapeutic relationship indicates that such contacts would be beneficial. By *attitudinal* we mean the attitude the worker conveys of personal availability, receptiveness, and responsiveness to the patient's needs on an ongoing basis, even though he may have difficulty accepting the worker's approaches.

One of the underlying assumptions in using this approach is that the worker needs to reach out to the client in order to overcome the client's apathy, resistance, and lack of motivation, whatever their sources might be. Reaching-out was felt to be indicated when the client was inaccessible, either physically or emotionally, so that the worker needed to exercise aggressiveness (in the literal sense of *moving to*) or "intrusiveness" (intruding oneself into the family situation) to bring services to him.

This entailed a revision of the prevailing philosophy of agency help and called for a new spectrum of approaches and techniques, including, predominantly, the worker's seeking out of the client in every way possible, by meeting him at unusual times and places, working with him as required in his own physical environment rather than the office setting, and by maintaining evening office hours. It was agreed that all forms of reaching-out should be based on individualization, flexibility, and most important, a sound assessment of the client and his family in their social situation. It should never be applied mechanically. There were limits to its use and occasions when this approach would be contraindicated from a treatment standpoint. For example, it was conceivable that the case situation would at times not require reaching-out in the sense of visits or other contacts with the patient and his family. This might apply in cases where further contact or too persistent pressure would upset the precarious balance achieved, or where a patient's improved functioning suggested, as an indicator of our confidence in him, placing greater trust in his increased controls and reliability and allowing him to assume greater responsibility and initiative for planning the frequency and nature of contacts.

In terms of historical perspective, early caseworkers or "home visitors" as they were called, leaned heavily on such visiting, but the practice was largely discarded by private agencies in the thirties and forties, and emphasis was placed instead on weekly office contacts. The expectation in major private casework agencies was that their clientele would come voluntarily to the agency (usually located in a central part of the city at some distance from the actual residence) on a regular basis; adjust flexibly to a sharply defined agency structure; and meet the strict criteria of eligibility and the goals outlined by the agency, which often included resolution of the problem within a limited period of time. In the main, therefore, rehabilitation in social agencies was geared to the treatment of persons who had achieved a reasonably high level of personality and ego integration, were motivated to seek help of their own accord, and were prepared to engage in a sustained, long-term treatment relationship. What became clear, however, was that the majority of clients in many communities had

MULTI-PROBLEM FAMILIES

It was increasingly understood by social agencies that the majority of potential clients and patients fall into the category of "impulse-ridden" character disorders, and present very complex and long-standing problems because of the extreme degree of social pathology in all their familial and community relationships. In 1948, in the three-city study conducted by the Community Research Associates under Bradley Buell, it was learned that some 6 percent of St. Louis families accounted for 77 percent of the public assistance case load, 51 percent of the health service recipients, and 56 percent of the case loads in mental health and correctional agencies. In other areas, "problem families," as they began to be called, accounted for up to 88 percent of agency time in public assistance case loads and 90 percent in the health services.[1-3]

These families, subsequently described as *multi-problem families,* constituted sore spots in most cities, contributing heavily to the severe social pathology (including delinquency, drug addiction, alcoholism, chronic physical illness, prostitution, unwed motherhood), and accounting for a large part of the expenditures by welfare agencies, police departments, correctional systems, mental hospitals, child placement facilities, and other institutional and welfare programs. These were the marginal human beings who lived on the edge of the poverty line of failure, defeat, and rejection. In his book *Five Families,* Oscar Lewis subsequently discussed the concept of "the culture of poverty" in describing the intergenerational and self-perpetuating marginality of these families.

Multi-problem families were defined by the St. Paul Family Unit Report Study as having serious problems in *more* than one of the four basic areas of family life: social, health, economic, and recreational.[4] Elsewhere, the criteria for defining *multi-problem* were listed as: (1) a multiplicity of problems; (2) chronicity of need; and (3) resistance to treatment and handicapping attitudes,[5] to which we would add inability to cope with problems.

These deprived families appeared to be living in a perpetual state of crisis, too apathetic to seek help of their own accord or come to an agency unless driven by extreme necessity or by the law, or to continue contacts with any agency for more than a few visits. Though they could not be involved easily, it was useless to postpone working with them until the situation settled down, because this never happened. One needed to relate to them in the midst of their crises or not at all. These families also found it difficult to enter into any discussion of their feelings and behavior; their way of communicating seemed to be symbolic, through actions.[6] Reaching-out was the inevitable response of the helping professions, for it seemed the only means of involving these persons in treatment.[7]

NEW YORK CITY YOUTH BOARD PROGRAM

Following publication of the reports of the St. Louis study, the New York City Youth Board initiated efforts to "reach the unreached." In the monograph issued under this title and released by the Board in 1952,[8] one of the fundamental elements stressed was prevention; namely, recognition of the need to reach out, detect the behavior and personality problems of children and youth at the earliest possible time, and secure adequate treatment services for them in the incipient stages of their problems when they could best be helped. This, of course, ties in with our more recent conceptualization of a public health approach and primary prevention. The Youth Board program developed at this time was actively devoted to going out to help parents and children in some kind of trouble. Referral units and a casework service for families and children were established by the Youth Board in cooperation with the Bureau of Child Welfare of the Department of Welfare and with groups set up to work with youth gangs through use of "detached" or "street-gang" workers. The rationale for the new programs was, as indicated, the realization that many persons in need of services would not come in on their own and that agencies needed to go forcefully to them.

STUDIES OF MULTI-PROBLEM FAMILIES

Studies of these multi-problem families were later undertaken on a wide scale by different disciplines and in various countries. A survey by the Community Chest and Councils of the Greater Vancouver, British Columbia, area revealed that, by 1962, at least 143 communities of 260 surveyed in the United States and Canada were engaged in activities involving multi-problem families.[9] More recent efforts have tended to focus on the need to get at some of the chronic underlying social factors such as discrimination, lack of opportunity, and feelings of powerlessness and alienation; and to attempt regulation through such devices as guaranteed minimum income, medical insurance, and extension of social insurance, as well as elimination of urban and rural slum conditions.

REACHING-OUT TO FAMILIES

How to deal with these resistive clients in large numbers presented a considerable problem for the Youth Board in New York City. Although the children experienced difficulties, their parents seemed unable to come to school or to other agencies to discuss their child's behavior. Youth Board workers were convinced these parents were not "bad" or uninterested in their children, despite their lack of involvement or motivation.

In utilizing the techniques of reaching-out in these difficult cases, the first step, once the agency became aware of the family, was a home visit, to be followed by repeated home visits, if necessary, until the client was reached and able to acknowledge the existence of a problem. Reaching-out also became a part of every interview in that the worker assumed a more active and supportive role than was customary in the casework relationship. This was continued until the families indicated their willingness to be helped. However, because the units usually did not offer services themselves and relied on referral to outside treatment agencies, families often either failed to follow through on keeping appointments or else came only once or twice and then disappeared. It was learned that these clients were already known to many agencies, but their cases had been closed because of the severity of their social pathology. The philosophy eventually evolved by the Youth Board was that families which had been in severe need could not, in the beginning, accept an abstraction such as casework and its goals as being helpful. They could come to value it through direct experience, however, but that experience had to be brought to them with an intensity beyond that of mere case-finding. The investment of genuine interest in these families on the part of the caseworker was an indication of the worker's confidence in them and their capacity to change.

The caseworkers had previously had long practice in corrective intervention, but only after overt destructive acts detrimental to the community had occurred. The hope now was to intervene effectively in situations where breakdown would ultimately occur if no aggressive reaching-out were offered. Along with this practice, a philosophy needed to be developed regarding the social worker's responsibility, right, and authority to try to reach people in need of the services which the community was making available through the Youth Board. What resulted was a redefinition of the usual casework idea of client readiness or motivation, and a revision and modification of the traditional processes required to reach these families. Though home visiting had been considered a thing of the past, except for diagnostic evaluation, it gained importance as the first essential step in relating to these families. The Youth Board brochure, entitled *How They Were Reached*,[10] describes these initial approaches as follows:

> Resistance can stem from many sources; thus the strength of the original resistance does not necessarily signify untreatability, either through casework or psychiatric methods. A real contribution of the Youth Board approach is that it recognizes this fact and refuses to surrender in the face of the initial suspicion, distrust and hostility found in families which have suffered so terribly and for such a long time. The Youth Board refuses to equate resistiveness with untreatability; it accepts the community's responsibility to exhaust all constructive means of reaching such families, for the sake of the children, if not the parents themselves. While, admittedly, there are many who cannot be helped, there are also considerable numbers who require this kind of "reaching-out" if they are to be made accessible to the treatment methods that are offered.
>
> Sound community mental health demands the development of such programs wherever these families exist. These programs should help materially in the eradication of breeding areas of delinquency, ill health, emotional conflict and illness. New methods must be found to diagnose these families early and recognize beginning stages of social pathology, which if untreated would develop into family disorganization. Communities must be alerted to the urgent need for programs dealing with family breakdown. They must be prepared to

meet the cost of these programs. Unmet needs within the community will be discovered through the intensive work with disorganized families and these must be made available as they are needed in treatment planning.[11]

The Youth Board operated under the assumption that the children likely to come into contact with authority had primarily aggressive difficulties. Their brochures described these children as difficult to reach, suspicious of the authority represented by adults, and therefore unlikely to respond to traditional methods of help. It had also been anticipated that the families in which these children lived would display a multitude of social and emotional problems in such forms as serious economic stress, wretched housing, disturbed marital relationships, conflicts with the community, and physical and mental illness, and yet would be unable or unwilling to seek help for their children or themselves. It was also believed that very few of these children or their families had in the past been served consistently by the established voluntary agencies. The aggressive delinquent child and the disorganized family had often been considered "untreatable" or at least not amenable to treatment, and had largely gone unserved.

The findings of the Youth Board studies subsequently indicated that their initial conceptions were valid. It was discovered that several of the children in each family referred often had serious problems. Constant effort was required by both the referral unit worker and the workers in the contractual agencies to help families understand the need for service and to use it purposefully and constructively. In spite of the severity of the children's problems and the multiplicity of pressures from family groups, a surprisingly large proportion of these children were found to achieve a better adjustment at the time of the Youth Board's follow-up study. It was learned that, although the majority of these patients presented problems of a predominantly aggressive nature and had not been considered amenable to treatment, they did respond to appropriate reaching-out help. While much more needed to be learned about effective methods of work with these children and their families, ways could be found of communicating with them and helping them use available services.[12]

Reaching-out was thus designed to serve unwilling clients whose needs were very great, who were so damaged and deprived that they were a threat to the community, and who looked with suspicion and distrust on all efforts to help them. The objectives of preventing further deterioration, promoting cohesiveness, and enabling the persons concerned to discover and use their capabilities more effectively—all worthwhile goals in themselves—were dependent upon the creation of a climate in which motivation could be encouraged. This called for the utmost in terms of perception, flexibility, resourcefulness, and determination; achievement was not to be easily attained. The work itself was arduous, both physically and emotionally, with few of the satisfactions that ordinarily accompany competent casework performance. The work did, however, present a challenging opportunity to meet a substantial need and it did attract some adventurous, experimental, and capable social workers.[13]

HOME VISITS

Insufficient orientation of the total family, with associated inability to separate out of a maze of difficulties those which were fundamental to the functioning of the family, often led to indiscriminate home visiting and too little long-term planning, without effective results. This was caused, in part, by an erroneous impression of the concept of reaching-out. While it is true that the majority of multi-problem families were unable at first to travel to the agency, reaching-out does not only mean home visiting. It is much more comprehensive than the worker's physical attendance alone. To reach an unwilling client, to get at the person barricaded behind defenses, and to make contact, require time and a warmth and generosity of spirit which elicits responsiveness. Home visits simply constitute one of the first steps in this process.[14]

In recent years, the concept of reaching-out has been greatly expanded to include services, techniques, and perspectives not contemplated by the original home visitors to needy families or the agencies involved in the 1950's. For example, psychiatric teams may now fairly routinely visit the home for diagnostic and treatment purposes and even involve members of the extended family such as gardeners, neighbors, maids, and relatives, as well as the children themselves, in their family conferences. Such visits may consume a morning, a day, or a whole weekend.

INDIGENOUS WORKERS

Regarding narcotic addiction itself, the use of indigenous workers, ranging from ex-addicts and ex-criminals to residents of the local community itself (who are in a better position to understand and communicate the needs of local residents and assume leadership roles) has been greatly extended. The "Career Development Program" of Douglas Grant in Sacramento, set up in conjunction with the California Department of Correction several years ago, has used ex-addicts and ex-criminals in at least two important ways: (1) as a means of reaching-out into the community and bringing other addicts and criminals into existing programs, thus serving as a bridge from community to agency; and (2) working inside existing agencies to interpret the needs of their associates and to make these agencies more accessible by eliminating red tape and administrative obstacles.[15] Dr. Ramirez, the former New York City Narcotics Coordinator, has also used ex-addicts in Puerto Rico and New York City as a means of bringing addicts into his model programs[16] and as directing staff for his Community Orientation and Day-Night Care Centers as well as for his group "encounters."

NEIGHBORHOOD SERVICE CENTERS

Another recent major focus of reaching-out has been the establishment of Neighborhood Service Centers. The Youth Board had earlier established such a center in Harlem, and the Lincoln Hospital Mental Health Services Division later created three such centers in the South Bronx. These centers represent a significant advance from the original concept of reaching-out and deserve a detailed description. For this section, we shall cite below the work of Emanuel Hallowitz, former Director of this program.

> The Neighborhood Service Center is based upon the view that an effective community mental health program must not only provide services to those whose pathology has reached critical proportions, but also early direct assistance to those individuals and families who are under psychological and social stress before less reversible pathology sets in. An effective mental health program must identify and support those forces in the community conducive to the develop-

ment of mental health and combat those community forces destructive to the well-being of the community's inhabitants. The Centers' location, staffing and programs are specifically designed to assist in meeting these obligations. The sponsors of the Centers believe these Centers provide an opportunity for anyone in the neighborhood with whatever problem or trouble to walk in, immediately talk to someone about his concerns and get some degree of assistance. Thus the Center becomes the neighborhood first-aid station and a port of entry into various service systems. No appointments are required and there are no waiting lists. The first contact is not with the receptionist, but directly with the indigenous nonprofessional who is the main service agent. The fact that it is located in the midst of the neighborhood it is to serve provides a visibility and relatedness to the community. In addition, employment of neighborhood residents (nonprofessionals), their naturalness and the informal atmosphere confirm the "open door policy," and enable freer contact and communication on the part of the "clients" from the area.[17]

For the Lincoln Hospital, the Neighborhood Service Centers and the use of indigenous nonprofessionals have a potential value that goes far beyond that of a first-aid station or port of entry into the service system. Because the Center has become the place in the community to which residents can turn in time of crisis, it can keep abreast of the kinds of psychosocial problems with which the residents have to cope, the services needed and their availability. Similarly, the gaps, limitations and deficiencies in the formal service structure and the informal alternative arrangements currently employed by the community are detected more readily. Therefore, by documenting the specific needs of the neighborhood, the Center can stimulate existing agencies and institutions to modify their practices and programs or to develop new service models. The Neighborhood Service Center itself can initiate and demonstrate new kinds and patterns of service. Equally important, the Center becomes an important source of information on the nature of social changes needed as well as the focus from which action to implement the needed changes can arise. In other words, the Neighborhood Service Center and the indigenous nonprofessionals not only provide immediate help to individuals and families, but also stimulate or initiate on their own, the development of new patterns of service and mobilize and stimulate residents to engage in self-help efforts and community action.[18]

According to this report, it was decided to undertake a series of home visits to reach the persons in greatest need of help, those not in contact with some mental health or some social agency. A mental health team went directly into the neighborhood, knocked on doors, and talked with the families, inviting them to come to the Neighborhood Service Center with their problems. Instead of canvassing the neighborhood at random, however, these teams directed their efforts to families one or more of whose members were hospitalized. The mental health team that visited these homes consisted of a professional psychologist and a Neighborhood Service Center Aide. This arrangement had the advantage of combining the aide's sensitivity to the culture and familiarity with the people in the neighborhood with the professional's skill in interviewing and assessing psychological problems. To develop total participation in the team, the program and visits were discussed at length with the aides and their suggestions were incorporated into an overall plan of action.

The Neighborhood Service Centers were geared toward:

1. Increasing the competency of residents to cope with stressful situations.
2. Fostering an attitude of service to others and to neighborhood service.
3. Informing residents of services now available and how to make appropriate use of them.
4. Supporting, whenever possible, resident organizations dedicated to improving community services (recruiting members for their organizations, providing them, where feasible, with meeting space either at the Center or at the Lincoln Hospital, and assisting them with mimeographing, stationery, etc.).
5. Stimulating social and fraternal organizations to take an interest in community affairs (church groups, ladies auxiliaries, Puerto Rican home town groups, etc.).
6. Where necessary, organizing residents into groups to tackle specific community issues (e.g., block organizations, tenant councils, welfare client organizations).
7. Where community councils exist, assigning a professional and nonprofessional staff member to become active in these organizations for the purpose of providing additional leadership (influencing the development of these councils, seeking broader grass-roots representations, feeding into the council and its appropriate committees information on unmet needs, assisting it in developing a strategy of action for the neighborhood).
8. Assisting the neighborhood-based agencies to fulfill their purposes more adequately.[19]

In the New York Demonstration Center experience, conducted by one of the authors (Leon Brill) and concluded in 1961, the workers had agreed that a very great degree of extending one's self (reaching-out) was required with addicts. The acute crises which so often occurred with addicts prompted workers to go out of their way. This ranged from making evening home visits to personally delivering a needed letter when the mail was too slow, calling a patient who was "kicking" at home several times a day, or expressing direct interest in a variety of other ways. While this kind of reaching-out might later expose the worker to a flood of new unrealistic demands, the patient was nevertheless left with the feeling that the worker was genuinely concerned and available to him, a feeling which might in the future provide the basis for a real relationship.

In the New York Demonstration Center, casework was accomplished through traditional approaches, but also included a variety of the reaching-out techniques used with hard-core groups. Those patients who became involved in more extensive casework contacts at the Center seemed to be those manifesting a more pronounced dependency. The specific techniques used were supportive, including reassurance, direct advice, doing things for the patient, guiding him more carefully and consistently through each community agency contact and referral, permitting the expression of hostility (which was primarily directed toward agencies in authority), fostering the development of trust, making decisions for patients in crisis situations, bolstering controls, setting limits, "nurturing" them, and offering immediate recognition for positive accomplishments, however small.

Although there were variations in individual worker's practices, all arrived at certain common methods: the use of crisis situations to establish relationships, some permissiveness about appointments and openly manipulative demands; the frequent offering of concrete services. In general, the reaching-out approach was a very active and directive one, in part because of the need to meet the many real problems confronting the patient as a result of his many years of drug use.

In contrast to hard-to-reach patients, we became more aware of hard-to-reach agencies. Family agencies were hesitant about accepting patients who required extensive reaching-out or displayed considerable acting-out behavior, promised to require long-term attention, and presented little guarantee of success. Then, too, a case which seemed most promising to the Center staff might appear bizarre to a family agency worker. This was due in large part to the community agency worker's unfamiliarity with addiction and the overwhelming nature of its symptoms, which tended to make addicts appear uncomfortably different from other clients.

RECOMMENDATIONS

At the conclusion of the earlier New York Demonstration Center,[20] the following recommendations had been made:

The casework approach needs to be acting, directive, and reaching-out to counteract the addict's deep-seated dependency needs, passivity, poor motivation for change, difficulties in communication, and low frustration tolerance. Specifically:

1. The worker should be flexible about appointment schedules since the addict lives from crisis to crisis and seeks help, for the most part, only during such periods of crisis.
2. The worker must capitalize on the addict's reaching-out for help during these periodic crises in the hope of eventually establishing an ongoing casework relationship. Active assistance with the patient's emergency problems to the point of sometimes making a decision for him when he is immobilized may help the addict view the worker as a strong reliable person interested in his welfare. Reaching-out efforts should include repeated home visits, the sending of follow-up letters when a patient fails appointments, telephone calls, and availability in times of acute stress to reinforce the addict's image of the worker as a person committed and able to help him.
3. Addicts can best be reached and helped, at least at the outset, on the level of concrete and tangible services. Center workers believed these services to be the only appropriate ones to help ease pressures on patient and family, build a casework relationship, and ultimately involve the addict more meaningfully.
4. Helping the addict to utilize appropriate community resources entails a supportive process, plus step-by-step guidance through each agency contact to ensure that his characteristic impulsiveness and low frustration tolerance do not push him back into his typical patterns of avoidance of assistance and relapse to drugs. Consultation and close cooperation with community agencies serving the addict, coordination, continuity, and comprehensiveness of services are essential to obviate his getting lost between agencies.
5. The action approach appears to be indicated, at least in the initial stages of treatment of the addict, rather than attempts

to focus on intrapsychic or interpersonal conflicts, to work through problems, or to elicit feelings and develop insight.
6. The intensity of the relationship with the addict needs to be diluted. His inability to tolerate closeness may endanger his already precarious balance and stimulate the acting-out behavior to which he is so prone.
7. Before any regular treatment can be initiated with the addict, a period of preliminary treatment should be maintained until a relationship can be built and the addict becomes a client who can assume some responsibility in planning the resolution of his problems.
8. The caseworker needs to recognize and learn to control her negative reactions to the addict since he poses greater problems than other clients in terms of unrealistic demands, self-defeating operations, tendency to test the limits of the relationship, and repudiation of the social values and standards with which the worker is identified. Without condoning his antisocial behavior, the worker should try to remain nonjudgmental. At the same time, she must cope with the constant drain on her energies represented by the patient's dependency needs, apathy, and continued acting-out behavior.
9. In view of the addict's impulsiveness and strong resistance to change, as evidenced by his unwillingness to seek out or sustain any rehabilitative endeavors, the role of authority in relation to rehabilitation warrants further investigation. Attempts should be made to find the optimal balance between help and compulsion which can sustain the addict in a rehabilitation program.[21]

At the Washington Heights Rehabilitation Center, which followed the New York Demonstration Center[22] in 1962, reaching-out was practiced both by public health nurses and social workers in terms of their individual and professional orientations. It was felt that reaching-out to the drug addict would need to be consciously, consistently, and discriminately applied, always based on a sound psychosocial assessment.

In accordance with our concept of "starting where the client is," it was often necessary that staff meet him in his own environment. Workers assumed the initiative for sustaining contacts outside the agency walls as long and persistently as necessary. By work and action, they attempted to demonstrate that they were interested and involved. They were flexible about appointment schedules, sent follow-up letters when he did not keep appointments, called him on the telephone, visited him and his family at home, particularly at times of acute distress. They showed their readiness to enter into and deal with the crisis situations in which he was so frequently embroiled. This entailed offering emotional support and concrete help in an effort to ease his stress. Because his problems were manifold, often involving assistance from many sources, they needed to take reponsibility for coordinating interagency activity to ensure the integration of all agencies into an effective helping service. Referrals were often a long and arduous process entailing very careful preparation and follow-through, especially in view of most agencies' unreceptiveness to these patients.

Because of the client's basic passivity and frequent problem with communication, they also took the initative in verbalizing their concern, desire, and ability to help. They assisted the addict to put into words his anxieties and hopes, and demonstrated to him their acceptance of his right to feel angry, frustrated, rejected, hostile, and ambivalent. While they accepted him as a person, they at the same time conveyed to him that his behavior was destructive, in order to make him aware of the consequences of his acts and thereby help him obviate his destructive activities.

Reaching-out also meant conveying their partnership or treatment contract with him by offering support and concrete services to help him achieve abstinence, greater independence, and a higher level of integrated functioning. This meant a sensitive awareness of, and relatedness to, his aspirations and hopes, no matter how unrealistic they might seem at the time. Reaching-out required conscious utilization of advice and information-giving and even education. Staff could, for example, on the basis of their experience and by their constant reality testing, cut into the addict's distorted thinking, poor reality testing, or feelings of hopelessness. In these ways they hoped to bridge the gap from the delinquent subculture to that of the "squares," teaching their client the forms of behavior expected in conventional society and the new gratifications to be achieved thereby.

Their reaching-out needed to be implemented by involving the addict's family as well in a family-centered approach. In many cases, the families represented the hard-core multi-problem families described earlier. Because its functioning was closely intermeshed with the addict's, they needed to reach out to the family as persistently as to the addict. They needed (1) to understand the family's role in his problems, past and current; (2) to help families become their allies in his rehabilitation and also to separate themselves from him and permit him to grow up; and (3) to prevent further family breakdown and intervene in the cycle of intergenerational maladjustment.

CASE ILLUSTRATIONS *

Reaching-Out, by Nurse: Hospital Visit to Mother of Probationer—Mrs. E.

Frequent visits to see the probationer or family member in the home, jail, or place of employment served as a further expression of our interest and involvement.

On learning that Mrs. E., mother of a patient, was in the hospital and that the family was worried about her condition, I offered to visit her. When I arrived, I could understand the family's concern since Mrs. E. was in great distress. I obtained permission to bathe Mrs. E. and change her bed linen. She expressed her gratitude for this and felt so comfortable that she was then able to discuss her concern about her son rather than dwell on her own discomfort. She had resisted the nurses' earlier efforts to reach her, and this was the first time she could permit discussion of her son's drug use. The nurse's spontaneous response in relieving her suffering epitomized not only a high degree of empathy, but nursing at its best, and immediately established a rapport that had previously not been possible.

In another instance, Mrs. E. called in panic to say that her son was lying unconscious on the bathroom floor. The nurse advised the mother to call an ambulance immediately, indicating also that she would be right over. When the nurse arrived, the ambulance had not yet been called. She ministered to the patient, and as he was gaining consciousness, gave him black coffee and walked him up and down until he was over the effects of what had been a moderate overdose.

Reaching-Out, Offering of Concrete Service by Accompanying a Patient to the Clinic—Chico

Initially, and for the first six months of our involvement with Chico, we were aware of a great deal of resentment and resistance on his part to us and

---

* Some of these follow-up case illustrations are from the report of the Supervisory Public Health Nurse, Mrs. Yetta Deutsch. The rest are from nursing staff records.

the program as well. In spite of our continued efforts to involve him, his relationship with us remained on a very superficial level. He tended to break his appointments both at the Center and Probation Office, and constantly needed to be called in and forced to appear by the coercive use of probationary controls. A breakthrough seemed to occur at the time when I personally escorted him to the Social Hygiene Clinic, when he seemed, for the first time, to be viewing me with less suspicion, and began to believe that my interest in him was genuine and to his advantage. He came to me a short time later, confessed to using drugs, and requested our help in being hospitalized for detoxification. I responded immediately, to the extent of personally escorting him, his mother and younger brother to the hospital, by picking them up in my own car and delivering the mother and brother back to their home. They all seemed very grateful for this service, and from then on, there has been a remarkable change and improvement in our relationship. I am certain that I have now gained their confidence and respect, and am optimistic that, by continued intensive work with him and his family, I may be able to effect a change for the better in his future behavior.

Reaching-Out Through Worker's Helping Probationer Effect Reconciliation with Family—Peter

The staff's presence with advice, support, and reassurance at times of crisis did much to consolidate relationships. It was at these times that the workers helped mobilize community resources to meet a problem, by supplementing and reinforcing where the probationer could not fend for himself. For the probationer immobilized by his problems, a demonstration of "how to" was necessary, so that in the future he could follow the example set by the worker.

Peter came directly from jail because he feared going home. He had no money, and nowhere to go. After talking with him for a while, I realized that, more than anything else, Peter wanted to be with his family. He was doubtful of his reception, for his father had warned him that, if he were arrested again, he could not return home. Since he could not proceed on his own, I agreed to accompany him to his home where he sat down to talk to the parents. After some discussion, Peter's father, who was hostile throughout, consented to Peter's return home, provided he got a job. It was at this point that Peter asked if he could work in his father's plant. This Peter's father refused to do for very valid reasons; he had worked for his firm many years, and was fearful that his job would be jeopardized should Peter's drug use be discovered. Then Peter asked his father for a loan to get a job through a commercial employment agency, which his father agreed to do. This was an example of intervention at a crucial time when Peter could easily have rationalized his return to drugs. By reaching out to Peter and his family at a time of crisis, the family resources were called into play. The visit was timed for the end of the day, when all the family members could be engaged in solving Peter's problem.

I continued my supportive and reaching-out role subsequently by accompanying Peter and his family to clinics for treatment, for psychiatric consultation and later to a hospital for medical treatment. Peter saw my willingness to extend myself as tangible proof of my interest in him. It was during these informal trips that I had many opportunities to observe the family interaction as a basis for my continuing work with them.

Further reaching-out efforts were continued with Peter to keep him reporting for his appointments, combined with close planning with the probation officer. This consisted, at one point, of sending a joint-management letter indicating his case might be put on the court calendar because of lack of response. Most lapses of appointments were handled by an informal note or telephone call. The probation officer saw the patient once a month, and I saw him once weekly.

Reaching-Out to Entire Family and Collateral Facilities (Two Cases)

DAVID

With this particular probationer, emphasis was placed on family counseling. Within the framework of active reaching-out in the home of the probationer and his parents, David's basic problem was one of dependence upon his wife and parents and fear of his father especially. In an effort to help him assume more responsibility for himself and behave as head of his household, repeated visits were made and family conferences held. David looked to the nurse and his wife for support and relied upon the two to express his feelings for him. With the help of weekly one-to-one conferences, he gradually asserted himself more until he was able to speak out and confront his father openly.

My reaching-out at times extended to individual counseling with all members of the family in the home. An outgrowth of this was a form of marital counseling with the patient and his wife. David did not always see how his father's business decisions affected his marital accord. This was evident when he could bring home only $30 per week and even this amount was not reliable. At first, he responded by saying he felt his wife should be willing to support him since he had supported her, but with further exploration he could admit to feeling "put upon" by his father. It was then easier for him to see why his wife frequently "caught an attitude." Other forms of reaching-out included hospital visits when minor surgery was performed, and help in locating their first private apartment.

SALVATORE

A handicap with Sal seemed to be his inability to move from one activity to the other without strong support which required further reaching-out efforts. The mother's major asset was that she maintained a highly structured household for the boys though this was also a liability since it generated a great deal of tension and resentment as they came of age. Upon evaluation, Sal appeared to be immobilized by conflicting dependency-independence needs. I felt this and tried to help him maintain a steady course by conveying my approval and acceptance and offering him support in his efforts by accompanying him to the new agencies to allay his anxiety and help him follow through. I partialized his problems by helping him confront one part of them at a time with concrete advice and assistance. Sal seemed to chip only when his level of frustration had reached a peak because of difficulties with the family or when he met with what he considered to be insurmountable odds in attempting to find employment after finishing school. It proved helpful to try to anticipate problems and try to work them through or think them through as early as possible.

Reaching-Out, Attempting to Overcome Barriers in Communication—Manuel

In attempting to institute reaching-out efforts, many home visits were made to Manuel and his common-law wife, Inez. There were also contacts with Manuel's sibling, Lucia, in their home, and visits to the Bronx House of Detention and Riker's Island while Manuel was detained. Letters were also sent at other times as a means of maintaining contact with the patient and structuring our meetings. In attempting to build a relationship with him, it was felt that his difficulty in communicating in the English language tended to hamper my efforts since I could speak Spanish only haltingly. Manuel stated that he felt more secure when he could converse or write in the Spanish language and an effort was therefore made to capitalize on this factor, but it was not always successful. He was therefore referred to agencies in the South Bronx, which dealt with the Spanish-speaking population, and when referred to employment or skilled-trained agencies, an attempt was made to have someone available who could speak Spanish. This apparently was not enough since Manuel always returned to his former employer. To consolidate the relationship, joint conferences were held with the probation officer, Manuel, and myself, to supplement the reaching-out techniques. Joint visits with the probation officer were also made to Riker's Island. Manuel's feeling about being placed on probation was expressed when he told me he did not like the idea of having to come to the Center. He did come in more consistently to the Center after our Riker's Island visit.

REFERENCES

1. Buel, B. et al. *Community Planning for Human Services*. New York: Columbia University Press, 1952.
2. Pattern of Changes in Problem Families. Family-Centered Project of Greater St. Paul Community Chest and Councils, St. Paul, Minn., 1957.
3. Overton, A., and Tinker, K. H. Casework Notebook. Family-Centered Project of Greater St. Paul Community Chest and Councils, St. Paul, Minn., 1959.
4. Pattern of Changes in Problem Families. *Op. cit.*
5. Social Research Service of State Charities Aid Association. *Multi-Problem Families. A New Name or a New Problem?* New York, May, 1960.

6. Reiner, B. S., and Kaufman, I. *Character Disorders in Parents of Delinquents.* New York: Family Service Association of America, 1959.
7. Geisman, L. L., and La Sorte, M. A. *Understanding the Multi-Problem Family.* New York: Family Service Association Press, 1964.
8. New York City Youth Board. *Reaching the Unreached.* New York: New York City Youth Board, 1952.
9. Geisman, L. L., and La Sorte, M. A. *Op. cit.,* pp. 18–19.
10. New York City Youth Board. *How They Were Reached.* Mental Health Monograph No. 2. New York: New York City Youth Board, 1954.
11. *Ibid.,* pp. 10–11.
12. *Ibid.,* p. 90.
13. New York City Youth Board. *Reaching the Unreached Family.* New York: New York City Youth Board, 1958, p. 5.
14. *Ibid.,* p. 44.
15. Hallowitz, E. The Role of a Neighborhood Service Center in a Community Mental Health Program. (Lincoln Hospital Mental Health Services.) Paper prepared for the American Orthopsychiatrist's Association, March, 1967.
16. Unpublished brochure of Addiction Service Agency, 1967.
17. Hallowitz, *Op. cit.,* pp. 1 ff.
18. *Ibid.,* pp. 3 ff.
19. *Ibid.,* pp. 14 ff.
20. Brill, L. Rehabilitation in Drug Addiction. Mental Health Monograph No. 3. National Institute of Mental Health, U.S. Public Health Service, May, 1963.
21. *Ibid.,* pp. 47 ff.
22. Brill, L. Three approaches to the casework treatment of narcotic addicts. *Social Work* 13:25–35, 1968.

6. Evaluation Design and Sample

THE GOAL of the evaluation of the Washington Heights Rehabilitation Center was clear, but the methods for achieving it required further thinking through. The problem was basically that previous programs in the rehabilitation of narcotics addicts had as their primary and often sole goal, total abstinence for the addict involved in treatment. While movement in this direction was certainly one of the objectives of the Washington Heights Rehabilitation Center staff, we were also highly oriented toward the goal of socially acceptable functioning of the addict.

Given the complexity of rehabilitation needs, the research staff needed to determine the varieties of behavioral changes occurring in a population of addicts. That is, it was not sufficient to gauge whether or not the program was instrumental in enabling the addict to abstain from drugs, but also whether rehabilitation was being effected in a number of areas.

A survey of the evaluative techniques used by numerous other agencies engaged in the rehabilitation of addicts indicated that suitable, standardized techniques to measure the degree of rehabilitation had not yet been devised. Consequently, we felt that, given the goals of the Washington Heights Rehabilitation Center program, we needed to develop our own instruments and indicators of rehabilitation. This was done in conjunction with the treatment personnel, who cooperated by defining and making explicit their treatment objectives.

These major objectives were:

1. To alter the drug-use patterns of the addict in the direction of abstinence.
2. To alter, where indicated, the attitudes and behaviors of the addict in the areas of:
   (a) Work
   (b) Friendship and heterosexual relationships
   (c) Family responsibility
   (d) Leisure time activities
   (e) Criminality

In order to achieve these objectives, it was believed essential to maximize the ability of the treatment staff to maintain a desired degree of contact between the addict and the treatment milieu. Hence a third major variable could be added, although on a somewhat different level, that of:

3. Holding the addict in the treatment milieu.

PROCESS EVALUATION

A second aspect of the evaluation entailed dealing with the process of working with addicts through reaching-out and the use of authority in a community agency setting. Here, more qualitative material was to be gathered, through observation and interviews, of the more subtle changes which might be operative, but could not be made quantifiable, such as the new kinds of relationships being established with family, friends, etc. Of particular interest would be a description and examination of the functions and impact of the special rehabilitation efforts of workers in the Center as well as those used by the Office of Probation. This evaluation could be accomplished by directing attention to several general research questions:

1. What is the nature and content of reaching-out techniques as they are used in the Rehabilitation Center?
2. What are the forms of authority, and how may they be used in a rehabilitation program?
3. How does a staff develop and work with the techniques of authority and reaching-out?

This information was intended primarily for the use of the Project Director in following the development of the program. Much of this qualitative material has already been presented in previous chapters, and more will be presented in subsequent chapters.

In order to achieve the evaluation goals, various questionnaires and forms were developed to measure these areas of interest both quantitatively and qualitatively. The following is a brief description of the materials used in the evaluation (see Appendix A for Questionnaires and Forms):

1. *Initial Screening Form.* This form was designed to collect the information necessary to determine whether or not the probationer fulfilled the criteria for acceptance into the program. The probation officer completed this before sentencing.

2. *Intake Questionnaire.* This was administered by a research interviewer at the point of admission of each probationer into the program. The questionnaire covered the background data about the probationer, his work history, use of drugs, criminal involvements, peer group and addict relationships, and other base line data.

3. *Follow-up Questionnaire.* Like the Intake Questionnaire, this was administered by a research interviewer. Ideally, this was done one year after the probationer entered the program. This instrument collects data similar to that of the Intake Instrument so that change over the period of one year may be evaluated.

4. *Termination Questionnaire.* This was the same as the Follow-up Questionnaire and was administered by a research interviewer at the point of the probationer's termination of probation.

5. *Worker's Initial Evaluation.* Center workers filled in this form within the six-week period after a probationer began treatment. The data reflect the workers' evaluation of the patient in such areas as work, family, drug use, and health.

6. *Worker's Bimonthly Evaluation.* Like the Initial Evaluation, this was completed by each worker for every member of his case load, and provides data comparable to that of the Initial Evaluation, assessing changes over a period of time.

7. *Worker's Final Evaluation.* This provided data indicating how the worker viewed the progress of the probationer, or lack thereof, over the entire period the probationer was in the program. It covered the same areas as did the Initial and Bimonthly Evaluations. Each probation officer also filled out one for every case.

8. *Case Activity Analysis Form.* These were submitted each month by every worker. The data entered on it gave a picture of all the contacts (face-to-face or other communication) which took place each day of the month for each case. All contacts with the probationer, his family, his employer, his probation officer, other agencies, etc., were recorded, providing information regarding the purposes and the results of such contacts.

9. *Daily Drug Use Form.* These were kept each month by every worker. This instrument was designed to give information which indicated the worker's knowledge (or conjectures) of the probationer's drug use for each day of the month.

10. *Termination Status Form.* This form, completed by both the worker and the probation officer, indicated the summary status, at time of discharge, of each probationer in areas such as drug use, work, and school.

11. *Medical Reports.* These were filled out by the doctor who did the physical examination of the probationer.

12. *Psychiatric Evaluation.* All probationers were required to see the consultant psychiatrist for an initial psychiatric evaluation.

13. *Workers' Case Records.* These are the usual case records common to each of the disciplines (Social Work and Public Health Nursing). These records contained the workers' records of all material, interview and agency contacts, conferences, etc., relevant to the case, including their psychosocial assessment, periodic evaluations, and terminal impressions.

14. *Probation Officer's Case Records.* Like the Workers' Case Records, these provided an ongoing record of each case. The probation officer kept these records according to the methods common to his profession.

15. *Records of Thin-Layer Chromatography Tests.* These records report the results of urinalysis tests done at varying intervals for each probationer, and indicate whether the individual had used any

drugs of the opiate class (and certain others) in the previous seventy-two hours.

16. *Records of Arrests and Convictions.* These are also obtained from city and state sources to validate the evidence of reported interview data.

Behavioral changes were to be measured at three time intervals for all groups. An initial interview would be conducted at the time the probationer first came into the program, in order to derive base line information regarding each of the major areas in which behavioral modification was desired. Subsequent interviews were to be held one year later and at the termination of the program to learn whether these behavioral changes had, in fact, occurred. The qualitative data would be gathered routinely throughout the entire program, essentially in the form of case records. Since this material was not to be rigorously quantified, but was intended rather to provide an overview of certain areas of interest, we were spared many difficult problems that would otherwise have arisen.[1,2] In order to have a common time unit for comparison, it was the one-year follow-up which became the main source of evaluative data.

SEQUENCE OF STEPS FOLLOWED BY PATIENTS FOR TREATMENT AND EVALUATION

The following outline summarizes the various steps through the treatment and research program followed by patients.

1. Having been alerted to the program, the judge determines on the basis of the current charge and the prisoner's prior criminal record whether or not the prisoner should be considered a candidate for probation.
2. For those deemed by the judge to be potential candidates, a presentence investigation is ordered to determine eligibility for probation.
3. The presentence investigation is assigned to a member of the Special Narcotics Unit of the Office of Probation.
4. The probation officer conducts his investigation and also completes the Initial Screening Form to determine whether or not the individual is eligible for the program.

5. The probation officer recommends to the judge that the individual be placed on probation.

6. If the judge accepts the recommendation of the investigator, the individual is then placed on probation. At the same time, the judge makes known to the individual the general and special conditions of probation required by the program.

7. The case is routed to a probation officer in the Special Narcotics Unit for assignment to either Group I or Group II. The probationer is assigned to Group I if he resides either in the Washington Heights area or its environs, and to Group II if he resides in other sections of the city.

8. The probation officer notifies one of the two supervisors at the WHRC (social work or nursing) who assigns a social worker or a public health nurse to the case. Cases are assigned randomly to either discipline.

9. The Center worker meets with the probation officer, probationer, and any member of the latter's family who may be present for a prearranged initial structuring conference. This meeting serves to establish the joint-management relationship between the Center worker and probation officer.

10. The worker, probation officer, probationer, and family members review all the conditions of probation; the probationer is also advised of his responsibilities in the program.

11. An appointment is made for the probationer to come to the Washington Heights Rehabilitation Center for an initial intake session with his Center worker.

12. An appointment is made for the probationer to see a member of the research staff within one week from the initial structuring conference so that an intake questionnaire can be administered.

13. At the initial structuring conference, it is determined whether the patient is drug-free. If he is using drugs heavily, arrangements are made to hospitalize him for detoxification.

14. The probationer comes to the Center for his first meeting usually within a week after the structuring conference. At this point, for treatment and evaluation purposes, he is officially classified as a patient. Social Service Exchange clearance is initiated.

15. Within the same week, a researcher sees the patient for the research intake interview.

16. Within a few weeks from the first meeting the patient is seen by the psychiatrist for a psychiatric evaluation.

17. The patient is also seen by a medical doctor for a physical

evaluation. If a further medical work-up is indicated, he is referred to outside medical facilities.

18. As part of the worker's psychosocial assessment of the case, the family is visited.

19. Within six weeks after a patient's admission the workers are expected to complete a research Initial Evaluation Form for him (see Appendix). Similar forms are to be subsequently filled out on a bi-monthly basis.

20. Daily Drug Use and Case Activity forms are turned in to the research staff by the workers each month.

21. As part of the continuing treatment, the addict and his family are seen by the worker on a regular basis, usually at least once weekly.

22. When indicated, further thin-layer chromatography tests are given on a spot-check basis.

23. In cases in which this is indicated, patients are referred to other agencies for help with such specific problems as employment, welfare, housing, vocational rehabilitation, and so on. The Center worker maintains primary responsibility for treatment and coordination of services.

24. After a year, the patient is seen by a member of the research staff for a one-year follow-up interview.

25. At the termination of the program, the patient is discharged from probation as well as from treatment at the Washington Heights Rehabilitation Center. Referral is made to an outside agency if indicated.

26. The patient is seen by a researcher for a termination interview.

PHASING OF EVALUATION

The evaluation procedures began with the initiation of the main phase of the demonstration program on December 1, 1964. It was felt that patients should be exposed to the Washington Heights program for as much as a two-year period before a final evaluation was executed. Though it was hoped that the rehabilitation efforts would be carried out for at least two and one half years, this later needed to be modified to at least one year because of the extreme initial difficulty in obtaining referrals through the courts due to the reluctance of judges to place addicts on probation. This was to be followed by a period of final follow-up, preparation of data, analysis, and final report-writing. Though the evaluation functions had begun simultaneously with the program, it was necessary that they exceed the treatment phase by approximately one additional year (later modified to six months). During this evaluation phase, it was planned to terminate treatment and make arrangements for referrals of patients to other agencies. Evaluation thus became an integral part of the total demonstration program to be carried out during each phase.

CRITERIA FOR ADMISSION

The sample population under study was to include two groups of 100 male patients each:

1. The "Joint-Management" Group (Group I) described previously, in which service was to be given by the Center and supervision shared with Probation. This group was to be recruited from the Washington Heights area.
2. "Specialized Probation" Group (Group II). Services and supervision were to be provided solely by the Special Narcotics Unit of the Office of Probation. This group, which was to serve as a control for the main experimental group (Group I) at the Center, was to receive traditional probationary attention, but was to be grouped in small case loads.

Apart from considerations of residence, the program required that each prospective probationer meet certain definite criteria. These were outlined on the Initial Screening Form administered to each potential probationer by a probation officer. These criteria, which applied to both Group I and Group II, were specified on the Initial Screening Form as follows (see Appendix A):

Minimal Criteria for Consideration for Program

1. Client must appear to be a likely candidate for probation.
2. Heroin or other acceptable drug is drug of choice.*

* Acceptable drug of choice: heroin, morphine, pantopon, methadone, dolophine, demerol, paregoric, hycodan, percodan, dilaudid, codeine, cocinol, dicodid.

3. Has used heroin or other acceptable drug in daily continuous use for at least two weeks at some point during the last year in the community.
4. Has experienced withdrawal symptoms at least once.

If the answer to all these items was "yes," the client was eligible for the program.

Because the inflow of probationers to the program was very slow at first and threatened the ability of our program to continue, these criteria were changed as follows:

1. Client must appear to be a likely candidate for probation.
2. Anyone who has used heroin or other acceptable drug either in the past few years or currently.
3. Group I clients should be residents of the Washington Heights area or neighboring areas fairly accessible to public transportation.

Clear indication that these persons were increasingly being caught up in the addiction system was also required; e.g., delivering or selling drugs, hanging around with addicts, and so on.

Arrangements were made to ensure that patients were abstinent at the time of their admission to the program. This was important for providing common base line data. Most addicts, newly released from prison, were not taking drugs at the time of their referral. When initial interviews with the social worker revealed drug use, the patient was sent to the Metropolitan or Manhattan General Hospital for detoxification. Thus, all patients at the Washington Heights Rehabilitation Center began the program in a drug-free state.

PROFILE OF THE WASHINGTON HEIGHTS EXPERIMENTAL GROUP

Out of over 6,000 convictions involving narcotics in the Criminal Courts of New York City during the seventeen-month intake period from November, 1964, to March, 1966,* approximately two hundred

* We wish to acknowledge our indebtedness to Abraham Ford, Director of Analysis of the Criminal Court of the City of New York, who provided us with the data to make this estimation.

addicts were placed on probation.* This group of probationers provided the 94 cases for the Center's demonstration program (Group I) as well as the 86 cases in the control group (Group II), which was supervised and seen exclusively by the Special Narcotics Unit probation officers.

The procedure for the construction of the two groups was to be as follows: at the time of a prisoner's presentence investigation, his name was recorded in a central file at the Office of Probation. A listing was therefore available of all persons undergoing presentence investigation. From this list, the two groups were derived. Probationers for assignment to the joint-management group of the Washington Heights Rehabilitation Center were to reside in the Washington Heights area. Probationers for assignment to the "Probation only" control group would be drawn from the city-wide population.

We soon discovered that this strict division by residence could not be implemented, since relatively few of the probationers referred to us (7 percent) actually came to us from the Washington Heights area. We therefore needed to extend our boundaries to Harlem, East Harlem, and the South Bronx. Harlem and East Harlem provided us with 44 percent of the total Group I; and the South Bronx, an area in which there has been recent rapid growth of the addiction problem, produced 27 percent of our cases. The remaining cases (22 percent) came from other parts of Manhattan, principally those having direct public transportation connection with the Center as specified in the modified proposal.

Because of the differences in residence integral to the formation of Groups I and II, we were aware from the beginning that there would probably be some differences in population characteristics between the patients in the two groups. Awareness of such differences is important, for it is commonplace in the field of narcotics addiction to assume that whites are more likely to do better in treatment than Negroes or Puerto Ricans; older patients than younger patients; and the better educated than the less educated. These assumptions, although they have not been demonstrated in the past, tended to be borne out in our findings. Since many workers in this field believe that these variables may affect treatment outcome, we decided to control for these variables and present them later in our

---

* This figure was provided for us by the Office of Probation through Hy Efron, Supervisor of the Special Narcotics Unit, who asked the probation officers throughout the city to check their case loads, not only for those probationers placed on probation for a narcotics conviction, but also those placed on probation concerning whom the probation officer did not learn until later that they were narcotics users.

analysis. In comparing the differences between Group I and Group II, the results, although not striking, are nevertheless noticeable. Group II is somewhat different from Group I in having the advantage of an older (median age 21 years 3 mos. *versus* 18 years 11.5 mos.) and more predominantly white (52 percent white *versus* 11 percent white) population. No significant difference in educational background could be ascertained.

In light of this, the researchers decided that, since they could not stratify the sample on intake in order to balance out the experimental and control groups, they would instead derive a matched stratified sample through elimination of cases which were not matched in Group I and Group II. Consequently, in the different types of evaluation data that will be presented in subsequent chapters, Group I and Group II will also be compared after they have been stratified and matched on variables of age and race. (For results, see Table 6.)

SAMPLE GROUPS

We turn now to a brief description of Group I at the point of intake.* This is the group which was treated at the Washington Heights Center.

Sex

In order to reduce the number of variables, intake was restricted to males.

Age

Although we placed no age limitations on the probationers to be accepted, there was an automatic built-in restriction as a function of the legal system which, in New York State, ordinarily prohibits a minor under age sixteen from being convicted of a crime. Since all our cases had to be addicts convicted of crimes, those referred could not be under this age.

The age range of the patients entered into treatment as Group I at the Center thus ranged from the legal minimum of 16 years to a

---
* Appendix B presents selected characteristics for Groups I and II combined.

high of 51 years. They were a predominantly younger group, with a median age of 18 years 11.5 months. As may been seen in Table 1, only 29 percent were over the age of 21. This is in contrast to Group II, whose median age was 21 years 3 months.

TABLE 1. GROUP I, AGE OF PROBATIONERS ENTERING PROGRAM

Age	No.	Percent
16–17	23	24
18–19	31	33
20–21	13	14
22–25	12	13
26–30	7	7
31 and over	8	9
Total	94	100

Place of Birth

Fifty-four percent of our addicts in Group I were born in New York City and 16 percent in other parts of the United States; 28 percent indicated their birthplace as Puerto Rico, and 2 percent were born elsewhere.

When the Center patients were asked where they were raised, 84 percent described themselves as products of New York City. Addiction was, most certainly for this group, very much a result of these young persons' involvement with the New York scene.

Ethnicity

Racial characteristics have often been viewed by social scientists as a most important variable. As with social class, one can better understand group behavior on the basis of racial group identification. While we acknowledge the dubious value of the concept of race as far as its biological validity, we must recognize its social reality and influence on interpersonal interactions.

Prior to the 1930's, addicted persons were, in the main, white.[3-5] There were variations, depending upon geographic locale. In California, for example, the arrest records for narcotics violations from July 1 to September 30, 1930, show that 49 percent were Anglo-Saxons and Latins, 4 percent Negroes, 8 percent Chinese, and 39 percent Mexican.[6] This ratio, of course, largely reflects the relatively high proportion of Mexican-Americans in California. Generally, it would appear that populations in transitional status are those far more likely to seek out narcotics addiction as a technique of personal and social adaptation. Ball[7] has observed a marked change in the racial distribution of patients admitted to the Lexington Hospital between 1935 and 1965, in the direction of greater proportions of Negroes than before. The reasons for this are complex and not too clearly understood, but the general trend of certain minority groups in some large urban areas toward narcotics addiction appears clear.

The New York City Narcotics Register Project collects information on users of narcotic and other drugs. Their information indicates that in New York City, the largest racial group contributing newly reported cases to their registry is the Negro.[8] Of the cases registered, 46 percent were Negro, 27 percent were white, 24 percent were Puerto Rican, and no information was obtained on the remainder of cases. Negroes thus represent almost one-half of the addict population if we assume a close relationship between growing incidence and prevalence, with whites and Puerto Ricans each contributing one in four addicts to the population.

TABLE 2. GROUP I, RACE OF PROBATIONERS IN PROGRAM

Race	No.	Percent
White	10	11
Negro	43	46
Puerto Rican (white, Negro, and mixed)	41	43
Total	94	100

As seen in Table 2, the social characteristics of the patients referred to the Washington Heights Rehabilitation Center matched closely the figures available for the city for Negroes, while we received proportionately fewer whites and more Puerto Ricans. It is possible that this was due to the city's statistics being based on newly reported cases whereas ours were not, but it more likely reflects our desire to receive those probationers living closest to the Center, where whites are less likely to reside. This is in striking contrast to Group II, which was composed of 20 percent Negroes, 28 percent Puerto

Ricans, and 52 percent whites. If popular theory is correct, it would appear that in terms of response to therapeutic regimens, Group II, being largely white, should have enjoyed a large advantage.

A further breakdown of racial characteristics was made. The Puerto Rican community utilizes the term *trigueño* to describe mixed Negro and white physical appearance. Of the Puerto Ricans in our population, one-half were classified as *trigueño*, about a third were classified as white Puerto Rican, and the remainder as Negro Puerto Rican. These three categories are used because we feel the social definitions related to each are maintained both within the Puerto Rican community and outside it, and are likely to affect the way in which the person adapts to his world.

Religion

The Washington Heights Center group was weighted with persons who indicated that they were raised as Roman Catholics (57 percent). This is due to the fact that the Puerto Rican is heavily represented in our population and is likely to have come out of a tradition of Caribbean Catholicism. About four out of ten of Group I patients were raised as Protestants; and, within this group, the most prevalent denomination was that of the Baptist Church. The

TABLE 3. GROUP I, RELIGION IN WHICH PROBATIONERS WERE RAISED

Religion	*No.*	*Percent*
Catholic	54	57
Protestant	36	38
Jewish	3	3
None	1	1
Total	94	99*

* Because of rounding, the sum of the component percentages is not exactly equal to 100 percent.

explanation in this case is equally simple: the largest ethnic group in the Center's program was Negro, among whom there is a tradition of identification with the Baptist Church.

The religious composition of Group II was slightly different: 65 percent were Catholic, 23 percent were Protestant, and 9 percent were Jewish. Since religion is so clearly related to ethnicity in our sample we felt that it is not a particularly relevant variable for analysis.

It is difficult to say whether addicts continue to maintain contacts with religious institutions as much as their peers. What is more important, and this derives from our own past experience as well as the present data, is that some addicts appear to continue their contacts with the church as a significant force in their lives. The highly tolerant, social problem-oriented, store-front churches of the deprived areas are geared to meeting people in the contexts with which they are familiar. Similarly, there is a growing awareness in the Protestant and Catholic Churches that work with addicts must be a focus of their efforts.

Education

As Table 4 will indicate, only 16 percent of patients in Group I have completed high school or gone beyond. Data from Group II are not significantly different.

TABLE 4. EDUCATION LEVEL OF PROBATIONERS IN GROUP I

Level	No.	Percent
Elementary, incomplete	3	3
Elementary, graduated	12	13
High school, incomplete	64	68
High school, graduated	11	12
College, incomplete	4	4
Total	94	100

An 84 percent dropout rate may seem high when one notes that the dropout rate in all of New York City's public schools ranged from a high of 41 percent in 1951–1952 to a low of 36 percent in 1960–1961.[9] However, when one looks at the ghetto areas from which most of our patients come, such as, for example, Central Harlem, we find that 53 percent of the students in academic high schools and 61 percent of those in vocational schools dropped out without receiving a high school diploma.[10] If we add to this rate the dropouts in junior high schools, then the low educational backgrounds of our sample appear more normal in view of the ghetto backgrounds.

Family Situation

What was the composition of the childhood families in Group I? In 44 percent of the cases one or both of the parents were absent before the youth reached his sixteenth birthday. If a parent disappeared for any reason, this was most likely to occur before the youth reached his tenth year (80 percent of those cases in which parent was absent before the sixteenth birthday). In the main, it was the father who was absent, because of separation, desertion, death, and divorce (in that order). In the few cases where the mother was absent before the addict was sixteen, we were told by the addict that this was because of the death of this parent. About one-half of the mothers who "lost" their husbands continued on without remarrying or establishing a new relationship.

Four of the Center patients were "only children." The median number of siblings was two, yet we find the range varies considerably, with 21 percent of our addicts having five or more siblings. At the time of admission into our program, 71 percent of the patients continued to live in the homes in which they were raised. An additional 10 percent were living with their wives. One myth that has had some popularity is that addicts are migratory, moving constantly from rooming house to rooming house and seeing very little of their families. Ball has cast substantial doubt on this conception of the addict's residential patterns in a study of patients treated at the United States Public Health Hospital at Lexington.[11] His findings indicate little difference in addict mobility when compared with that of the general population. We questioned our patients about the amount of contact they had with their families in their homes, which included their families of orientation and procreation, and other relatives as well. In 96 percent of the cases, we found that they had a high degree of contact, i.e., that they saw most of the other household members on a daily basis. This is not to suggest that they were essentially "homebodies" bound to the activities of the household, but rather that they had homes in which their identity and membership were evidently established, and to which they could return in most cases, should this be therapeutically indicated.

We have already indicated that our patients came from socially and economically deprived areas. Many of the families were composed of dependent children without a male wage earner. It is not surprising that one-third of the Group I families received financial support from the New York City Department of Welfare. A further examination of the socioeconomic status of these families was made by the application of the Hollingshead Index of Social Position.[12] On the basis of information about the education and occupation of the father, we were able to place these families in a social position relative to the larger population (Table 5).

TABLE 5. GROUP I, HOLLINGSHEAD INDEX OF SOCIAL POSITION

Class	No.	Percent
Class I	—	—
Class II	4	5
Class III	4	5
Class IV	25	30
Class V	49	60
Total	82*	100

* There were twelve families for which information concerning the father's occupation and/or education was unavailable.

Class I on the Hollingshead scale approximates the position of the upperclass, more affluent members of our society. Class II represents the upper-middle class, and III is the lower-middle class. Class IV approximates the upper level of the lower class, and Class V brings us to the lowest socioeconomic level. When we use this device to isolate the positions of these families, it becomes clear that we are dealing with families likely to have economic problems of substantial magnitude.

Early Drug Use

The age at which an individual begins to experiment with drugs and the age at which he becomes addicted are likely to set certain behavioral patterns in motion that will determine his subsequent addiction behavior. This will be discussed in later chapters.

As seen in Table 6, 44 percent of the Center's patients indicated that they began to use some form of drug by the time they were 14. Thus the median age for onset of drug use was 14.6 years, whereas for Group II it was 16.0 years. Most began their experimentation with drugs in the classic pattern; 79 percent of our addicts began by smoking marijuana. Heroin was the first drug used by 12 percent

TABLE 6. AGE AT WHICH CENTER PATIENTS FIRST TRIED ANY DRUGS*

Age	No.	Percent
10–13	22	23
14	20	21
15	15	16
16	8	9
17	12	13
18	9	10
19	5	5
20 and over	4	4
Total	94	101†

* Alcohol was not to be considered for purposes of analysis of drug use.
† Percentage does not total to 100 percent because of cumulative error in rounding.

of our patients, with glue and barbiturates among the substances used by the others. Eighty-one percent of our patients indicated that heroin was the drug most often used after they became addicted. When asked what drug was used during the period in which they considered themselves most intensely involved with drugs, virtually all (98 percent) indicated heroin as the drug of choice for such periods.

At the point of initial referral to our program, a few of our patients protested that they were not heroin addicts. Some contended that they had taken only a few shots and were then caught. If we use the criterion of addiction, as defined by the Lexington Hospital, as two weeks of continual daily use, then all but a few of our patients were addicts. In these few cases, sufficient preoccupation with drug use was evident to justify our considering them as already involved in the addiction subculture, with a strong likelihood that their denial of regular drug use was not justified.

DRUGS AND CRIME

Most of the patients referred to the Center had arrests prior to the one for which they had been currently convicted and referred. For only 22 percent did the present charge represent a first arrest. In 10 percent of the cases, our patients had in excess of five arrests prior to the current charge. These addicts admitted to a wide variety of criminal activities in support of their habits, but generally conveyed the impression that these activities were motivated by the search for drugs. We sought to examine this claim, at least partially, by determining the number of arrests that preceded drug use. For Group I, only 27 percent of the total showed arrest on criminal charges prior to the onset of drug use; this was only slightly higher than in Group II. Although these data are not conclusive, they raise a question regarding the assumption that all addicts are criminals before entering into narcotics use.

READINESS OF PATIENTS FOR REHABILITATION

At the end of the research intake interview, our newly referred clients were asked, "Do you want any kind of help with anything at all?" (See Table 7.) *One-third* of all the patients said they could not think of any help they wanted. In view of the fact that in most cases these individuals had what we considered serious problems in many areas of living, this could only be interpreted as resistance to our efforts to bring about change. We might ordinarily assume that any person just arrested and convicted should feel he needed some help.

TABLE 7. AREAS OF HELP REQUESTED BY CENTER PATIENTS

What do you want help with?	*No.*	*Percent* *
My drug problem, help me stop using	23	36
Psychotherapy, to understand my problems better	7	11
Job	24	38
Get into school, educational problems	13	21
Other	5	8
Don't know	2	3
Do not want help	31	33

*Figures do not add to 100 percent since some addicts mentioned two or more categories.

It is interesting to note that, among those patients who expressed a desire for help, the request for employment assistance loomed as large as that for help with drug use. We did not necessarily interpret such requests at face value, for evaluative purposes. It has been observed that addicts will often tell treatment personnel the things they believe these persons want to hear, or else will verbalize their problems in terms of socially acceptable requests. For treatment purposes, however, we often felt it helpful to accept this request for job referral at face value and use it to help the addict move slowly toward the conventional goals of society within the context of a strongly structured therapeutic relationship. The attitude of this population to psychotherapy is indicated by the fact that only 11 percent wanted help that could be interpreted as conventional psychotherapy.

In summary then, what did the Washington Heights Rehabilitation Center have as its target population? These were poorly educated young men from economically deprived neighborhoods, whose drug use began at an early age, with concomitant involvement with crime. Most showed little motivation to change. From all we know about recidivism in addicts, as with other offenders, they constituted poorer prognostic risks since they were more likely to be nonwhite, reared in broken homes, and youthful.[13] They were, in brief, well suited for our experiment in the use of rational authority.

REFERENCES

1. Donabedian, A. Evaluating the Quality of Medical Care. Health Service Research Series, U.S. Public Health Service. May, 1966; pp. 166–196.
2. Kiesler, D. J. Basic methodologic issues implicit in psychotherapy process research. *American Journal of Psychotherapy* 20:135–153, 1966.
3. Kolb, L. Drug addiction, a study of some medical cases. *Archives of Neurology and Psychiatry* 20:171–183, 1928.
4. Lambert, A. *et al.* Report of the Mayor's Committee on Drug Addiction to the Honorable Richard C. Patterson, Jr., Commissioner of Correction, New York City. *American Journal of Psychiatry* 10:433–538, 1930.
5. Treadway, L. D. Further observations on the epidemiology of narcotic drug addiction. *Public Health Reports* 45:541–553, 1930.
6. California State Narcotic Committee. *The Trend of Drug Addiction in California.* Sacramento: California State Printing Office, 1931.
7. Ball, J. C. Two Patterns of Narcotic Drug Addiction in the United States. *The Journal of Criminal Law, Criminology and Police Science* 56:203–211, 1965.
8. Narcotics Register Project, *Report No. 1,* Office of Research, Department of Health, New York City, January 15, 1966.
9. *The Annual Report of the Superintendent of Schools in the City of New*

York, Board of Education. Quoted in *Youth and the Ghetto,* New York: Harlem Youth Opportunities Unlimited, 1964.
10. *Youth and the Ghetto. Op. cit.,* p. 181.
11. Ball, J. C., and Bates, W. M. Migration and residential mobility of narcotics drug addicts. *Social Problems* 14:56–69, 1966.
12. Hollingshead, A. B., and Redlich, F. C. *Social Class and Mental Illness: A Community Study.* New York: John Wiley & Sons, 1958, pp. 390–391.
13. England, R. W. A Study of Postprobation Recidivism among Five Hundred Federal Offenders. In N. Johnson *et al., The Sociology of Punishment and Correction.* New York: John Wiley & Sons, 1962, pp. 239–246.

7. Construction of Indices for Evaluation

IT IS AXIOMATIC in evaluation research that the criteria which one selects to evaluate a program must of necessity be related to the goals of the program as well as to the means employed.[1-5] In this light, it becomes extremely difficult, if not impossible, to compare the present experimentation in the use of rational authority with any other program, including those, such as the New York State, California, or Philadelphia projects, which use authority in the form of probationary supervision. Our program is not comparable with these in the first place because our primary goal was not abstinence, but rather "working in the direction of abstinence." Hence, recidivist rates alone could not become a meaningful criterion of success. However, even if our program had stipulated initially that abstinence alone was to be the goal, it still would have been impossible to compare our abstinence rates with those of any other program since the definition of recidivism varied considerably from program to program. A fuller discussion of the problem of using recidivist rates will be presented later.

Second, we did not have as a primary goal the lessening of conviction rates, since we felt that arrest and conviction rates in a population of narcotics addicts would be to a large degree a function of drug use. It is generally acknowledged that criminality in addicts is very often related to the need to procure large sums of money to purchase drugs from criminal sources.

Despite the difficulties and weaknesses inherent in using the conventional concepts of drug recidivist rates and arrest or conviction recidivist rates, we shall nevertheless attempt to present them as tradition dictates and provide some basis for comparisons with other programs. At the same time, we shall use these as two criteria of change when we compare the experimental group with the control group.

While the reduction of drug use, either through abstinence or by working toward abstinence, constitutes a worthwhile goal for a rehabilitation program, as is the reduction or elimination of antisocial and criminal activity which may result in arrest and conviction, there are always other individual goals explicit or implicit which emerge, related to the individual needs of each patient. In the Washington Heights Rehabilitation Center, as well as in the probationary control group, there were other areas of change that were considered desirable. Some of these areas overlap with the two criteria mentioned previously, namely, drug and criminality recidivist rates, but different standards and different criteria have been developed for them in the form of indices.

DEVELOPING BEHAVIORAL INDICATORS

Constant discussion was required between the treatment and research staffs to clarify the program goals so that their measurement could be researched. The researchers' insistence that the workers verbalize the criteria by which they evaluated the progress of their patients was usually responded to with vague intuitive statements. The problem of developing behavioral indicators was acknowledged by everyone to be difficult because of the treatment orientation, which required that the goals defined for each patient, as well as the methods employed, vary with each patient's needs. For example, the area of "Family Relationships and Involvements" had to be quickly abandoned as a variable for which behavioral indicators could be devised. The treatment personnel pointed out that for one patient the goal might be to return him to his family while for another it might mean separating him from them. This was further complicated by the fact that this might vary from time to time with any single patient. For all areas, we rejected the use of psychological indicators as not tapping the major concern of our treatment: moving the patient toward socially acceptable and desirable behavior. Another reason for this is the absence of evidence that we have as yet developed reliable psychological indicators which can measure progress in therapy, especially for lower-class patients.

After considerable discussion, the treatment and research staffs agreed that not all goals of treatment for addicts could be evaluated, but that a few should be considered. These included not only those which lend themselves to behavioral indicators, but also those in which the goals would be essentially the same for all. The four areas which were finally decided upon were drug use, criminality, work, and social conventionality (other than in the other three areas).

Criticism may be made of the middle-class bias of our criteria. However, we feel that this criticism would be true of most rehabilitation programs which attempt to move the patient in the direction of middle-class attitudes and behaviors even though they may be manifested in a lower-class context.

These four areas would, of necessity, have to be measured at different time periods. That is, in order to determine whether or not successful change has taken place in, for example, drug use over a period of time, one would need to know the status of drug use at time of admission into the program and the status of drug use at a specified time period after the patient had been exposed to the program. As noted previously, the time period chosen was the period of one year. Hence, the follow-up study of the patients engaged in the experimental as well as control programs was completed after a one-year period. In addition, the same data were collected from patients at approximately the time they were discharged from the program as well as at discharge from probation. The main purpose of these termination data was to provide base line data for a later follow-up of the patients.

SOURCES OF DATA

The sources of the data to be used for the criteria of movement in the four areas were standard stimulus instruments administered by the research staff. It was noted by the research staff at the very outset of the program that the perspective of the clinician is often different from that of the researcher. The clinician in this field, as well as many of the others discussed earlier, has great difficulty in establishing objective criteria to determine whether or not his own patient has progressed.[6] Although attempts have been initiated by some clinicians and rehabilitation workers, the application of an instrument which administers standard stimulus items is not a generally accepted practice in the field of rehabilitation. Even less so is it a practice in the field of probation and parole.

HEROIN MOVEMENT INDEX

The first movement index utilized was the Heroin Movement Index. All items selected for the index of heroin use movement were obtained for time period I, i.e., intake, from the researchers' intake questionnaires. The movement index was a function, therefore, of the status of the patient's heroin use at the time of admission to the program and his status one year later. In order to determine the status at intake, an index of heroin use was developed from the intake questionnaire by a combination of items in two antecedent time periods. First, the amount and frequency of drug use in the week immediately preceding arrest of the addict was determined. We then added the amount and frequency of drug use for a longer period of time, i.e., three months preceding arrest.

During the intake interviews, the addict was asked by our interviewer to tell what drugs he was using in the week prior to arrest. For each drug, he was also asked to explain how he took the drug; that is, whether by injection, sniffing, or oral use; how often he used the drug during the week; and how much he used during a given day on the average. The interviewer was thus carrying out instructions to ascertain the pattern of daily drug use. By this we meant, on the average, the amount of drugs used per day and the number of times during the day the drug was injected. It should be noted at this point that answers were not always given in terms of five-dollar bags, but in terms of three-dollar bags as well. In these cases, the coding personnel converted the three-dollar bags to their proportionate five-dollar bag equivalents. Although the information we obtained concerning the frequency of drug use during the week prior to arrest was detailed, we were unable to take frequency (i.e., number of times per day) into consideration because it proved too cumbersome to work with.

The data on drug use three months prior to arrest were determined through a reconstruction of the twelve-month period the addict had spent in the community prior to his arrest. The interviewers spent considerable time eliciting from the addict a detailed month-by-month account of his drug use for this twelve-month period; descriptions of his work history for the twelve months; the range of institutional involvement, such as hospitals, jails, treatment centers; arrests; convictions; as well as absences from the community. The research analyst then made the decision through an analysis of this material on the twelve-month chart in order to determine the extent of drug use for the period prior to arrest.[7]

The two sets of information from the two time periods (week preceding arrest and three months prior to arrest) were combined in the following manner, to be given rank positions ranging from low to high, for the index of heroin use at time period I, time of admission to the program.

The combining of the two time periods results in the Index of Heroin Use showing the number of persons fitting each category at time of arrest (see Table 2).

The decision to draw the data on heroin use from the period preceding arrest rather than the period preceding entrance into the program was based upon the knowledge that there is a time gap between the point of arrest and the time of sentencing by the court. During this period, the addict is often on bail and frequently either curtails or gives up completely his drug habit in order to impress on the judge that he has "mended his ways." To use this period would not provide meaningful base line data since most of the addicts were not using drugs during this time.

TABLE 1. CREATION OF HEROIN USE INDEX AT INTAKE

Drug use, three months prior to arrest	Drug use, week before arrest	Category on Heroin Use Index at intake
None	None	None
Low[a]	None	Low
Low	Low[d]	Low
Low	Moderately low[e]	Low
Low	Moderately high[f]	Medium low
Low	Heavy[g]	Medium low
Moderate[b]	None	Medium high
Moderate	Low	Medium high
Moderate	Moderately low	Medium high
Moderate	Moderately high	High
Moderate	Heavy	High
Heavy[c]	None	Medium high
Heavy	Low	Medium high
Heavy	Moderately low	Medium high
Heavy	Moderately high	High
Heavy	Heavy	High

NOTE: The criteria for classification of heroin use were as follows:
[a] less than one five-dollar bag of heroin per day.
[b] one to two five-dollar bags of heroin per day.
[c] over two five-dollar bags of heroin per day.
[d] less than one five-dollar bag of heroin per day—sporadic use.
[e] less than one five-dollar bag of heroin per day—regular use.
[f] one to two five-dollar bags per day.
[g] over two five-dollar bags per day.

TABLE 2. INDEX OF HEROIN USE AT INTAKE

Use	Number of patients					
	Group I	%	Group II	%	Total	%
None	5	5	4	5	9	5
Low	42	45	35	41	77	43
Medium low	5	5	4	5	9	5
Medium high	8	9	7	8	15	8
High	34	36	36	42	70	39
Total	94	100	86	101	180	100

HEROIN USE MOVEMENT SCALE

The same index was constructed from data gathered at the time of the one-year follow-up. Since identical items were used at both time periods and the same values were assigned to each item, it was possible to compare each patient's drug use during the two time periods and ascertain whether he had moved in the direction of greater or lesser involvement in drug use, or whether any change had taken place at all.

It was essentially the change that had taken place between the two time periods that was to be considered the evaluation variable in the area of drug use. This final evaluation scale we called the *Heroin Use Movement Scale*. It was constructed by comparing a patient's rank (low, medium low, medium high, or high) from the intake questionnaire and at the time of the one-year follow-up. Thus, for every patient for whom we had a follow-up, we were able to decide whether or not he had improved; that is, moved in a direction of a lessening of the extent of heroin use; whether he had deteriorated, that is, moved in the direction of greater involvement in drug use; or whether no movement had taken place at all. For this latter category, it was necessary to distinguish between two types of patients at the time of admission. One type of patient had come into the program using very little drugs, i.e., rated low on the drug-use index. For these patients, there was obviously little room for movement in the direction of lessening the extent of the drug habit, except for the possibility of abstinence itself. Since we did not necessarily take abstinence into consideration as a criterion for evaluation, it became difficult to compare this case; that is, a patient who showed no movement, but had started off doing well and had ended up doing well, with another type of patient who also showed no movement, but had, for example, started off as a heavy user and ended up as a heavy user.

In order to distinguish between these two types of patients, we decided that those patients who had started off well and had not deteriorated at all during the course of a one-year exposure to the program were to be placed in the category of those known as *stay-well*. In many cases, the category of stay-well was treated in a similar fashion as those who improved during the course of their exposure to the program. The rationale for this, in the area of drug use as well as in the three other major areas of evaluation, is that one of the major tasks of a rehabilitation program, particularly a program which treats a patient while he is in the community and is exposed to the distinctive social influences which may have originally precipitated his involvement with drug use, would be to act as a brake on the continuance or deeper immersion into socially disapproved behavior. Consequently, if we could prevent a person from becoming more deeply involved in criminality or the addiction system, which would appear from our previous experiences to be the more general trend of movement of an addict when there were no brakes on his activities, this would be considered a plus for this particular kind of program. In addition, since we viewed narcotics addiction as a chronic illness which must be treated for a lengthy period of time, it would appear reasonable to assume that a dramatic reversal of behavior is not very likely in the earlier stages of rehabilitation. Merely to stop deterioration of behavior becomes an accomplishment in itself. Table 3 presents the method by which the intake and follow-up indices of heroin use were matched in order to score the individual cases on the Heroin Use Movement Scale.

TABLE 3. CREATION OF HEROIN USE MOVEMENT SCALE

Rank at point of intake	Rank at point of follow-up	Category on index of heroin use movement
Low	Low	Stayed well
Medium low	Medium low	Stayed well
Medium low	Low	Improved
Medium high	Low	Improved
Medium high	Medium low	Improved
High	Low	Improved
High	Medium low	Improved
High	Medium high	Improved
Medium high	Medium high	Stayed poor
High	High	Stayed poor
Low	Medium low	Deteriorated
Low	Medium high	Deteriorated
Low	High	Deteriorated
Medium low	Medium high	Deteriorated
Medium low	High	Deteriorated
Medium high	High	Deteriorated

AN INDEX OF TOTAL DRUG USE

It should be pointed out that the Index of Heroin Use is specifically for heroin and not for any other kind of drug. Various attempts were made to construct an index of total drug use rather than heroin use only, but they presented problems analytically. How would a general drug index evaluate changes in drug of choice? One could consider, for instance, that if a person reduced the use of heroin while increasing the use of marijuana, this would be a measure of success. From one perspective, it is a success in that the cost of needed drugs is reduced, along with a reduction in many of the antisocial activities entailing criminal behavior. Also, since marijuana is far more accessible in the community than heroin, there is less likelihood of arrest. However, it is doubtful that most conservatives in this field would in any way respond favorably to this approach.

A similar consideration in the creation of a general drug index would be the additional problem of dealing with such drugs as amphetamines and barbiturates. Since it is generally accepted that, from a physiological point of view, barbiturates and amphetamines may be far more dangerous and harmful to the body than heroin, how are we to evaluate the decrease in heroin use and a concomitant switch to barbiturates or amphetamines? From the vantage point of some police forces, one might consider that this is more desirable, since it indicates movement in the direction of more legal drug use. From a physiological point of view, one would say that far greater damage to the body accrues from barbiturate and amphetamine use. For these and other reasons, we decided to consider the secondary drug use separately, and not to use it as a criterion for evaluation.

INDEX OF CRIMINAL INVOLVEMENT

The second evaluative area of improvement for which it was necessary to develop criteria was that of criminal involvement. Again, since one of the goals of the program was the reduction of criminal involvements, it was not sufficient to use only the usual criteria of either number of times arrested or number of times convicted to determine whether or not a reduction in criminality had occurred. To develop other criteria required more knowledge of an addict's criminality than official arrest records would show. Previous experience with addicts in other research projects had convinced us that, contrary to common sense expectations, we could rely to a great degree upon the reported information of addicts to give us a fairly truthful picture of such areas as criminality and drug use. In order to verify this, the research staff compared the pertinent information given to our interviewers with the fact sheet obtained from the files of the Office of Probation, which listed the addicts' arrests and convictions. We found, as we had expected, that in many instances the research staff had information concerning criminality which far exceeded the information known to both the Probation Officer and the official reporting of bureaus designed to keep track of arrests and convictions.

One might question the reasons why an addict would discuss previous criminal activities with our interviewers in such great detail. The reasons are several. First, we relied heavily upon quickly establishing rapport, which we consider essential for the utilization of a survey research-type instrument with this kind of population. The interviewers were all researchers, sociologists primarily, who had had at least several years of experience with drug addicts at various other installations in the New York City area and were aware of the problems of interviewing this population. The interviewers were thoroughly familiar with the terminology of the addict sub-culture, and all interviews that required even a minimal amount of sophistication in the Spanish language were conducted by one of our full-time research assistants who was a Ph.D. candidate in Human Relations at New York University and was fluent in the Spanish language. Such techniques as role-playing and role reversal were reviewed at the beginning of the program, as well as other methods for the training of interviewers, including tape recording of practice sessions and playback analysis of mistakes.

A second reason for the addict's willingness to cooperate with us was that, in this particular situation, he very often had no idea of the extent of information that had already been collected about him from official sources. Since this program was an alternative to the possibility of several years' imprisonment, the addict would very often try extremely hard to recall the finest details of his arrest and conviction record in order to impress upon us his willingness to cooperate with the program.

Information concerning criminality which had not resulted in arrests and convictions was also obtained. We stressed to the patient that we would in no way violate the confidentiality of the data. This contrasted with the position taken by the treatment staff who indicated to patients that for therapeutic reasons they would be sharing information with the Probation Officer. We also stressed that we did not want any details that could be incriminating. In other words, we were not interested in where a particular crime was committed or the names of other individuals involved in particular acts of criminality, or any other kind of information which would in any way be construed as evidence to be used for prosecution. The admission of the type of criminal act was obtained more readily than if we had asked for the specifics of any criminal act. It is for this reason, we believe, that most of the addicts were willing to tell us the different types of criminal involvements in which they had engaged.

After numerous experimentation with the kinds of information we would need for the variables for the index of criminal involvement, we finally decided upon four variables and four items of information. The first and most obvious of the variables was the number of times the addict had been arrested. The time periods of one year prior to admission into the program and one year of program involvement were selected for review, as opposed to the three-month time period used in measuring drug involvement. Whereas in a three-month period, one might get a fairly good indication of the involvement of an individual in the extent of drug use, the criminality picture would be less likely to emerge clearly during the three-month period. The number of times arrested during the past year became, therefore, a first-level indicator of criminal involvement.

This is not an absolute indicator, however, and one certainly must take into consideration the fact that, in the particular relationship the drug addict maintains with the law enforcement segment of society, it is likely that on several occasions during the period of one year a drug addict may be arrested and may not necessarily be found guilty of the crime for which he had been arrested. As is well known to researchers in this field, an addict who is identified as such in the community by the police may be arrested, even though there are no charges placed against him, merely to harass him or to use his presence to intimidate another person with the possibility of being charged with consorting with a known criminal. False charges, lack of evidence, and unconstitutional arrests are so frequent in the life of the drug addict that, in the last few years, more than one-half of all arrests of drug addicts did not result in a conviction. For example, as reported by the Criminal Courts of the City of New York, in 1965, of 10,557 misdemeanor arraignments for drug crimes, only 4,597 convictions were upheld by the courts; and, of 3,302 felony arraignments for drug crimes, 1,580 were held for Grand Jury.*

As a consequence of this fact, we believed that it was also necessary to include in the Index of Criminal Involvement the number of times convicted during the past year, on the premise that if a conviction did take place, it was probably an indication that a criminal act had indeed also taken place. It would appear reasonable, therefore, that the greater the number of times an addict is convicted during a one-year period, the more likely he was to have been involved in criminal activities.

It should be noted, however, that arrests and convictions may be indicative only of those addicts who are "failures" in the addiction system; successful criminals may not get caught so frequently. This theory has been advanced by psychoanalysts in the field of criminology, in particular by Abrahamsen[8] who has suggested that criminals who get caught may represent failures as criminals in the sense that, under the influence of emotional conflicts and guilt feelings, they wanted to get caught as a means of alleviating these feelings.

Consequently, to extrapolate to the entire population of drug addicts the knowledge that we have obtained from those who have been convicted or institutionalized as a consequence of being caught, may present an erroneous bias about the nature of addiction. However, since little other data are available at the present time other than those concerning addicts who have either been arrested or institutionalized voluntarily or involuntarily, we cannot speculate about the possible differences between addicts as failures and addicts who do not come into the public view through prisons or institutions. By extension of this notion, should a criminal avoid detection through extremely devious methods or because he is able to pass as a middle-class individual and hence incur less suspicion in a community, this would again cast doubt on the use of arrest and conviction reports as an absolute indicator of the degree of criminal involvement.

* We wish to acknowledge our indebtedness to Abraham Ford, Director of Analysis, of the Criminal Court of the City of New York for providing us with these figures in a private correspondence.

For this reason, a third variable was added to the Index of Criminal Involvement: the number of types of illegal methods used for support of a habit during the past year. The rationale for including this item of information was that getting funds to obtain drugs very often entails that the addict become skillful at several kinds of criminal activities. This is necessary because the likelihood of obtaining sufficient funds from a single kind of criminal activity appears to be rather slim. The addict population found in such urban areas as New York is not likely to be involved in the kind of criminal activities for which they might obtain large sums of money as a consequence of a criminal act. They are not bank robbers, extortionists, white collar criminals, or kidnappers. The kinds of criminal activities that our addicts engage in tend to be crimes against property, for which the amount of money acquired may be only a few dollars. As a result, the more varied the skills of an addict in different types of criminal activities, the more likely he is to be successful in obtaining the money he needs.

While it is somewhat fashionable among reformers in the field of narcotics addiction to believe that the criminality of narcotics addicts may be solely related to the necessity of having to steal in order to obtain the funds for the high cost of illegal drugs, many others are well aware of the fact that, in a number of cases, these addicts were criminals or serious delinquents long before they became addicted. In addition, intimate knowledge of the activities of drug addicts in urban centers indicates that many addicts will steal even though they may not be using drugs for a given period of time. As a consequence, a fourth variable was added to the Index of Criminal Involvement which would indicate whether or not an addict had been engaged in illegal criminal activities unrelated to his habit. It was our belief that the more likely an addict was to engage in criminal activities when off drugs, the more deeply involved in criminal activities he would be in general.

The data for all four variables came from the researchers' intake and one year follow-up questionnaires. Information regarding the number of times arrested and number of times convicted was in many cases verified by examination of the files at the Office of Probation. More important, however, the arrest and conviction information, as well as data for the Index of Drug Use, were obtained from a chart which reflected the twelve-month period in the community prior to the arrest which brought the patient into the treatment program. This period was reconstructed by the research interviewer with the patient. It represented a different method of gathering information, one in which it would be somewhat difficult for a patient to lie. This device served as an internal check on arrests and convictions. Wherever there was a discrepancy between the two parts of the questionnaire and/or the information from the Office of Probation, the data from any one of the three sources which indicated an arrest or conviction were used. This was done to maximize the amount of information concerning arrests and convictions under the assumption that if such information appeared in any one of the three places it was probably correct.

The number of types of illegal methods used for the support of narcotics habits came from two different questions in the intake as well as the follow-up questionnaires. One was an open-ended question which instructed the research interviewer to ask the addict "How were you supporting your habit at the time of your arrest?" In addition, we asked "How were you supporting your habit in the last six months?" and "How were you supporting your habit since you have been addicted?" The second type of question we asked in order to get a standard stimulus list was a specification of the various kinds of criminal activities or generally unacceptable methods one might employ to obtain funds for drug use. The list of specific activities to which the patient was to respond was gambling, begging, running numbers, having sex with men for money, conning, pimping, loaning works, copping (buying drugs for someone else), selling drugs, mugging, breaking and entering, and shoplifting. At the end of this list, in order to get any responses that had been previously missed and that he might have been reminded of during the reading of this list of twelve activities, we asked whether he had been involved in any other type of activity.

The fourth variable of the types of illegal methods used for reasons other than support of habit was obtained in a manner similar to that used to obtain the third variable. For the reasons specified previously, the weights of the scores assigned to the number of convictions differed slightly from those of the arrests. In addition, the weights assigned to illegal acts performed for money obtained not to support the habit were somewhat different from those of acts for money obtained to support the habit. The scores assigned for the four different variables are listed in Table 4.

The scores for each of the four variables were then added for

TABLE 4. INDEX OF CRIMINAL INVOLVEMENT AT INTAKE

Variable	Number	Score
1. Number of arrests during past year	1	1
	2	2
	3 or more	4
2. Number of convictions during past year	1	1
	2	3
	3 or more	5
3. Number of types of illegal methods engaged in to support habit during past year	0	0
	1, 2	1
	3, 4	3
	5 or more	5
4. Number of types of illegal methods engaged in for reasons other than to support habit in past year	0	0
	1	2
	2 or more	5

each addict, with resulting scores ranging from an actual computed low of 2 through a high of 17. The potential maximum was 19. This range of scores was collapsed into four divisions to facilitate the analysis of data. This collapsing is indicated in Table 5.

TABLE 5. INDEX OF CRIMINAL INVOLVEMENT AT INTAKE

		Number of patients					
Score	Rank	Group I	%	Group II	%	Total	%
2–4	Low	18	19	20	23	38	21
5–7	Medium low	27	29	22	26	49	27
8–9	Medium high	20	21	17	20	37	21
10–17	High	29	31	27	31	56	31
Total			100		100		100

The determination of which scores would go into the different categories was based upon an attempt to maintain a four-point scale and consequently to maximize the number of cases in each of the categories. It was acknowledged by the researchers that the determination of which scores constituted high as opposed to low marks is arbitrary in the sense that this is a function of the way in which the scores were distributed throughout the entire population. However, there did not appear to be any other reasonable method by which we could group the cases together which would enable us to utilize conveniently the index for analytical purposes, and which would not be the function of some sort of arbitrary decision related to the relative ranking of an addict in the total distribution of scores.

The only difference in the Index of Criminal Involvement at the one-year follow-up resulted from the fact that, in the course of one year's exposure to the experimental or control group programs, it is possible that a patient did not have any arrests or convictions. This had been an impossibility at the time of intake, since it was an arrest and a conviction which rendered the patient eligible in the first place for admission into this particular program. Consequently, at the time of the one-year follow-up, we changed the scoring for variable one to utilize a score of zero for no arrest and a score of zero for no convictions. Other than that, the scores were the same and the cutting points of the additive scores were exactly as they were at the time of intake.

The main evaluation index in the area of criminality, for the area of heroin use, was to be the Index of Criminal Involvement Movement. The construction of this index was accomplished in the same manner as for the Index of Heroin Use Movement. The relationships of the ranking at point of intake and ranking at point of follow-up and the subsequent scores of the index of movement are identical for the criminality movement and heroin use movement as indicated in Table 3.

INDEX OF WORK

A third major area for evaluation was the area of work. Since in this area, as in most of the evaluation, we decided upon the use of behavioral criteria as opposed to attitudinal indicators, it was evident that the amount of work—that is, the number of months worked in a specific period of time—as well as the stability of the work could become meaningful indicators of whether or not change had taken place in the patient population. To determine this, we

CONSTRUCTION OF INDICES FOR EVALUATION

decided to compare two variables in the area of work for two different time periods. Since work involves behavior which is best measured over a longer period of time, the first time period, as in the case of criminality, is a period of twelve months. The first variable in the area of work is very simply the number of months worked by the patient during the last twelve months he was available to work in the community. If, however, the patient was not available for work during the full twelve months prior to his admission into the program, by dint of the fact that he had spent several months or more in either a hospital or a prison, then the reconstruction on the chart for the twelve-month period was extended backward in time, so that a total of twelve months in the community was accounted for.

It was understood that the total number of months worked during a given period of time is not the only indication of work behavior that may be utilized for this particular index. Although there were many others, such as job satisfactions, income received, evaluation on the part of the employer, or advancement within the job, it was finally agreed that the second variable which would best indicate success or movement in this particular area would be that of job stability. Those persons, for example, who had eight jobs in a twelve-month period would, hopefully, as a consequence of the kind of rehabilitation they received through this program, be able to hold a job more continuously. Continuous employment over a nine- or ten-month period would indicate what appears to be a higher degree of adaptation to the work situation. The maintenance of an ongoing relationship with the concomitant possibilities of job advancement, as well as the satisfactions of being identified in a particular job role, would be a reasonable goal in rehabilitation. The notion of job stability is, however, a difficult one to define operationally. Upon examination of what it meant to us, we concluded that there were two aspects which must be taken into consideration simultaneously. These were the number of jobs held during the twelve-month period and the number of months spent on each of these jobs.

In Table 6 the final decision is indicated as to the method for assigning weights to take into account the stability of work performance over the twelve-month period the addict had been in the community prior to his arrest.

The procedure for scoring of stability requires some explanation. If an individual did not have a job and therefore did not work any number of months, he received a zero score. If the addict worked

150 AUTHORITY AND ADDICTION

TABLE 6. ASSIGNMENT OF WEIGHTS FOR JOB STABILITY

No. of months worked	No. of jobs held	Weight assigned
None	None	0
One	1 or more	0
Two	1 or more	0
Three	1	1
Three	2 or more	0
Four	1	1
Four	2, 3	*
Four	4 or more	0
Five	1	2
Five	2–4	*
Five	5 or more	0
Six	1	2
Six	2 or more	*
Seven	1	2
Seven	2 or more	*
Eight	1	2
Eight	2 or more	*
Nine	1	3
Nine	2 or more	*
Ten	1	3
Ten	2 or more	*
Eleven	1	3
Eleven	2 or more	*
Twelve	1	3
Twelve	2 or more	*

NOTE: In those cases marked by an asterisk, the score which was assigned to the case depended upon the weight the research analyst thought to be appropriate to the manner in which the jobs were distributed during the total number of months worked. The following table gives some examples of the possibilities of scoring these cases.

for one or two months in the community, he received no extra weight for job stability irrespective of the number of jobs held. It was our belief that, if a person worked only two months out of the twelve, even though those two months were on one job, this would not warrant any extra weight for stability. If, on the other hand, the addict had worked for three months on one job in a community, in one continuous three-month period, we gave an extra score of one to his Work Index.

In the category of four or more months worked out of the twelve months available in the community, however, we ran into

TABLE 7. SAMPLE SCORING OF JOB STABILITY WEIGHTS
FOR CASES MARKED BY AN ASTERISK IN TABLE 6

Months worked	Jobs held	Number of months on each job	Points scored for stability
Four	2	Less than 3 months on longest job	0
		3 months or more on longest job	1
Four	3	Less than 3 months on longest job	0
		3 months or more on longest job	1
Six	3	2, 2, 2	0
		1, 1, 4	1
Seven	2	3, 4	1
		1, 6	2
Nine	3	3, 3, 3	0
		1, 2, 6	1
		½, ½, 8	2
Ten	2	5, 5	1
		3, 7	2
		1, 9	3
Twelve	3	4, 4, 4	0
		2, 3, 7	1
		1, 1, 10	3

the difficulty of considering the length of time worked on the jobs in proportion to the total number of months worked. For example, an individual who had worked twelve months out of the twelve, but had five jobs during the twelve-month period might have had quite a different pattern of work stability than another individual who had also held five jobs and worked the full twelve months. In the former case, for example, it was conceivable that he had worked one month on each of four of the jobs and then held the fifth job for a continuous eight-month period. This would indicate to the evaluators a greater degree of stability for this person than for another addict who worked three months each on two jobs and then two months each on the remaining three jobs. The former should obviously get more added weight in the determination of stability than the latter.

We did not, however, find that it was possible to develop a completely mechanical way of scoring the stability which would give fairer representation in terms of an additional weight to the wide variety of patterns that emerged once the number of months worked went to four months of the twelve or beyond. Consequently, for each of the cases indicated in Table 6 by an asterisk, the decision as to what added weight should be given to the factor of job stability was made on a judgmental basis by the research analyst after much consideration. Since the possible combinations are obviously of an extremely high order of magnitude, it becomes impossible to specify every single situation which could be scored. We could specify what the scores would be for each of our cases, but this would not provide any more information about the method of judgment that we employed. We have, therefore, indicated for some of the possibilities the kind of weight we would assign to this particular combination and thus given a picture of the manner in which the judgment was made. Absolute replicability of judgmental material is never an easy task, nor is it very likely to be possible. We believe that in this case the decision on scoring should necessarily be a function of sound judgment on the part of a research analyst, rather than based on an artificially created system of scoring.*

The Index of Work at Time of Intake was constructed by combining the number of months worked during that past year in the community with the additional score for job stability. This is indicated in Table 8.

The two scores for number of months worked were combined and resulted in the distribution of scores seen in Table 9.

The work index at the time of the one-year follow-up was constructed essentially in the same manner as the Intake Work Index. There was, however, one exception which had to be taken into consideration. In all cases, the twelve-month period was a twelve-month chronological period from the time of admission into the program until one year later. It is possible that, in some cases, the addict may have been in an institution for part of the twelve months. He may have been in prison or in a hospital for a month or two, and consequently would not have had twelve months' time in the community

---

* The use of judgmental materials has had a long and respectable history in social and psychiatric research. Quite frequently, as criteria for judgment, examples are given rather than specific criteria. We find this method utilized, for instance, in C. F. Chapin's Social Status Scale in which interviewers rated "good taste" in home furnishings; Bales' interaction process analysis in which judgments of group interaction were made by observers; and also Lennard's *Anatomy of Psychotherapy,* in which judgments of the quality of statements made by the patients and therapists were made by coders rather than observers. Although the use of judgmental material may not be precise enough to satisfy some strict methodologists, we nevertheless believe there are situations in which it represents the most reasonable as well as the most accurate reflection of the phenomenon being observed. Without this sort of judgmental material, it would be well-nigh impossible for therapists to ever report their clinical observations in terms of attempting to find patterns of characteristics among their patients.

CONSTRUCTION OF INDICES FOR EVALUATION

TABLE 8. CONSTRUCTION OF WORK INDEX AT INTAKE

Variable 1—Number of months worked during past year in community		Variable 2—Job stability	
No. of mos. worked	Score	Possible score for stability	Total score
None	0	0	0
Under 3	2	0	2
		1	3
3 to less than 5	6	0	6
		1	7
5 to less than 9	8	0	8
		1	9
		2	10
9 or more	11	0	11
		1	12
		2	13
		3	14

TABLE 9. INTAKE QUESTIONNAIRE INDEX OF WORK

		Number of patients					
Score	Rank	Group I	%	Group II	%	Total	%
0–3	Low	30	32	17	20	47	26
6, 7	Medium low	25	27	25	29	50	28
8–10	Medium high	25	27	26	30	51	28
11–14	High	14	15	18	21	32	18
Total		94	101 [a]	86	100	180	100

[a] Errors due to rounding off of percentages.

available for work. For these cases, the amount of time worked was made proportional to the amount of time available in the community. In this manner, a person who worked ten months out of the ten months he was available in the community was treated in the same manner as a person who worked twelve months out of twelve months.

Following our earlier procedures, we then constructed the Index of Work Movement in the same manner as the Index of Heroin Use Movement and the Index of Criminality Movement, with the consideration that High on this index is the desirable end, whereas Low on the Indices of Heroin Use and Criminality was the desired end.

INDEX OF SOCIAL CONVENTIONALITY

In the initial structuring of the evaluation design, the research staff in consultation with the rehabilitation workers decided that one of the important areas which affect the rehabilitation of the addict is the area of conventional leisure-time activities. It has been observed by us in past programs that one of the important contributing factors which play a role in the return to drugs after an addict has been detoxified is boredom.

Participant observation with addicts over longer periods of time, such as several days, impressed upon certain members of our staff the problems that face an addict after release from a hospital for detoxification when there appears to be very little to do to occupy his time. When this is the case, one is often tempted to revert to an earlier behavior pattern which was pleasurable and which provided relief from the anxiety which often accompanies boredom. It is also fairly well accepted by vocational counselors and other rehabilitation workers that if an individual can be kept busy during specified time periods, there is less likelihood that he will begin to dwell upon himself in terms of problems and frustrations. The examination of leisure-time activities provides an additional dimension of addict adaptation which goes beyond the activities themselves. As clinicians are well aware, the ways in which individuals occupy leisure time provide clues to their values, goals, motivations, etc. Our task then was to select indicators of conventionality primarily related to leisure-time activities for a population which comes predominantly from the lower class.

A previous study reported by one of the authors indicated that the traditional notions of conventionality, which equate criminality with unconventionality, are not realistic in the population of drug addicts.[9] It was observed that addicts may be conventional and at the same time highly involved in criminality. Similarly, an addict may be conventional, although he is greatly involved in drug use, while another addict may be considered, using the same instruments and measurements of conventionality, just as conventional, even if he is not using drugs or is at the earlier stages of drug use. The notion of conventionality, then, is not a clear one when applied to addicts.

The kinds of items to be used in the measurement of conventionality should not reflect the ever-present class bias of rehabilitation workers. For example, one item we finally decided upon, after rejection of many others, was whether or not the patient contributed money to the household. Although this might be considered to be very likely a function of work, interviews and discussions with addicts frequently disclosed that this was not the case. True, some addicts who did work turned over part of their earnings to pay for the rent. But there also were some addicts who obtained all their money through illegal sources, primarily stealing, yet felt that they were obligated to pay for the rent, even though they were using stolen money for this purpose.

Other items were combined to create subindices within the Index of Conventionality.

The Index of Conventionality proved to be the most difficult to construct. Of the various questions related to conventional activities (see Appendix A, Intake Questionnaire), an index was finally constructed, consisting of three parts:

1. Part I. In itself an index of conventional activities.
2. Part II. Based on information about the respondent's contribution to the household expenses.
3. Part III. Based upon efforts at finding nonaddict friends.

Part I

In order to obtain the numerical indicators for this part, respondents were asked what they did in their spare time prior to arrest when both on and off drugs. These were open-ended questions and probed. Their responses were then scored as follows:

Activity	Score
Conventional social relationships outside the home	3
Sports outside the home	2
Various work in the household	1
Hang around, walk around, etc.	0
Other category	Range from minus 1 to plus 2, depending upon degree of conventionality

Since a respondent was asked to report five activities each when on drugs and when off drugs, the maximum score possible was 30. In following our principle of grouping to maximize the number of cases in each category, the cutting points and new scores assigned were as follows:

Conventionality	Raw score	New score
High	21–30	3
Medium high	16–20	2
Medium low	12–15	1
Low	0–11	0

In addition, a checklist of conventional activities engaged in was read to the respondent to determine whether he had done any of them during the past month in the community. These consisted of:

1. Go to any parties or dances.
2. Have a few drinks with friends.
3. Visit a friend who does *not* use drugs.
4. Read a book.
5. Play some sports.
6. Go out on a date with a girl.

A score of 1 was given for each "yes" answer, and these were scored as follows:

Conventionality	Raw score	New score
High	5–6	4
Medium	3–4	2
Low	0–2	0

These scores were combined with the previous scores of spare-time activities on and off drugs to provide a numerical indicator for the first part of the Index of Conventionality. The combination of the two scores resulted in a third score ranging from zero to seven. These scores were further collapsed into four categories, with a new numerical indicator given for each category.

Part I of the Index of Conventionality, therefore, was scored as follows:

Conventionality	Raw score*	New score
High	6–7	3
Medium high	5	2
Medium low	3–4	1
Low	0–2	0

* Spare-time activity plus checklist.

Part II

Part II of the Index of Conventionality emerged from our discussions around the area of growing responsibility on the part of the addict. The workers' views were that, in a lower-class population, each adult member or older child is usually asked to contribute toward the support of the household; or, even if an addict is living on his own, there is the expectation that he should pay for his rent rather than depend upon welfare. This item was held to be independent of work since many addicts will contribute a portion of their illicit funds to the household. Thus, a movement from noncontribution to contribution was believed by us to be a fairly sound indicator. This item, therefore, was based on information regarding whether or not the addict paid any of the family's rent or gave any other financial contribution to the household. Those who had contributed were scored "high" (2) and those who had not were scored "low" (0).

By comparison with Part I, it is obvious that we are giving fairly heavy weight to this single indicator. Since the entire problem of weighting is frequently based upon feelings or impressions about the real value of an indicator, there is no mechanical method by which we assign this relative weight compared with the totality of weights in Part I. Experimentation with higher or lower weights may be of some methodological interest, but we did not believe that it would significantly alter an individual's relative ranking in most cases.

Part III

Part III of the Index of Conventionality revolved around the importance for the addict of finding new friendships with persons who have never been addicts in order to emerge from the addiction system. It was our belief that the impact of addict friendships during the process of rehabilitation was decidedly detrimental to achieving our goals. Therefore, movement in the direction of finding new friends was considered a fairly important indicator in the area of conventionality. The information was obtained from an open-ended question, which was probed, as to where he went to find new friends. Those who had made the attempt to find new friends were scored "high" (2) and those who had not were scored "low" (0).

Total Score of the Index of Conventionality

Parts I, II, and III were then added to form the Index of Conventionality, with index scores ranging from 0–7 as shown in Table 10.

TABLE 10. INTAKE QUESTIONNAIRE INDEX OF SOCIAL CONVENTIONALITY

Score	Rank	Number of patients					
		Group I	%	Group II	%	Total	%
0–1	Low	25	27	25	29	50	28
2	Medium low	13	14	19	22	32	18
3–4	Medium high	23	24	26	30	49	27
5–7	High	33	35	16	19	49	27
	Total	94	100	86	100	180	100

The conventionality index at the time of the one-year follow-up was constructed in the same manner.

REFERENCES

1. Borgatta, E. F. *Research Problems in Evaluation of Health Service Demonstrations.* Health Services Research Series, U.S. Public Health Service, 1966. Pp. 182–199.
2. Donabedian, A. *Evaluating the Quality of Medical Care.* Health Service Research Series, U.S. Public Health Service, 1966. Pp. 166–196.
3. Herzog, E. *Some Guide Lines for Evaluative Research.* Washington, D.C.: U.S. Dept. of Health, Education and Welfare, 1959.
4. Shlien, J. M. Cross-theoretical criteria for the evaluation of psychotherapy. *American Journal of Psychotherapy* 20:125–133, 1966.
5. Wilkins, L. T. Research methods in criminology: A critical note. *International Review of Criminal Policy,* United Nations, No. 23, 1965. Pp. 47–55.

6. For another perspective on this problem, see D. J. Kiesler, Basic methodologic issues implicit in psychotherapy process research. *American Journal of Psychotherapy* 20:135–153, 1966.
7. For a similar handling of the problem, see J. A. O'Donnell, Research Problems in Follow-up Studies of Addicts, in *Rehabilitating the Narcotic Addict.* Washington, D.C.: U.S. Government Printing Office, 1966. Pp. 321–334.
8. Abrahamsen, D. *The Psychology of Crime.* New York: John Wiley & Sons, 1960; and lectures on Criminology at the Graduate Faculty of the New School for Social Research.
9. Brotman, R., Meyer, A., Freedman, A., and Lieberman, L. A Community Mental Health Diagnosis of Narcotics Addiction: A Preliminary Report on Social Types of Addicts. Presented at the meeting of the National Research Council, Ann Arbor, Michigan, February, 1963.

8. Comparison of the Two Groups

IN THIS CHAPTER, we shall compare the success of patients in the experimental and control groups. The comparison will be based on data regarding patients at time of intake into the program and at the one-year-in-program follow-up period. We shall first present the findings for our four main indices and then compare the absolute drug and criminal recidivist rates.

HEROIN USE

When we compare the two groups for progress made in this area, we find practically no difference between the experimental and control groups: 44 percent improved in Group I compared with 42 percent in Group II. An additional 17 percent and 16 percent for Groups I and II, respectively, who were doing relatively well in this area at time of intake continued to do well after one year. Those who were doing poorly at time of intake and did not improve, plus the patients who actually deteriorated amounted to 39 percent for Group I and 41 percent for Group II.

Since the usual pattern of the life cycle of addiction leads the addict from mild involvement in the addiction system to greater and greater involvement in terms of drug use and criminality, one indicator of success for a program which treats addicts who live in the community is the ability to apply brakes to their increasing deterioration as a consequence of drug use.

In this context, we can view patients as a kind of "success" who were not deeply immersed in the addict way of life when they came into the program and who did not deteriorate. These we have called the "stayed well" group, and they will be presented repeatedly in all our tables. If we combine this group with the "improved," then 61 percent of the cases in Group I were successes compared with 58 percent in Group II (see Table 1).

TABLE 1. INDEX OF HEROIN USE MOVEMENT

	Group I	Group II
Stayed well	15 (17%)	12 (16%)
Improved	38 (44%)	31 (42%)
All others	33 (39%)	30 (41%)
Totals	86* (100%)	73 (99%) †
Successes	53 (61%)	43 (58%)
Failures	33 (39%)	30 (41%)

* Number of cases based on those for whom we were able to obtain follow-up data. A later discussion will treat the other cases as failures (although we found that a number of these were doing well in some other program).

† Percentages may not add up to 100 percent due to rounding error.

In treating the data, whether by adding the category of "stayed well," or not, we would still conclude that the impact of the additional services provided by caseworkers and public health nurses appears to have made no appreciable difference in effecting a greater success rate for Group I. Both groups experienced a considerable amount of success in moving the addict in the direction of total abstinence. We shall later discuss our success with total abstinence.

CRIMINALITY

As in the area of heroin use, there appear to be little differences between Group I and Group II in reduction of criminality. In Group I, 67 percent improved, while in Group II, 63 percent improved. In combining the "stayed well" and "improved" categories as we did for the Heroin Use Movement Scale, we note that Group I could be considered successful in 77 percent of the cases and Group II in 78 percent of the cases. In brief, a considerable number in both groups improved (see Table 2).

TABLE 2. INDEX OF CRIMINAL INVOLVEMENT MOVEMENT

	Group I	Group II
Stayed well	8 (10%)	11 (15%)
Improved	57 (67%)	45 (63%)
All others	19 (23%)	15 (21%)
Totals	84* (100%)	71* (99%)
Successes	65 (77%)	56 (78%)
Failures	19 (23%)	15 (21%)

* Two cases could not be scored in each group because of lack of data for the significant items.

This apparent success in reducing criminality in a population which is usually heavily involved in crime is understandable when we consider that a new arrest and conviction would not only bring on a new sentence, but would be compounded by a violation of the addict's current conditions of probation. In addition, the intensive relationships established by both groups because of the small case loads permitted the probation officers in Group II and the joint-management teams in Group I a far closer scrutiny of the addict's activities. The value of small case loads to permit this kind of surveillance cannot be minimized with this kind of population.

WORK

In the area of work, Group I appears to have done somewhat better than Group II (see Table 3). Although there is no difference in the percentage that did well at time of intake and continued to do well—14 versus 15 percent, respectively—38 percent improved in Group I while only 23 percent improved in Group II. This additional 15 percent "improved" in Group I might have been expected in view of the more intensive efforts caseworkers make in this area as a consequence of their training and knowledge of vocational resources and training facilities available in the community.

TABLE 3. INDEX OF WORK MOVEMENT

	Group I		Group II	
Stayed well	12	(14%)	11	(15%)
Improved	33	(38%)	17	(23%)
All others	41	(48%)	45	(62%)
Totals	86	(100%)	73	(100%)
Successes	45	(52%)	28	(38%)
Failures	41	(48%)	45	(62%)

CONVENTIONALITY

In this area as in those mentioned previously, there appears to be very little difference between the two groups, although a higher percentage in Group I continued to stay well than in Group II (see Table 4). Successes in Group I, therefore, would be 71 percent compared with 60 percent in Group II.

TABLE 4. INDEX OF CONVENTIONALITY MOVEMENT

	Group I		Group II	
Stayed well	26	(30%)	13	(18%)
Improved	35	(41%)	31	(42%)
All others	25	(29%)	29	(40%)
Totals	86	(100%)	73	(100%)
Successes	61	(71%)	44	(60%)
Failures	25	(29%)	29	(40%)

SUMMARY

In looking at the four areas of movement for Group I and Group II, we note that the area of greatest improvement was that of criminality. This could be anticipated since it is in this area that social retribution is most usually borne out among our patients; that is, there was probably a greater incentive for a patient to reduce his criminality than to reduce his heroin use or increase work or conventionality. However, Group I is not more effective than Group II. For the other three areas—heroin use, work, and conventionality—we find that, although there is some difference between indices for the two groups, these differences are not great enough to indicate that either Group I or Group II had been considerably more successful in any given area of program goals. A good deal of success was achieved in all four areas, however. Considering the fact that these patients lived in the community for twelve months (or that portion of the twelve months which was later controlled for), the success in the reduction of heroin use or moving the patient in the direction of abstinence is to be taken as a hopeful sign that, if the program had continued longer and the patients had had more treatment, there would have been further increases in the extent to which patients could be moved toward abstinence. We shall consider the movement in all four areas as an indication that the program had a considerable impact on the addicts while they were under the jurisdiction of the probation officers in Group I and Group II.

In this program, we tried to get as far away from a unidimensional evaluative criterion as possible. Our research design called for separation of different areas of evaluation, according to the goals of the program. We took into consideration the fact that some programs may be successful only in certain areas of a person's life and not in others, and we distinguished the four areas which we consider particularly relevant in the rehabilitation of narcotics addicts. These areas have been analyzed separately previously. There is an advantage, however, from an analytic as well as descriptive point of view, in combining the various areas in which movement had occurred in order to obtain some sort of profile of movement for the entire population as well as for the different areas of change.

The need for this is obvious. While some patients may have done well in only one area, such as heroin use, they may not have improved in the areas of criminality, work, or conventionality. From the perspective of program goals, such a person would not be considered a successful case except in the limited area of drug use. By the same token, there are individuals who might have moved in a desirable direction in all four of the areas. To combine these, we decided to develop a simple Combined Movement Index by noting whether or not a person moved in the desired direction or stayed well in one, two, three, four, or none of the areas of change. This index is presented in Table 5.

TABLE 5. COMBINED MOVEMENT INDEX (FROM INTAKE TO ONE-YEAR FOLLOW-UP)

Success on number of indices	Group I	Group II
4	21 (24%)	14 (19%)
3	24 (28%)	23 (32%)
2	29 (34%)	16 (22%)
1	10 (12%)	15 (21%)
0	2 (2%)	5 (7%)
Totals	86 (100%)	73 (101%)

The Combined Movement Index again reflects what appears to be indicated in the individual areas of movement; that is, while Group I does not appear to have produced a dramatically better program in terms of results than Group II, there are certain differences in the results which indicate that Group I had a slightly greater impact than Group II. This may be discerned from Table 5 where we note that 86 percent of the Group I patients were considered successful on two or more of the four indices, as compared with 73 percent of Group II. It is possible that the impact of the more intensive casework did not become sufficiently developed in the brief period of one year as indicated here.

EFFECT ON MOVEMENT OF CONTROL FOR MATCHED VARIABLES OF AGE AND RACE

Group I seemed to perform slightly better than Group II, possibly as a consequence of the additional utilization of the intensive casework services. It is likely that, had Groups I and II been more closely matched on the variables of age and race which are commonly assumed to have a bearing on treatment outcome, Group I might have come out significantly better than Group II. In order to test this, a selected number of cases were chosen from both Group I and Group II which were now matched on these two variables. Matching Groups I and II in this way resulted in a reduction of the size of each group by approximately 25 percent. The movement indices were then run by the new matched samples. Table 6 presents the comparisons of Group I and Group II for the four movement indices as well as the Combined Movement Index.

TABLE 6. COMPARISONS OF EXPERIMENTAL AND CONTROL GROUPS FOR MOVEMENT OF PROBATIONERS BETWEEN INTAKE AND FOLLOW-UP FOR ALL INDICES WHEN GROUPS ARE MATCHED ON RACE AND AGE

	Group I		Group II	
	No.	%	No.	%
Heroin Use				
Success	36	59	30	59
Failure	25	41	21	41
Criminality				
Success	49	80	39	76
Failure	12	20	12	24
Work				
Success	30	49	21	41
Failure	31	51	30	59
Conventionality				
Success	43	70	30	59
Failure	18	30	21	41

A comparison of the tables for the stratified sample with the original sample indicates that there is practically no additional gain made by Group I when the two samples are matched. Therefore, in order to maximize the number of cases available, the analysis continued to use the original samples rather than the selected stratified samples.

TABLE 7. EFFECT ON COMBINED MOVEMENT INDEX (FROM INTAKE TO ONE-YEAR FOLLOW-UP) OF CONTROL FOR MATCHED VARIABLES OF AGE AND RACE

Success on number of indices	Group I		Group II	
	No.	%	No.	%
4	14	23	9	18
3	15	25	18	35
2	24	39	11	22
1	8	13	9	18
0	—	—	4	8
Totals	61	100	51	101

LOST CASES

Tables 1 through 4 presented findings of movement along different indices for those cases in which we were able to interview the patient at the time of entry into the program as well as one year later. For certain cases, however, this was not possible. Some patients, both in Group I and in Group II, had either absconded or disappeared during the course of the year and could not be located by either probation officer, research staff, or the police, so that bench warrants were issued. Some had moved to other cities (where other treatment agencies may have been involved) and consequently were beyond the scope of involvement in this particular program. Two addicts died, and one went to Synanon in California. In the presentation above, we left these cases out of the analysis of movement for the obvious reason that, unless we knew where they stood at the second time period, there was no means of comparing them with their position in the first time period and hence, no way to ascertain movement. It may be conjectured that people who abscond, disappear, or go into another treatment facility are not likely to have been doing very well while they were in the program. In order to acknowledge this likelihood, Table 8 will include the cases left out of the previous tables and will consider these cases in all instances as "failures." As a result, the percentage of "successes" will decrease somewhat for both groups in all areas. Although Group I still shows

TABLE 8. COMPARISON OF EXPERIMENTAL AND CONTROL GROUPS FOR MOVEMENT OF PROBATIONERS BETWEEN INTAKE AND FOLLOW-UP FOR ALL INDICES WHEN LOST CASES ARE INCLUDED AS FAILURES

	Group I		Group II	
	No.	%	No.	%
Heroin Use				
Success	53	56	43	50
Failure	41	44	43	50
Criminality				
Success	65	69	56	65
Failure	29	31	30	35
Work				
Success	45	48	28	33
Failure	49	52	58	67
Conventionality				
Success	61	65	44	51
Failure	33	35	42	49

up as being somewhat more successful than Group II, the difference is not impressive.

RECIDIVIST RATES

One of the more difficult tasks in the evaluation of probation or postprison behavior is the determination of the meaning and interpretation of the concept of recidivism. Although this may be viewed by some as an absolute, i.e., either a person is arrested in a given period of time, or he is not, goes back to the use of drugs in a given period of time or does not, etc., when one looks a bit more closely at such a phenomenon as drug use, the absolute criteria quickly dissolve into a set of value judgments.

Let us take, for example, a hypothetical program, in which 50 percent of the population after treatment returned to narcotics within the first month, an additional 20 percent the following month, an additional 10 percent in the month after that; so that by the third month 80 percent had gone back to drugs. Let us assume that the remaining 20 percent did not go back to drugs during the remainder of the year. Consequently, one might assume that the recidivist rate of this particular program was 80 percent in the first year on the basis of the statistic that 80 percent of the population had gone back to drugs during the first year. This is, of course, a usable statistic that could be compared across programs, but a closer examination will prove that it is, by and large, a meaningless statistic, as many often are.

Suppose, for example, that of the 50 percent who relapsed to drugs in the first month, 45 percent out of the 50 percent had experimented with heroin immediately after leaving prison, or whatever the program was; but, as a consequence of treatment, no longer felt that drugs had the same meaning for them and consequently discontinued use after trying it once or twice. On the basis of using the recidivist rate as a criterion for evaluation of the program, these cases, although they had not used drugs at any time for the remainder of the year, and had only "chipped" once or twice immediately upon exposure to the community, would nevertheless be regarded as failures and would be part of the 80 percent that would be classified as failures. Thus, using the number of persons who went back to drugs in a specific period of time can be an extremely deceptive indicator.

Another problem which emerges in the attempt to use drug-use recidivism patterns as the criteria for evaluative success is the absoluteness of the concept "on-off" drugs. While abstinence is certainly a desirable goal, it is conceivable, and it appears very likely on the basis of what we already know about addicts, that many, if not most, addicts will have an extremely difficult time remaining abstinent while in the community. This may even be independent of the effectiveness of any program in bringing about changes in other areas such as social behavior or changes in insight or any other changes that may be warranted. We may then have individuals who have been working "toward abstinence" rather than having become abstinent themselves. That is, an addict may, as a consequence of his involvement with the treatment program, alter his drug-use patterns so that he no longer uses as much drugs as in the past; or he may begin to use only sporadically, or his period of continuous drug use may be shortened with concomitant increased periods of abstinence. Other kinds of changes in drug use may have taken place, e.g., moving from heroin use to marijuana which, from the perspective of the law, may not be any more legal, but from the perspective of a therapist would indicate an increased ability on the part of an addict to cope with his problems,[1] although he may not yet be absolutely "cured."

O'Donnell[2] addressed himself to this problem in his "Research Problems in Follow-up Studies of Addicts." Pointing up objections to the absolute classification of addicts as abstinent or relapsed, he suggested that such a dichotomy biases findings toward relapse, groups very different patterns of behavior together as relapse, and minimizes the chances of learning about the actual factors associated with relapse and abstinence. Since most addicts alternate between abstinence and addiction, a more realistic pursuit would be to discover the variables that determine abstinence and relapse.

Another thoughtful approach to the problem of therapeutic change is that of Raymond Cattell. "It is naive to measure therapeutic change on a single dimension of sickness-to-health," he suggests.[3] "We are dealing with the totality of a complex personality change, which is multidimensional and should be treated as such." Cattell believes that research should, for the time being, concentrate on a broad spectrum of dimensions on the basis of which change can occur.

Another fact which merits attention in the evaluation of a treatment program is the considerable period of time required before new techniques can be successfully developed and their full impact exerted on the target population. Recidivist rates, therefore, must reflect not only the number of persons in a drug rehabilitation program who have returned to the use of opiates, but also the proportion of drug users in any given month who are presently using drugs. For example, it is hypothetically possible that, in a narcotics program treating 100 addicts, which opens its doors in January, all of the patients may use opiates during the month of February. Using the absolute criterion for recidivist rates, this program might be viewed as a failure insofar as 100 percent of the addicts treated returned to opiates within two months. It is also hypothetically possible that, from the month of March until the end of the observation period (one, two, three, or more years), none of these 100 addicts touched opiates again. Nevertheless, through the perspective of absolute criteria, 100 percent returned to opiates within two months. For these reasons, the absolute rate is of dubious value and should be presented with caution.

In reporting the recidivist rate, we need to make some qualification. In the first place, we should reiterate that, in our program, complete abstinence in itself was not considered to be a goal. Instead, the goal of developing a tolerance for abstinence and *working toward* abstinence was considered to be of major importance within the framework of the general rehabilitation of the addict in the limited period of only a year. Consequently, as long as a patient was moving in the direction of abstinence through the reduction of drug use and the alteration of his drug-use patterns, we regarded this as a sign of success. We feel that the notion of recidivism must be defined more realistically to indicate the beginning of a continuous pattern of drug use behavior comparable to the pattern of use for which the individuals were admitted into the treatment program, as compared with a specific act of drug taking which may be performed by the individual after treatment, but which does not coalesce into a regular pattern of drug use.

Second, the discussion of the problems of abstinence mentioned earlier in this chapter is equally valid here. Therefore, the cumulative rates for patients who returned to the use of opiates are highly deceptive figures. We present them here for the interest of the reader, with the conviction that even though they have been the predominant focus of all treatment programs and have caused more frustration and anxiety on the part of treatment personnel than any other, recidivist rates can be misleading in defining what constitutes progress in treatment and "success."

A much more reasonable indicator would be the number of "clean man days" an individual has, i.e., was drug-free while in the community and with access to drugs. Unfortunately, we could not locate another study utilizing this technique so that we could compare our findings, although we did have this data for our Group I patients. We recognized the difficulty of obtaining such data as well as the difficulty in determining "clean man days." Our evaluation attempts to deal with a modified version of this concept without using it as one of the mainstays of the evaluation.

HEROIN RECIDIVIST RATE

Thus far we have said very little about how many of our patients remained abstinent. This is in keeping with our desire not to overemphasize the criterion of abstinence alone as a goal in a rehabilitation program for narcotics addicts. We nevertheless realize that our colleagues in the field of narcotics rehabilitation are interested in learning to what degree we were successful in keeping our population from relapsing to the use of drugs. Certainly the governmental agencies, such as the Federal Bureau of Narcotics, which have committed themselves for the most part to the concept of total abstinence as the ultimate goal in the rehabilitation of addicts, are also interested in determining whether or not the treatment modality of rational authority is any more or less effective than the variety of other modalities used over the last forty years.

TABLE 9. MONTHLY RETURN TO FIRST SHOT OF HEROIN FOR GROUPS I AND II

Month*	Group I			Group II			Groups I and II		
	No.	%	Cum. %†	No.	%	Cum. %	No.	%	Cum. %
1	38	44	44	30	41	41	68	43	43
2	12	14	58	8	11	52	20	13	56
3	5	6	64	5	7	59	10	6	62
4	5	6	70	5	7	66	10	6	68
5	1	1	71	1	1	67	2	1	69
6	3	3	75	2	3	70	5	3	72
7	1	1	76	1	1	71	2	1	73
8	2	2	78	2	3	74	4	3	76
9	—	—	78	1	1	75	1	1	77
10	—	—	78	2	3	78	2	1	78
11	—	—	78	1	1	79	1	1	79
12	—	—	78	—	—	79	—	—	79
(Did not use heroin)	(19)	(22)	(22)	(15)	(21)	(21)	(34)	(21)	(21)
Base	86		100	73		100	159		100

* Each month represents patient month rather than program month, e.g., the patient's first month in the program.
† Cumulative percent using heroin at least once.

Table 9 presents the recidivist rate for the return to heroin use during the first twelve months in the program for each individual probationer. This information was obtained from the workers and probation officers, as well as from the results of the thin-layer chromatography urinalysis tests and the researchers' reconstruction of the twelve months in the program for each case. All relevant pieces of information on each case were collated by a research analyst who kept a separate weekly chart of drug use on each patient.

Table 9 indicates that there is no significant difference between Group I and Group II in regard to the rate of return to heroin or other opiates despite the slight differences in composition of the two groups. Over 40 percent of both groups used opiates within the first month. (This does not mean that they continued their drug use for the remainder of their year.) By the end of their first year, more than three-quarters of the patients in both groups had used heroin at least once. It is worthwhile to note, however, that the increase from the fifth through the twelfth months for Group I is 7 percent and, for Group II, 13 percent. That is, if our probationers used heroin, this occurred by and large within the first few months.

This might indicate to future rehabilitation programs that the crucial months for return to heroin are the first four months of treatment; in particular the first month when almost half used heroin after being detoxified. Consequently, if abstinence is to be considered a goal, treatment programs cannot be designed which attempt to build up the patient's strength to resist heroin over a gradual period of time. On the contrary, our data seem to indicate that the most intensive efforts, irrespective of traditional rehabilitation orientation toward drug addicts, should be directed toward the first one or two months of a patient's involvement in a treatment modality. This, of course, is contrary to general psychotherapeutic considerations. In most psychotherapeutic relationships, the first few months represent a development of the socialization of the patient into the relationship with the therapist, defining the role of the therapist to the patient as well as orientation of the therapist to the needs and aspirations of the particular patient. Presumably, therefore, the fullest impact on social behavior may not be reached until fairly late in the therapeutic relationship. If, however, society insists on immediate abstinence, more attention must be paid to the period of the first few months of the relationship.

It is interesting to note that the rate of return for Group II is extremely close to that of Group I. While the percentage of persons is high for both groups in the first month, the percentages are close and remain close throughout the entire year. We cannot at the present time explain why the rates should be so similar for both groups. Some factors which are relevant to relapse are apparently at work. They are probably crucial in explaining the reasons for the return to drugs when individuals are in the community after detoxification or hospital treatment. This observation is underscored when we compare the rates with those of other programs for which reasonably accurate data are available. For example, when we compare our rates of recidivism (combining Groups I and II in order to present the treatment modality of rational authority) with those of Riverside Hospital,[4] in which patients were treated for varying lengths of time in an institutional setting, the similarities are noticeable for the first six months.

TABLE 10. RATIONAL AUTHORITY CASES (GROUPS I AND II) COMPARED, BY MONTH, WITH RIVERSIDE HOSPITAL CASES

Month	Percent of cases returned to opiate use	
	Rational authority cases	Riverside Hospital cases
1	43	31
3	62	62
6	71	76
9	77	88
12	79	92

We note from Table 10 that the recidivist rates show a striking degree of similarity, although by the end of the twelfth month the use of rational authority appeared somewhat more effective. This is particularly interesting when we realize that, in the former case, the patients were being treated in the community through intensive casework and under probationary supervision in all cases. In the latter, the period in the community, although following intensive inpatient treatment, they had little intensive follow-up or probationary supervision. In spite of the differences in type of program involved, there appears this consistency of recidivist rates for the first six months. It would have been very useful to compare our data with those of other programs in which patients were being treated or followed up in the community after institutionalization. No such data was available, however. One might hypothesize that, at the present time, barring the use of drug-maintenance programs such as methadone maintenance, the rates of return to drug use may be fairly constant when addicts are returned to the community, regardless of treatment methods employed, whether it be the Public Health Service Hospital at Lexington, Synanon, prison, or treatment which maintains the patient in the community only.

This similarity of rates is also noticeable when we later examine the arrest and conviction rates.

The difficulty of comparing drug rates is evidenced by the differing criteria, methods of presentation, etc., of various other studies. For example, in the New York State Division of Parole study "Recent Developments in the Treatment of Paroled Offenders Addicted to Narcotic Drugs" by Meyer H. Diskind and George Klonsky (Albany: New York State Division of Parole, 1964), the authors state that ". . . *36% of all Parolees supervised in the six-year period were never involved in drugs*" (their italics). One could interpret this as suggesting that, compared with our findings, by the end of twelve months only 21 percent had not used opiates, and the New York State program was therefore more successful. If all patients had been in the program for the six-year period this would be likely. However, as noted on page 74 of the study, "The average period on Parole for the entire group was one year and two months." As a result, considerable numbers must have been under supervision for a good deal less than one year and it is therefore conceivable that if they had been reported on for a full twelve months, the percentage remaining abstinent would have decreased.

Similar problems are presented in an addendum to the Civil Narcotics Program *Five Year Progress Report* of the California Rehabilitation Center, Corona, California (October 27, 1966), in which the following statement appears: "A recent tabulation indicates a total of 265—206 men and 59 women, have been drug-free in the community for 18 months or longer." It does not indicate the total number originally committed to the program who subsequently did return to drugs, nor does it indicate the rate by month of return to drugs.

One of the best-known follow-up studies conducted by one of the authors was described by Hunt and Odoroff ("Followup Study of Narcotic Drug Addicts after Hospitalization," by G. Halsey Hunt and Maurice E. Odoroff, Public Health Reports, Vol. 77, No. 1, January, 1962, pp. 41–54). In their study of all the drug addict patients successfully completing withdrawal at the Public Health Service at Lexington, Kentucky, who lived in New York City, it was learned that 90.1 percent were readdicted. What they do not report is the rate of return by month.

When we look at the recidivist rates for all drugs, and not only for opiates, we find that the recidivist rate becomes higher for Groups I and II. This is because many addicts will use alternate drugs, including marijuana, amphetamines, and barbiturates, as a device to head off their return to opiates. We have not included alcohol in our consideration of return to drugs, even though it is a drug, since there is no social stigma attached to the use of alcohol for conventional or "straight" people. We are aware, however, that it is conceivable that a person who is addicted to narcotics and who subsequently abstains from narcotics, for one reason or another, over a long period of time, may at the same time have reverted to alcoholism as an alternate form of adaptation. We believe that this kind of data must be taken into consideration. However, since evaluation or follow-up studies generally do not include return to alcohol as a criterion for recidivism in a population of narcotics addicts, we shall not pursue the matter here. Table 11 presents the recidivist rates for return to all drugs:

TABLE 11. MONTHLY RETURN TO ILLICIT USE OF ANY DRUG FOR GROUPS I AND II

Month*	Group I			Group II			Groups I and II		
	No.	%	Cum. %†	No.	%	Cum. %	No.	%	Cum. %
1	45	52	52	33	45	45	78	49	49
2	15	17	70	8	11	56	23	14	63
3	6	7	77	6	8	64	12	8	71
4	6	7	85	7	10	74	13	8	79
5	1	1	86	1	1	75	2	1	80
6	3	3	89	2	3	78	5	3	83
7	1	1	90	1	1	80	2	1	84
8	2	2	92	2	3	82	4	3	87
9	—	—	92	1	1	83	1	1	88
10	1	1	93	2	3	86	3	2	90
11	1	1	94	1	1	87	2	1	91
12	—	—	94	—	—	87	—	—	91
(Did not use any drug)	(5)	(6)	(6)	(9)	(12)	(12)	(14)	(9)	(9)
Base	86		100	73		100	159		100

* Each month represents patient month rather than program month.
† Cumulative percent using some drug at least once.

As is evident from Table 11, practically all patients returned to some form of drug use by the twelfth month. There would seem to be some indication here that the need to use drugs even while in a treatment program may be so overwhelming for the addict population that, even though heroin is not being used, some drug is nevertheless needed to alleviate anxiety or help the addict face his perennial crises. In essence, then, the return to drugs of any sort very likely represents a repeat of the situations in which the drug user initially turned to drug use. This will be expanded upon in the following chapter.

We believe that the continued use of drugs by narcotics addicts represents a solution perceived by them, either on a conscious or unconscious level, of certain kinds of problems, primarily emotional in origin, with current social ramifications. This may suggest the need to sustain addicts upon some sort of medication or use a variety of techniques, including rational authority, while engaging with them in a therapeutic and rehabilitation relationship. If we assume that the drug serves the function of meeting rather strong needs on the part of the individual addict, then it is not surprising that, when an addict is exposed to the pressures of the community, where drugs are readily available, he will again turn to the device which meets his needs. The implications of this are discussed by Alksne, Lieberman, and Brill in a recent paper.[5]

PROGRAM DRUG USE INDICATORS

As noted earlier in this chapter, the percentage of patients who went back to the use of opiates at least once by the end of the twelfth month was approximately 80 percent. The deceptiveness of this statistic, even though it is of the type frequently cited in all follow-up studies, is that if a patient had gone back to drug use at the end of the first month, but abstained for the next eleven months, he would be treated no differently than a patient who had abstained for eleven months and had gone back in the twelfth month. Both would be considered failures in a given twelve-month period. However, it is conceivable that although considerable experimentation or chipping had taken place, the bulk of the patients did not go back to regular, continuous drug use.

To evaluate the effectiveness of a program, it is also necessary to gauge its capability for curbing the use of heroin in a specific population of addicts for a given time period. That is, was the program any more successful after treating a patient for twelve months than it was at the time he first came into the program? This is particularly important in an experimental program such as the W.H.R.C., in which workers were trying to learn and to develop new techniques during the same time period in which they were treating. In view of our finding that most patients had used heroin by their twelfth month in the program, one might conclude that the staff was less and less capable of treating successfully toward the end of the evaluation period than they were at the beginning.

In order to determine the relative ability to keep a population free of drugs over an extended time period, what we needed was a comparison for each of the months of the twelve-month period to ascertain whether an increasing proportion of patients were using drugs. That is, if a patient went back to drugs at the end of the third month and continued using them through the twelfth month, he would be recorded as using drugs during each month from the third through the twelfth of the program. If, as our findings in Table 9 indicate, an increasing number of our patients used heroin during the evaluation period, this should be reflected in our calculation of the percentage of patients using drugs in each patient month of the program. This is presented in Table 12.

TABLE 12. PERCENTAGE OF PATIENTS USING HEROIN IN EACH PATIENT MONTH

	Percentage using heroin	
Month	Group I	Group II
1	46	42
2	55	47
3	56	46
4	66	50
5	58	49
6	62	49
7	62	54
8	48	52
9	49	53
10	62	59
11	59	55
12	54	62

However, when we look at the percentage of patients using heroin each patient month (all those who were in the program for their first month, etc., until their twelfth month, while controlling for those patients not in the community), we find that there was not a steadily increasing amount of opiate use during the patients' twelve months in the program for Group I patients, while there appears to be for Group II. Group I fluctuates extensively from a low of 46 percent in the first month to a high of 66 percent in the fourth patient month, while Group II ranges from a low of 42 percent in the first month to a high of 62 percent in the twelfth month. When these percentages are graphed, they provide an interesting contrast, as shown in Figure 1.

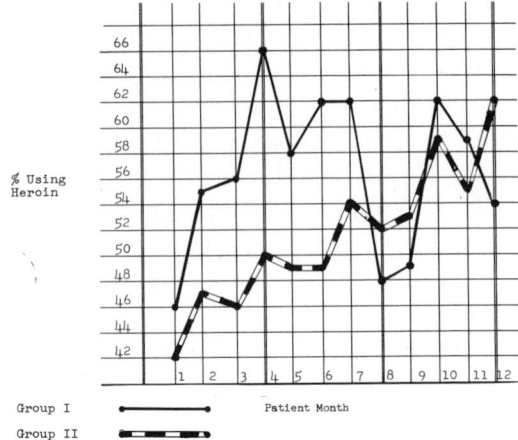

FIGURE 1. PERCENTAGE OF PATIENTS USING HEROIN IN EACH PATIENT MONTH

Group I ———
Group II ▬ ▬ ▬

Group II patients showed a steady rise in the proportion of patients using heroin each month, reaching Group I by the end of the twelve-month period, whereas for Group I there is a great deal of fluctuation. The variation in Group I may be attributed to the patients' testing of the rehabilitation workers to determine whether or not they would be as traditionally tolerant of the patients' drug use as they had been in other programs. The sharp drop from the fourth to the eighth month might be attributed to the awareness of the patients that the workers in Group I would not easily tolerate drug use, but since it would be unreasonable to assume that addicts would readily accept this awareness of the control of the worker over them, a new testing might ensue by the tenth month and then show a decline by the twelfth month. Had the program continued longer, it would have been of great interest to learn whether the slope would have approximated the low point of the eighth month, or perhaps have gone even lower.

For Group II, the lack of really sharp variation from month to month with a steadily increasing curve may indicate that the probation officers were not as demanding as our own rehabilitation workers in exercising effective controls. This is supported by our observations and the reports of the rehabilitation workers that, even in Group I, the rehabilitation workers had to exercise persuasion over the probation officers, so that they would be more authoritative and less permissive with regard to drug use.

When we compared Group I and Group II on marijuana use, we discovered an interesting fact. In every one of the twelve months, Group I had a larger proportion of its patients using marijuana without using heroin than Group II. The proportion varied from one-and-one-half times as large to five times as large in any given month, with the average approximately two-to-one. While it is difficult to explain why this should be so, the most likely reason is the lower age level of Group I patients who because of their age are more likely than Group II patients to associate with others who still use marijuana.

NUMBER OF CLEAN MAN MONTHS

Still another way of evaluating rates of success for a treatment program is the computation of the number of man months patients used drugs out of the total number of man months available for the patient to have used drugs while in the community. In other words, if 100 patients were treated for twelve months in the community, there would be a base of 1,200 man months during which the addicts might have used drugs. To compute this rate, we merely need to total the number of months each patient used drugs out of the twelve months in the community. The value of this sort of computation lies in its more realistic representation of the amount of drug use for a given period than the recidivist rate alone.

As noted earlier, the problem of how to treat two individuals, one using drugs only during the first month of treatment in the community and the other using drugs only in the twelfth month of treatment, remains a difficult one since, in the former case, he would ordinarily be considered to have relapsed during the first month of treatment and in the latter during the twelfth, whereas in actuality, each has used only one month during a twelve-month period. The way out of this difficulty lies in the use of the man-month concept.

Unfortunately, we were able to present the data only for the Group I patients since records were not kept with sufficient accuracy for Group II patients. Of the ninety-four persons in Group I who spent a year in the program, a number did not have a full 12 months, but only 11 months in the program, while others were in the program only a few months before they were terminated either because of long-term imprisonment or institutionalization in another treatment center such as Synanon. This reduced the total to 1,112 man months. Also, there were twenty-four man months for patients regarding whom we had no information, plus seventy-three man months of patients who were out of the community due to short-term hospitalization or prison. This left us with a base of 915 man months during which patients could have used drugs while they were in the community.* Of these months, 252 (28 percent) were months in which there was regular opiate use.† In an additional 254 months (28 percent), there was some "chipping" with heroin.‡ This leaves a total of 409 (45 percent) months in which there was no opiate use at all.

This success rate must be compared with our earlier findings (Table 9) in which, by the twelfth month, 22 percent had not used heroin; and the presentation in Table 12 in which, during the twelfth month, 54 percent were not using heroin. This emphasizes the complications in attempting to use abstinence as a criterion for evaluation. Which criterion is the best? Perhaps the drug movement scale is a better measurement? This cannot be answered with any degree of certainty, since the values and goals of the treatment program obviously have a bearing as to which indicator is more realistic. This is certainly something which should receive more attention in the field of narcotics addiction, and criminal recidivism generally.

CONVICTION AND ARREST RECIDIVIST RATES

As indicated in Table 13, there is little difference in arrest rates between Group I and Group II. However, a 48 percent arrest figure for the first year is not necessarily indicative of the extent of criminality of this particular population. As we know from previous analysis of statistics, convictions upheld by the court normally number only half the number of arrests. As noted in Chapter 7, less

---

* A *man month* is here defined as more than a half month in the community.
† *Regular opiate use* is here defined as using during half of the month or more.
‡ *Chipping* is defined as some opiate use for less than half of the month.

TABLE 13. ARRESTS BY MONTH FOR FIRST TWELVE MONTHS OF PROBATIONERS' INVOLVEMENT WITH PROGRAM

Month*	Group I			Group II			Groups I and II		
	No.	%	Cum. %†	No.	%	Cum. %	No.	%	Cum. %
1	6	7	7	10	14	14	16	10	10
2	7	8	15	1	1	15	8	5	15
3	3	3	18	3	4	19	6	4	19
4	4	5	23	3	4	23	7	4	23
5	4	5	28	5	7	30	9	6	29
6	4	5	33	1	1	32	5	3	32
7	2	2	35	2	3	34	4	3	35
8	1	1	36	1	1	36	2	1	36
9	4	5	41	2	3	38	6	4	40
10	2	2	43	1	1	40	3	2	41
11	4	5	48	2	3	42	6	4	45
12	1	1	49	3	4	47	4	3	48
(Was not arrested)	(44)	(51)	(51)	(39)	(53)	(53)	(83)	(52)	(52)
Base	86		100	73		100	159		100

* Each month represents patient month, rather than program month, e.g., the patient's first month in the program.
† Cumulative percent arrested during year.

than half of drug arraignments result in convictions. This attrition of 50 percent is reflected in our data; only half of the arrests in our sample resulted in convictions. Table 14 presents the rates for convictions on all charges.

This finding raises a question which bothers many professionals in this field and concerns the degree to which there is harassment by the authorities of persons known as addicts in the community. As public reaction to the addict increases, not only is the addict's self-image as deviant and criminal augmented, but the gap increases as well between the conventional traditional world as represented by the police, and the addict who feels and sees himself as persecuted by the authorities. This, of course, cannot be gone into more deeply in this study, but the degree to which the perception of authority as a prosecuting and persecuting institution may be instrumental as a self-fulfilling prophecy in maintaining the addict in the addiction system is something that should be explored in future research.

TABLE 14. CONVICTIONS BY MONTH FOR FIRST TWELVE MONTHS OF PROBATIONERS' INVOLVEMENT WITH PROGRAM

Month*	Group I			Group II			Groups I and II		
	No.	%	Cum. %†	No.	%	Cum. %	No.	%	Cum. %
1	4	5	5	7	10	10	11	7	7
2	4	5	9	2	3	12	6	4	11
3	2	2	12	—	—	12	2	1	12
4	2	2	14	1	1	14	3	2	14
5	1	1	15	4	5	19	5	3	17
6	—	—	15	1	1	21	1	1	18
7	3	3	19	—	—	21	3	2	19
8	1	1	20	—	—	21	1	1	20
9	3	3	23	1	1	22	4	3	23
10	—	—	23	—	—	22	—	—	23
11	1	1	24	1	1	23	2	1	24
12	—	—	24	1	1	25	1	1	25
(Was not convicted)	(65)	(76)	(76)	(55)	(75)	(75)	(120)	(75)	(75)
Base	86		100	73		100	159		100

* Each month represents patient month rather than program month, e.g., the patient's first month in program.
† Cumulative percent convicted during year.

As with our other statistics, it would have been of great value if we could have compared our arrest and conviction rates with other programs. However, the paucity of the data in this area as well as the noncomparability of statistics makes this almost impossible. However, we were able to compare our rates with the data from the Riverside Hospital follow-up. As in the case of the drug recidivist rates,[6] we again noticed a striking similarity between the two programs. This is clearly seen in Table 15.

TABLE 15. COMPARISON OF ARREST RATES BETWEEN RATIONAL AUTHORITY AND RIVERSIDE HOSPITAL

	Percent arrested	
Months	Rational authority	Riverside Hospital
6	33%	25%
12	48%	46%

REFERENCES

1. Shlien, J. M.   Cross-theoretical criteria for the evaluation of psychotherapy. *American Journal of Psychotherapy* 20:125–133, 1966.
2. O'Donnell, J.   Research Problems in Follow-up Studies of Addicts. In *Rehabilitating the Narcotic Addict*. Washington, D.C.: U.S. Government Printing Office, 1966.
3. Cattell, R. B.   Evaluating therapy as total personality change: Theory and available instruments. *American Journal of Psychotherapy* 20:69–87, 1966.
4. Alksne, H., Trussell, R. E., Elinson, J., and Patrick, S.   *A Follow-up Study of Treated Adolescent Narcotic Users*. Unpublished report of the Columbia University School of Public Health and Administrative Medicine, 1959.
5. Alksne, H., Lieberman, L., and Brill, L.   The life cycle of addiction. *International Journal of the Addictions* 2:221–240, 1967.
6. Alksne, Trussell, Elinson, and Patrick. *Op. cit.*

9. Prospectus for the Future

OUR EXPERIENCES at the Washington Heights Rehabilitation Center elicited a number of interesting and hopeful findings. Of greatest import to us was learning that desired behavioral changes may take place either before or independent of abstinence. This confirmed our belief that the process of moving an addict from the condition of addiction to that of complete abstinence necessarily entails a lengthy procedure which requires a tolerance on the part of the rehabilitative agency for repeated relapses to drugs, whether heroin or other. While the addict is being treated as an outpatient in the community, he is obviously going to come into contact with the conditions which initially precipitated his entry into the drug world and subsequently sustained his involvement in the addiction system.

The transition from drug use to abstinence, as well as the physiochemical components of addiction itself, are still not too clearly understood. As noted earlier, in Chapter 1, operant conditioning factors may be at work in the addict which compel him, even after detoxification, to return to drug use; or, as Dole and Nyswander have indicated to us, there may be some evidence of prolonged or possibly permanent changes accompanying intensive use of opiates, which produce a craving for the drug of physiogenic rather than psychogenic origins. In any case, the ability to transform an addict into a person who does not experience the craving for heroin has been notoriously difficult to accomplish.

Even for those treatment modalities such as Synanon and Daytop in which residents have been off drugs for varying lengths of time, constant reinforcement appears to be needed, primarily through keeping a person within the institution or affiliated with the facility by working for it and advancing the "movement." In these cases, we cannot help but question the validity of the claims of cure for the products of these institutions who appear compelled to remain forever involved, or obsessed with the problem of drugs, even though they may no longer actually use drugs. From a rehabilitation point of view, the cure of an addict should lead to his movement into the larger normative society in which he takes his place as any other human being would, engaged in any one of a wide variety of occupational and social roles which are present. The necessity to remain in a role structurally linked to the addiction system raises question as to whether a cure has indeed taken place or, rather, a strange alteration of behavior which represents a compromise between the undesirability of heroin use and a legitimate cure.

A second major outcome of the Washington Heights Rehabilitation Center experiment was the finding that the added services of the social workers and public health nurses (Group I) along with the probation officers did not appear to add significantly to the group using the authority by the probation officers alone (Group II). The reasons for this are difficult to adduce. It is conceivable that if the demonstration had been carried on for at least another year and the addicts had had a minimum of two years' exposure to our staff instead of one, the more intensive relationship carried in the joint-management teams might have become more productive. It is also possible that a serendipitous effect due to learning experiences by the probation officers while working with our staff canceled out any initial advantages our staff might have had by virtue of their prior professional training. It would be interesting to control for this in a future study in which one of the groups contained probation officers who were not also part of joint-management teams.

One possibility that cannot be ignored is that the main factor which produced the changes for both groups was the consistent and self-conscious use of rational authority in probation officer–probationer relationships. The effective use of probation mechanisms should receive a good deal more research and evaluation, not only in the case of narcotics addicts, but for the full range of offenses for which persons are now being imprisoned. The reasons for this are as follows:

1. Incarceration does not appear to be an effective deterrent to future antisocial behavior.
2. Rehabilitation efforts in prisons take place in an artificial setting in which the resources and strengths of the community cannot be utilized while their training is taking place.
3. Keeping a person in prison is extremely expensive—as compared with probation or parole supervision—without any indication that this added expense produces more socially desired results.
4. The prison subculture frequently serves as a reinforcing agent for the negative aspects of the offender's self-image, and may only serve to alienate him still further from the normative larger society.
5. Resocialization efforts in an isolated setting do not allow the offender to develop his strength slowly and in a realistic manner which will allow him to cope with the everyday world. Whatever social factors initially contributed to his antisocial behavior are presumably still in the community awaiting his return.

Our experiences at Washington Heights indicate to us that effective rehabilitation for addicts is not only a slow process but also a complicated one, involving the interaction of the addict with his social world. We believe that strong and consistent controls will help the addict through a most difficult period. Without the controls, he will tend to flee to the comforts of drugs at the first crisis. However, isolation in prison or elsewhere will not even permit him to confront any crises. Just as we cannot raise emotionally healthy children by keeping them protected at home until maturity, we cannot realistically expect that the social maturation necessary for rehabilitation can be developed *in vacuo*.

Our experience at the Washington Heights Center and elsewhere leads us to believe that one of the major handicaps of any treatment program has been the rather naive lumping together of all patients into the category of "addict," without any rational differential diagnosis, thereby treating all addicts as similar. Common sense tells us that they are not only dissimilar psychologically, but also socially and in regard to their life styles. The variation of emotional and social types in the population known as addicts is so great as, at times, to approximate the general population of nonaddicts.

Historically, there have been changing patterns in drug use: narcotics addiction some fifty years ago was predominantly a problem of white, middle-class, middle-aged Protestants, rural rather than urban. In recent decades, it has been largely a problem of lower-class minority groups, beginning in early adolescence in the more dilapidated areas of our large urban port cities. Why have these changes occurred and what is their meaning?

There are also varying patterns of use in terms of class, economic levels, and stage of involvement in the addiction system; that is, the involvement may be with drugs alone or with the total "hustling syndrome," including a criminal way of life and exclusion of the square culture. We do not know what the similarities and differences in etiology are for addicts from different ethnic and class backgrounds. We would assume, for example, that a middle-class youth who has free access to society's success-goals would have greater psychological problems than a lower-class boy since he must renounce his family's standards and own aspirations and choose a sordid junkie existence.[1]

A thorough examination of the nature, psychology, and behavior of those we call addicts is missing. This has been an area clouded with irrationality and stereotyped thinking which serves as a pale substitute for the scientific information we require. There has been very little systematic research in the psychology, sociology, and etiology of narcotics addiction, which could provide this data. The major focus has been on pharmacological investigations; and even here, we do not yet fully comprehend the mechanisms in such basic phenomena as tolerance and dependence and the nature of the biochemical changes in central nervous system counteradaptations to drug use.

PROBLEMS IN ETIOLOGY AND DIAGNOSIS

In considering the questions of etiology and diagnosis, a number of difficult, still unanswered problems intrude themselves:

Why does a member of one family become an addict and his siblings respectable pillars of society? Why does not everyone in a high incidence area become an addict, but only a few? What causes some individuals to be so strongly attracted to, and highly tolerant of, narcotics addiction and its way of life, while others are highly resistant, in fact seem invulnerable?

Many individuals may experiment with narcotic drugs, chipping for briefer or longer periods, but then drop out and discontinue use. *What are the differences between these dropouts and the confirmed junkies, and what makes these "true" addicts go on forever, seemingly undeterred by the terrible consequences of addiction and the despised image of the street junkie?*

Is there a drug-prone personality common to all narcotics addicts? And, as part of this, are there antecedent psychological factors predisposing some individuals to drug use? Or are many of the characteristics believed to be causal really a consequence of drug use? Longitudinal studies could help us answer this, but regrettably these have never been done.

To anticipate, if we go back to our previous notion of a variety of addicts rather than "the addict," we must relinquish this idea of a common, drug-prone personality type. What would emerge rather is a pattern or cluster of different personality traits which could be found in the context of any clinical diagnosis. These traits may include the aspects so often cited in the literature; namely, a weak ego structure; defective superego functioning; inadequate masculine identification and psychosexual development; "oral dependency" and the need for outside narcissistic supplies; tense depression; fears regarding pain, aggression, and sexuality; impulsiveness and inability to postpone gratification; fears of success and assuming responsibility; poor controls; and confusion of role and personal identity. To these we would add also a "delinquent orientation" to life as defined by Chein; i.e., a lack of realistic orientation to the future and feelings of being a "loner" and a "loser" with a distrust of major social institutions.[2] Since these traits are found in many other kinds of maladjusted persons, however, we cannot state that they are unique or even causal in the etiology of addiction.

A word about the concept of addiction as a "sickness": just as there was formerly an exclusive emphasis on the criminality aspects, so was there later, among therapists, a preoccupation with the idea of sickness which we feel has interfered with their ability to help addicts. If we believe that addicts are psychologically disturbed, then the expected traits are sure to be found. There is much to be said for the Dole–Nyswander approach of seeing addicts primarily as "addicted persons" to be treated for their addiction (if psychological problems should emerge, these too can be treated); or for the Daytop Village concept of "inadequate persons," who need to learn to assume responsibility through a reality therapy approach. Some workers believe it at least conceivable that some of the psychological problems found may have little bearing on the addiction itself. We understand now that treatment can be accomplished without "insight," especially among lower-class patients; and, from the field of public health, we know that we do not need to understand all the etiological factors in order to treat and cure disease.

Are there any predisposing physiological factors? The existence of such factors has never been demonstrated. Contrary to popular belief, narcotics addiction is not inherently a euphoric or pleasurable condition. The pleasures and initial reactions need to be learned, and addicts have amply documented the sickness, nausea, and vomiting experienced upon taking the first few shots. Becker's classic study of marijuana use documented the role which the social situation, imitation of other users, psychological and social supports, and group interpretation of the effects of pot use play in creating a marijuana user.[3] Studies in opiates and placebo research by Lasagna and Beecher confirm that only a small minority of people find narcotics drugs initially gratifying, and this minority includes the most disturbed adolescents, whose traits resemble those of the confirmed street addict.[4] The danger of addiction to opiates lies therefore not necessarily in the drug itself, but in the person, since any alterations in drives, behavior, and emotions will be experienced with pleasure or alarm depending on the psychological and social needs of the user.[5]

This leads to the question of differences between occasional users or "chippies," medically or accidentally addicted persons, and confirmed addicts. One way to answer this is by using the concept of "craving," which we believe to be an essential hallmark for most, if not all, compulsive addicts. Craving does not appear for medically addicted persons, for neonatal babies born addicted of addicted mothers, or schizophrenics experimentally addicted, all of whom experience no desire for drugs once withdrawn. Craving appears to derive from the ability of the drug to reduce the perception of sources of anxiety and pain by increasing the individual's detachment and to allay distress regarding sexuality, aggression, and pain. Opiates, by relieving this anxiety, feed the craving for further relief of these continuing sources of tension and a new cycle of need and satiation—i.e., tension and drug relief—is thus created. The greater the distress satisfied, therefore, the greater the need to use drugs compulsively, one would assume. Further research is required to learn whether there are also constitutional differences in responsiveness to drugs and in the potential for the relief which they afford.[6]

Is drug addiction merely a symptom or a way of life? We can answer this by saying that, for most narcotics addicts, the symptom in the normal course of events becomes a way of life since their entire existence is eventually engaged. As Simmel remarked, "In the end, all reality resides in the needle."[7] The sources and reasons for becoming an addict may have initially been as varied and discrete as the individuals themselves, but the drug culture eventually exercises a flattening influence and many addicts begin to look alike. In great part, we believe this process is a result of our criminal definition of the problem, which eventually forces most addicts to steal or prostitute so that they are caught up in a new tribal subculture and "addiction system." Escalona, in studying children, showed that very similar behavior could be caused by very different factors. For example: lack of adequate mothering in autistic children could be attributed either to organic factors in the child itself which made it not receptive to mothering, or to environmental factors such as an absent or detached mother. The end effect was the same, however.[8]

What are the predisposing familial factors involved? Is there a specific family constellation? Studies of family dynamics by Ackerman,[9] Boszormenyi-Nagy,[10] and Bowen,[11] among others, demonstrate the very complicated interaction, modes of communication, including double-bind symbiosis going on which so often condition the child's functioning and relationships to the family and the world. Chein and Gerard thought that the families of addicts were, indeed, factors contributing to the various personality defects outlined earlier. Their studies described clear-cut differences between addict families and control groups. In almost all families, there was a disturbed relationship (emotional divorce) between the parents. The mother became the most important figure in the boy's life, with the father appearing as a more shadowy and inadequate, less involved figure. The homes were in numerous ways far less wholesome than those of the control groups.[12] The reports of our workers confirmed the existence of a great deal of emotional and social pathology in the families of the W.H.R.C. addicts.

The work of Murray Bowen at the Clinical Center of the National Institute of Mental Health is of relevance here. Dr. Bowen drew up a paradigm of schizophrenogenic families, i.e., families which nurture one or more schizophrenic children. The trouble with this model is that it seems equally valid for narcotic addicts, alcoholics, delinquents, and colitis and gastrointestinal cases as described by Dr. Melitta Sperling, and obesity cases as discussed by Hilda Bruch.[13] We enter here into the difficult question of choice of neurosis: Why, with seemingly similar family backgrounds and social situations, does one person become a narcotics addict and another an alcoholic or colitis case or schizophrenic?

SOME PREVIOUS EFFORTS AT DIAGNOSIS AND CLASSIFICATION

All efforts at classification of typologies of users, with the exception of that of Rado, assume varying degrees of disturbance and maladjustment, some addicts being fairly well integrated into society and only partially involved in the addiction system, others more clearly disturbed, and some totally immersed in all areas of the addiction system.

Some earlier attempts at classification now seem very dated, even irrelevant. Kolb's early diagnoses were purely descriptive and nondynamic, including such labels as psychopathic diathesis, inebriate personality, and psychopathic personality.[14] Ausubel[15] later distinguished between three basic categories of opiate addiction:

1. Primary addiction, in which opiates have specific adjustive value for particular personality defects.
2. Symptomatic addiction, in which the use of opiates has no particular adjustive value and is only an incidental symptom of behavior disorder.
3. Reactive addiction, in which drug use is a transitory developmental phenomenon in essentially normal individuals influenced by distorted peer group norms.

PSYCHODYNAMIC FORMULATIONS

Another framework used to understand etiology and, consequently, diagnosis and treatment is the three-fold psychological approach which includes the *genetic* based on early reaction and coping modes, the *psychodynamic* or current defense operations, and *diagnostic* or descriptive classification. Chein offers one example of such psychiatric classification:

1. Overt schizophrenia.
2. Incipient schizophrenic or borderline personalities.
3. Delinquency-dominated character disorders.
4. Inadequate personalities.[16]

Rado's adaptational approach postulated a "tense depression" as the basic emotional state relieved by opiate intoxication, and tended to universalize all types of drug craving as variants of one single disease, that is, *pharmacothymia*. He found that addicts respond to frustration in life with tense depression, marked by painful tension and, at the same time, by a high degree of intolerance to pain, a "condition remarkably improved by alcohol (drugs)."[17] However, this state was invariably followed by the rapid return of the tense depression and a renewed craving for elation. Not many people today accept the idea of the equivalent of a manic-depressive cycle, rather stressing the depressive underlay. Psychodynamic theories are often still caught between confusion of craving as an active seeking of pleasure or euphoria, and negative pleasure, i.e., relief from distress and tension. Thus, neurotic individuals are said to seek relief from anxiety (negative euphoria) while psychopaths use drugs for kicks (positive euphoria) and psychotic patients to relieve depression (negative euphoria).

LIFE-STYLE FORMULATION

An important recent innovation has been the effort to move away from psychiatric classification alone and to study the person in his social milieu. With Chein, we get into more dynamic configurations, since he intermingles psychological factors with four life-styles for addicts:

1. Those totally involved, but without craving.
2. Those craving, but not totally involved.
3. Those both craving and totally involved.
4. Individuals with a history of repeated dependence without in-

dications of total involvement or craving (the situational addict).[18]

These types obviously have different etiological backgrounds and prognoses and would pose different problems in treatment.

Workers at the New York Medical College[19] have, like Chein, also postulated four life-styles, although from a rather different standpoint, since addicts are rated on the basis of conventional behavior or criminal involvement:

1. *Conformists* are those who rate high in conventionality and low in criminality.
2. The *uninvolved* rate low in conventionality and low in criminality.
3. The *two-worlders* are high in conventionality and high in criminality.
4. The *hustler* rates low in conventionality and high in criminality.

Cloward's work [20, 21] derives from Durkheim's as well as Merton's studies of alienation and anomie, to the effect that, when individuals are denied access to the means of attaining society's culturally defined goals and success values, they may engage in criminal or retreatist behavior, including drug use as a direct or substitute form of satisfaction. Cloward agrees that the kind of opportunity structure in which young people find themselves is the central condition determining their behavior. Deviant behavior will occur more frequently among lower-class, urban, male adolescents because of their lack of access to these success goals. Cloward distinguishes three delinquent styles of life: the criminal, the conflict, and the retreatist orientation. He considers drug addicts retreatists who are "double failures" because they can neither resort to criminal behavior nor even to violence to succeed. While this theory has much to commend it, there has been some question recently regarding such aspects as whether addicts are truly "retreatists" and "double failures." It also leaves unexplained the specifics of exactly how blocked opportunity acts on some individuals in deprived areas and contributes to their becoming addicts, while others appear able to overcome their initial handicaps and achieve the socially approved goals.

FRAMEWORK FOR APPROACHING THE PROBLEM OF DIAGNOSIS AND TREATMENT

Learning theory affords an excellent springboard for elucidating many of the factors involved in etiology and consequently for rational diagnosis and treatment, building up from simple to more complex levels until we involve the whole person in his social situation.

As John Clausen stated:

> Narcotics addiction is both a psychophysiological state and a social category, a product of behavior learned within a social context which cannot be understood apart from that context. The prevalence and consequences of drug addiction in any society depend as much on the social and legal definitions as upon the nature and effects of the drugs themselves or the nature of the persons involved.[22]

As its simplest level, learning theory is a study of the circumstances under which a response and cue become connected. After learning has been completed, response and cue are bound together in such a way that the appearance of the cue evokes the response. The learner must be driven to make the response and then be rewarded for having responded to the cue. We can summarize the factors in learning, therefore, as drive, response, cue, and reward. The strengthening of the cue-response connection is the essence of learning. Learning theory places emphasis upon the conditioned response as a device for eliciting drive-oriented behavior in situations to which it was not at first appropriate, but to which it was transferred; for example, the way an addict learns to lean on drugs to satisfy a variety of needs. Conditioning, the making and breaking of stimulus connections, becomes a fundamental process of human thought and behavior as well as psychopathological phenomena.

This learning process becomes more complicated when we bring in motivational or psychodynamic factors—the psychological, physiological, and social reinforcements of drug use as well. In time, each individual develops a schema, an individual outlook and affectively toned approach for organizing all his responses, which gives meaning and continuity to his experiences. In this connection, we shall mention several learning experiences important for the development of a narcotics addict.

LEARNING FACTORS IN BECOMING AN ADDICT

Differential Association

This places emphasis on an individual's social associations in determining his motives, attitudes, and skills and preparing him for a specific role in society, whether legitimate or deviant. There are learning factors in becoming a criminal or narcotics addict as our later model will show. Narcotics addicts will have a high tolerance for certain experiences and for the self-image of an addict. Volkman and Cressy have shown how Synanon, by offering a reverse kind of differential association in a therapeutic community, can lead to extinction of this previous conditioning and the opportunity for new learning and conditioning with effective results for certain addicts.[23]

Lindesmith's Learning Theory

Lindesmith postulated that the neophyte user's realization of his physical or psychological dependence upon drugs was an essential precondition for the establishment of addiction. Knowledge of one's dependence upon drugs in alleviating the distress of withdrawal is to him an indispensable ingredient for the definition of a true addict.[24, 25] Lindesmith leaves out, however, other essential factors to be discussed in our model, i.e., the consequent change in one's self-concept; preoccupation with drugs and gradual assimilation into the addict culture; and development of the skills, customs, language, and rituals necessary to maintain oneself in the addiction system. At this stage, it is questionable practice to postulate a *single* learning experience as unique and most important when the actual factors are so numerous and complex.

Wikler and Operant Conditioning

Although we have touched upon this in Chapter 1, it is relevant at this point to elaborate Wikler's views on the problem of diagnosing various aspects of the problem of drug addiction in order to develop the various methods of treatment. One of the major contributions to our understanding has been Wikler's theory of operant conditioning. The idea is that, with the development of pharmacogenic dependence, a new and continuous cycle of drug-induced need and gratification develops which can motivate behavior in much the same way as the recurrent cycles of hunger, thirst, or other primary needs and gratifications. The choice of a particular class of drugs may be explained on the basis that it facilitates or hinders specific feelings and patterns of behavior which are acceptable to the user.[26]

Wikler doubted that a conscious desire for euphoria was the only, or even the major, motivation for the use of narcotics and for relapse after withdrawal. Instead, he emphasized the way in which two forms of learning, the instrumental (operant) and classic (Pavlovian) forms of conditioning could provide an unconscious motivation for both continued drug use and relapse. He pointed out that being hooked (physically dependent), rather than constituting an unwanted complication of drug use, could actually furnish the drug user with a motivational basis for continued activity (such as hustling for drugs) and attaining other goals such as secondary gains by belonging to a deviant subculture.

Wikler described the effects of the drug (relief of anxiety or depression) as producing a progressively stronger tendency to seek out and use the drug as each reduction in tension reinforced the preceding drug-seeking behavior. The development of physical dependence gave rise to a new fear (the distress of the withdrawal syndrome) that regularly appeared when the drug was not used, which could be dramatically alleviated by using the drug. The reduction of this new tension by the drug resulted in further reinforcement of drug-seeking behavior. Such strongly reinforced behavior could not easily be extinguished. A return to the situation, either geographical or emotional, in which the responses were originally made would be likely to call forth the customary drug-seeking behavior. Together with Lindesmith, Wikler brings to learning motivational factors which more and more require the emergence of a total personality structure built on narcotics, an associated self-image and a related way of life.

GENERAL PROBLEMS IN PERSONALITY STUDIES

All studies of personality are difficult since findings will vary with the population studied, the interests and prejudices of the investigator, and the methods used. We need to be constantly alert to the fact that most addicts we see are selected samples, largely the "failures" in the addiction system who continually come to the social agency's attention, while the successes escape us. This was particularly true of the clients we saw at the Washington Heights Rehabilitation Center, since they obviously had failed in the addiction system to the extent that their illegal activities became known to the police, with subsequent arrest and conviction. On the other hand, in our chemotherapy at the Albert Einstein College of Medicine, for example, we found a large number of middle-class, hidden drug abusers, with families, earning very large incomes, who had never been detected, arrested, or even hospitalized, some of whom were sniffers who had never used the needle and were highly motivated to seek help.

All work to date has been retrospective, which means that the addicts studied have been identified as such by other agencies; their drug use and their experiences as socially stigmatized persons have no doubt altered their behavior. This "masking" phenomenon in which apparent personality uniformity is the consequence of a long period of drug abuse and repeated institutionalizations is a serious impediment to our study of drug-dependent persons.

As we can see, there is no simple means of classification of addicts; in fact, the more elements we draw in, the better chance we seem to have of understanding the problem, including the here-and-now functional and adaptational purposes it is serving in the day-to-day life of the addict. We can only cite the consensus that among persons currently identified and studied as opiate-dependent in the United States today, personality plays a causal role for most if not all addicts, in association with other factors. But personality disorders no more than any other single factor can cause or explain addiction. For the larger number of identified addicts, it is part of the constellation of factors comprised in the socioeconomic deprivation of our large port cities.[27] We need to understand far more about the process of how psychological and social factors intermesh to contribute to addiction; and to differentiate between the long-term genetic and the current factors shaping the adolescent. There are also studies indicating a "maturing out" or increasing abstinence with the passage of time, and it would be important to document this.

The Task Force summary indicates that, irrespective of the diagnosis or conceptual framework used to diagnose an addict's condition, the vast majority of addicts who normally come to the attention of rehabilitation agencies will be involved in different stages of the addiction process. This awareness of developmental stages of addiction led the authors, together with an associate, Harold Alksne, to construct a model detailing the steps involved in becoming a narcotics addict. It was noted that this is an extremely complicated process which cannot be explained simply by using universal types and single motivations. We believe that it is necessary, in any therapeutic endeavors undertaken with addicts, to take cognizance of this movement through the life cycle of addiction.

A CONCEPTUAL MODEL OF THE LIFE CYCLE OF ADDICTION [28] *

The concept of different stages through which drug abusers appear to pass in the course of entering into an addict way of life has already been noted in the literature.[29] These studies support the notion that the entry into addiction entails initial experimentation followed by increasing involvement with drug use. Each of these studies has pointed out the presence of secondary supports for drug abuse and subsequent addiction in the social contacts of the abuser after his earlier experimentation with drugs. Although there is an implication in these works that drug dependence is cyclical in nature, a delineation of stages—from the perspective of a full cycle involving an identification of the conditions preceding initiation of narcotics use, movement toward addiction, addiction, and finally the exit from addiction when an exit does occur—has never been explicitly specified.

We believe that it is possible at this time, using evidence from the literature and the cumulative experience of the authors in addiction research and rehabilitation, to create a descriptive model which will elucidate not only the processes through which the drug abuser enters into the addiction system, but also the stages which would be necessary if he is to leave it. The dominant assumption guiding the construction of the model is that the process of becoming an addict and being an addict in our culture may well be as much a social process and condition as it is physical and psychological.

It should be noted that this paper describes the content of the life cycle of addiction as experienced by persons located in urban Ameri-

* Much of the following discussion of the life cycle of addiction is taken from the paper by Harold Alksne, Louis Lieberman, and Leon Brill, "A Conceptual Model of the Life Cycle of Addiction." *International Journal of the Addictions* 2:221–240, 1967. With permission of the editors.

can communities, addicts for whom the term "junkie" reflects the popular stereotype. It is not meant to imply that our observations are applicable to all addicted individuals. Some of the exceptions are noted in the description of the early stages of the model among those persons whom we consider to be the drop-outs from the life cycle of addiction, e.g., the physician-addict.

General Description of the Model

For purposes of analysis, we have divided the cycle into four phases. Each of these phases is further subdivided into several stages.

As shown in Table 1, there are four phases in the life cycle of addiction: Phase I: *Tolerance for Potential Addiction;* Phase II: *Tolerance of the Addiction System;* Phase III: *Tolerance for Potential Abstinence;* Phase IV: *Tolerance of Abstinence.* The logic of the division of the life cycle of addiction into four phases is based upon the premise that addicts do not go from non-drug use to addiction in a single step; or, at some later time, directly from addiction to abstinence. Within the first phase, there are also clearly noted stages which have been observed. The typical movement from non-drug use to addiction more nearly resembles this series of stages, which may in a few cases show a degree of individual variation. These stages are outlined as part of Phase I, Tolerance for Potential Addiction. They are: initiation, experimentation stage, adaptation stage, and physiological stage. The phase encompassing the addict's involvement with, and commitment to, the addiction system is called Phase II, Tolerance of the Addiction System.

The movement out of the addiction system to complete abstinence may also be viewed as a process encompassing several stages. On the basis of our own experience and that of other workers in this field,[30, 30a-30c] it seems apparent that, relative to the total number of individuals believed to be fully addicted, few reach the stage of complete abstinence. Our model suggests the kinds of stages within Phase III, Tolerance for Potential Abstinence, through which the addict must pass before complete abstinence is possible and if the addict is to function adequately in the more conventional society. These are similar to the stages in Phase I. The ultimate goal of rehabilitation as well as the final phase of the life cycle of addiction is designated as Phase IV, Tolerance of Abstinence.

The concept of tolerance is an essential element in all four phases. This concept is derived from the medical sciences. It is ordinarily

TABLE I. PHASES IN THE LIFE CYCLE OF ADDICTION AND THE SERIES OF STAGES WITHIN THESE

Phase	Stage	Types of drop-outs from the life-cycle model
Pre-drug condition	Addiction set: pre-disposing social and psychological factors	
I: Tolerance for potential addiction	Initiation to drug use	
	Experimentation: irregular drug use	1. Cessation of drug use 2. Long-term irregular use
	Adaptation: regular use	1. Cessation of regular use 2. Cessation of all use 3. Weekender
	Physiological: addicted	1. Hidden addict 2. Medically supervised addict 3. Physician-addict
Transitional Phase I		
II: Tolerance of the addiction system	Individual and sociocultural interaction system of addiction	1. Death 2. Maturing-out 3. Semi-permanent full-time treatment, e.g., Synanon
Transitional Phase II		
III: Tolerance for potential abstinence	Experimentation: recidivism Adaptation: chemotherapy or drug substitution Physiological: drug-free with supports	
IV: Tolerance of abstinence	Non-drug use with no need of supports	

used in a context where the normal condition is called upon to tolerate a disruptive or foreign force or influence. It is medically defined as the "capacity for enduring a poison or a food or drug which may be harmful if taken in excess; power of resistance to such, or point at which such resistance ends." [31] The concept of tolerance in this paper is, in large measure, based on the idea that an individual is capable of adapting to a system which was not originally normative for him. While this developing tolerance is usually considered only at the physiological level as one of the factors leading to the resultant addiction, our model includes the idea that the development of a secondary tolerance of the undesirable social consequences of drug use is also an important consideration.

The concept of tolerance may be carried over in understanding the movement toward abstinence, for the conditions of the abstinence system are in the same relationship to the addiction system as the addiction system was to the pre-drug state. This, we postulate, ultimately necessitates the development of a special kind of tolerance associated with abstinence from narcotic drug use. *Just as the nonuser builds a tolerance for the use of drugs while adapting to the addiction system, so must he build a tolerance for abstinence in order to adapt to the abstinence system.*

PRE-DRUG CONDITION: ADDICTION SET

Even in high-risk drug areas where most adolescents are aware of narcotics use and drugs are easily obtainable, only a small proportion of youths actually become personally involved with experimentation and still fewer with eventual addiction.[32] In the making of an addict, potential availability of drugs evidently must be supported by a combination of unique psychological and social factors.

As discussed earlier in this chapter, the psychiatric literature suggests that even prior to initial drug use, addicts were likely to have been socially inadequate individuals with weak egos and difficulties in coping with reality.[33] Such individuals may also be imbedded in a family constellation where a dominating, seductive mother increases her control through the pathological manipulation of a son in the face of a weak father or in the absence of a father. Further, there is evidence that intergenerational factors may play a role in the transfer of forms of illness from parents to children.[34] It is contended that such delinquency-prone children may be acting out the unconscious wishes of their parents.[35] This orientation may be reinforced through the delinquent orientation present in some of the community groups to which the individual relates.[36] The literature also documents[37] pervasive underlying depressions and difficulties addicts have in coping with their sexual and aggressive feelings.* Although the types of underlying emotional pathology present in those persons who later go on to drug use vary extensively, it is reasonable to treat them during rehabilitation treatment whether or not they are directly related to the drug use.

The social components are equally important. It has been observed that more deviance is likely to be present in areas where lower-class minority groups are not provided with the means to achieve socially defined goals.[38] One may infer from Merton's use of the concept of anomie that drugs and involvement in a deviant system may be accepted by some in the community as a way of circumventing the middle-class value system, within which there are limited opportunities for the means to reach success goals. Cloward and Ohlin[39] have elaborated on this in their description of drug addiction as "retreatist behavior." They further suggest that some individuals are given opportunities to enter into drug use by way of special associations they may develop in the community.

Another social factor that has received little attention is that the use of drugs is associated with a social setting in which there are unique opportunities for a kind of status achievement. This appears especially relevant to the addicts who come out of ethnic and class groups which often see legal authorities as oppressing agents. For them, defiance of the law can become an accepted fact of life. Fantasy-producing status achievements arising out of childhood cops-and-robbers games can, for a fourteen-year-old neophyte drug user, be turned into a real-life game with enormous opportunities for emotional satisfaction. The status recognition which has been denied him, reinforced by what he sees in his family, friends, and neighbors, can quickly be achieved within his own group of peers.

These factors are only a few of those which constitute the addiction set and which help to support a deviant orientation. They indicate that there is a vector of both emotional factors and social factors which account for who does or does not begin to experiment with drug use as well as who continues with it.[40] The specific content of the addiction set is likely to show some variability from user to user but this set must nevertheless be present and of sufficient

---

* As indicated earlier, a weakness of most psychological as well as sociological studies is that findings are based on studies of addict populations with inferences projected backward to the pre-drug state. More longitudinal research, as well as controls on comparable nonaddict populations, may someday eliminate this methodological difficulty.

intensity to permit a person to take his first "taste" of a prohibitive drug. A more precise examination of the content of the addiction set would be of great value for understanding the etiology of addiction. It is through the addiction set that the neophyte is sustained during his experimentation stage.

PHASE I: TOLERANCE FOR POTENTIAL ADDICTION

Addiction to narcotic drugs* is a process which must develop over a period of time. Although the length of the developmental period may vary from one person to another, the user customarily goes through these several stages before he enters into, and fully adapts to, the addiction system. It is the movement through these stages which represents the developing tolerance for addiction. We have called the first stage of this process the *experimentation stage*.

Experimentation Stage: Irregular Drug Use

A variety of substances have been available in most communities for use by those who are predisposed to drug use. Model airplane glue, ether, and nonprescription amphetamine-type nasal inhalators are commonly used, easily available substances in the United States. In addition, barbiturates and prescription amphetamines, as well as a variety of cough medications, have been fairly easy to obtain.† Estimates of the number of young persons using these legitimate pharmaceutical products are not available, but there is a growing awareness that the figure may be large. Marijuana is often readily available and inexpensive enough for many to use. It is our impression that a relatively large proportion of all drug users who have tried some drug at least once engage in the use of these substances without moving on to experimentation with heroin or other opium derivatives or synthetics. Therefore, it would be unreasonable to assume that use of these "soft" drugs caused a person to go on to the use of "hard"

---

* Although this model is conceptualized primarily in terms of the heroin user, this is not meant to deny the fact that many users will, at the same or different times, use other drugs simultaneously or sequentially.

† The Federal government and several states have recently tightened their regulations governing the distribution of these drugs. However, since the legitimate use of these medications is so extensive, easy access is assured.

drugs such as heroin or cocaine. To infer causation because one substance preceded another in time would suggest a greater likelihood that alcohol, aspirin, nicotine, caffeine, etc. "cause" one to move onto heroin since about 100 percent of all heroin addicts used all of these before they used heroin. The absurdity, apparent in this fallacious argument, of this reasoning seems to escape most people who attempt to impart this imaginary danger to the qualities of marijuana. Nor can it be supposed that the desirability of the marijuana "high" will lead to a desire for a heroin "high" any more than the "high" most of us receive at cocktail parties creates a desire for the use of drugs stronger than alcohol. A more realistic hypothesis is suggested by our model: when the addiction set (i.e., the predisposing social and psychological factors) is sufficiently primed, such an addiction-prone individual will seek out many substances until he arrives at heroin. The presence of alcohol, cigarettes, or marijuana is in no way necessary for the use of heroin. On the contrary, it may be that the use of these substances may *prevent* many from going on to other drugs because of the satisfactions gained from these. From a pharmacological standpoint, the only drug necessary for opiate addiction is an opiate. The possible dangers of marijuana use must be researched carefully and with suitable controls, but there is little to be gained by mistakenly linking, as a result of faulty logic, its usage to heroin use.

Although a few individuals begin their experimentation with drugs by direct intravenous injections of the opiate, our findings at the W.H.R.C. confirm other reports that this is not the typical pattern of entry into heroin use.[41] For most drug users, mainlining represents a commitment to a practice which is clearly seen as a violation of social norms and is therefore more representative of the stereotype of the junkie. For the neophyte, execution of this act is likely to be seen as directly symbolic of addiction. Sniffing the drug represents a point of lesser commitment to the self-image of being a drug user since it requires relatively little skill and no paraphernalia. In one study of adolescent narcotic users, it was reported that 51 percent began their use of heroin in this way.[42] Sniffing and skin-popping, sometimes in combination with the use of other drugs, will generally precede the intravenous injection of heroin during the experimentation stage.

As the novice user develops the physical need for larger doses to obtain the same effects as during the beginning of heroin use, a concurrent need for financial support of his habit becomes more pressing. Socialization into a criminal way of life for the future addict characteristically begins with an increase in drug use. The user must, of necessity, move toward the extensive knowledge, skill, and attitudes required to maintain himself in the criminal aspect of the addiction system if he wishes to continue drug use. In the United States, full involvement in the addiction system, almost by definition, incorporates an interrelated involvement with criminality.

It should be stressed, however, that this movement proceeds by stages. This first stage, the *experimentation stage* of irregular use, or chipping, may continue for a considerable period of time before the user moves on to the next stage of regular drug use, the *adaptation stage;* or, he may move away from drug use completely after very little experimentation. It is here hypothesized that those who drop out are those persons who cannot build up their tolerance for potential addiction. There may be a combination of several reasons for this: It may be the result of adverse reactions either to the effects of the drugs themselves, to the alteration of the accompanying self-image, or to the counterinfluence of more conventional, norm-supporting values; or it may be a consequence of internal needs. Unfortunately, the literature of narcotics addiction does not include an investigation of those factors which might account for an individual's being able to break away from drug use during this early stage of the life cycle. It may be profitable in this connection to examine drug-use dropouts in the light of Sutherland's "differential association" theory.[43]

For most drug users, it is during this experimentation stage that the immediate effects of the drug have a bearing upon the emotional component of the predisposing addiction set. By this we mean, for example, that an adolescent's inability to cope with a multiplicity of anxiety-producing situations may be resolved through the anxiety-reducing effects of the drug. Some benefits must accrue to the user through the use of drugs—whether perceived by him as euphoric or adaptational or the benefits are on an unconscious level—as a necessary step for enabling the tolerance for addiction to be developed.

Other users are able to control their use during this experimentation stage. Although no research reports are available for this kind of user, our own observations indicate that some persons continue with occasional or limited use for an indefinite period of time without going on to more regular use. However, it is more probable that experimental users will eventually take the step either into more regular involvement or else drop out of the life cycle of addiction.

Documentation to determine whether or not this is inevitable is certainly necessary.

Adaptational Stage: Regular Use

The adaptational stage is characterized by the regular daily use of drugs and a progressive increase in the amount of drugs used even though the user may not be addicted. There is great variability in the length of time involved in the adaptational stage just as there is in the experimentation stage.

Functionally, the adaptational stage prepares the addict for his later commitment to the addiction system. It is during this stage that the user appears to build his relationship to the addiction system.* As a consequence of this relationship, he begins to develop confidence in his ability to function as an addict as he acquires the necessary skills associated with the addiction system. The adaptational stage is delineated because it is during this stage that the user discovers how regular drug use may enable him to adapt and relate his particular emotional and social needs to the world via the use of drugs. In short, he learns that drugs, for him, provide the wherewithal to function with a minimum amount of pain.

However, not all the persons who enter into the adaptational stage go on to full physiological addiction. Some users cannot tolerate the reinforcement of the negative social and self-image aspects of regular drug use. If they cannot, this may enable them to stop at this point and withdraw from the life cycle of addiction. The others are likely to continue on through the process. One aspect which has not received sufficient attention is that of magical thinking and the counterphobic mechanism. The counterphobic mechanism entails a state of war with the thing feared: we must master the thing which threatens to master us;[44] that is, many addicts feel, "It can't happen to me; I am stronger than the drug," and are generally surprised when it does happen.

---

* Throughout this discussion, the term *addiction system* is used because we believe it represents a more pertinent descriptive term than *addict sub-culture*. It implies that the various components in the world of the addict—the hospitals, the police, the pushers, the pharmacists, rehabilitation agencies, the courts, the neighborhood, the family, and the addict himself, as well as others—are all enmeshed in a network of relationships such that a change in any of the components usually has varying degrees of effect on all the other elements within this system.

Physiological Stage: Addicted

It is generally accepted that regular daily use of analgesic narcotic substances leads to the physiological state of addiction. During the adaptational stage of regular use, the body develops an increasing tolerance for the addictive substance and requires greater quantities of the drug in order to achieve the previously desired effects. The addict's body develops a dependency upon the drug which makes it impossible for him to discontinue its use without suffering withdrawal symptoms. Patients have indicated that fear of withdrawal may be one factor maintaining them in the addiction system. Simultaneously, the addict's self-image develops an increasing tolerance for the stereotype of the "junkie." We would postulate that, if the drug user is to continue drug use to the point of physiological addiction, he will first have to build up his psychological tolerance for the accompanying negative self-image. Becker has indicated that this phenomenon is associated with marijuana use as well.[45]

Some persons who reach the stage of full physiological dependence on narcotics may still not progress into a full involvement in the addiction system, i.e., an addict life style. One such group is composed of medically supervised addicts who have available sources of drugs through legitimate medical personnel. Others may be physicians and nurses. Some, in fact, may never have entered into the life cycle of addiction as described here. They are similar to the kinds of persons who were addicted prior to the establishment of regulation of narcotics use by Federal authorities.

Others who control their habits through self-detoxification, and whose only involvement with the addiction system is in the weekly purchase of narcotics from a reliable and steady source, may be found in the population of "hidden addicts." Many in the latter group are able to avoid entry into the next phase because their financial resources do not require that they place themselves in serious jeopardy with the law in order to obtain drugs. These people purchase drugs from relatively safe sources and tend to go to private hospitals for detoxification, or are detoxified in the community with the aid of a private physician. Thus, because of unusual circumstances, the hidden addict is enabled to avoid entry into the addiction system, and in some cases the life cycle of addiction itself.

We are left with those addicted persons who possess neither a special protected status nor qualities which hold them to the more conventional social system. These, therefore, enter the addiction system.

TRANSITION TO ADDICTION SYSTEM: TRANSITIONAL PHASE I

The stereotype of the addict as a junkie or dope fiend implies a way of life involving the hustling syndrome,[46] the copping syndrome,* and a marked alienation from the more conventional subgroups from which the addict emerged. These factors play an important role in supporting the movement of the addict during the first transitional phase between physiological dependency and the addiction system. The addict usually realizes that he is addicted after withdrawal symptoms follow an attempt at not using, and he recognizes that the drug will alleviate these symptoms.[47] This realization leads to a complex of doubts and fears based primarily on the recognition that he has approached the border of full involvement with the addiction system. This is perceived by the user as a function of those activities of the drug world in which he is already partially involved. To continue as a drug user means an extension of the same behaviors into new areas. To remain involved in this way of life necessitates a self-image which is not in conflict with the addiction system. In effect, he will develop a self-image which incorporates the expectations of others in the addiction system and will help provide the basis for knowledge of how to act appropriately. As in the process of socialization described by George Herbert Mead,[48] one is able to function appropriately in the context of different social systems and groups within our society as a consequence of internalizing the various "generalized others" for all the roles involved in those systems or groups. In this sense, movement into the addiction system may be viewed and analyzed as a socialization process, with consequent implications concerning resocialization in order that the addict move out of this system again.

In the movement through the different stages of Phase I: Tolerance for Potential Addiction, the alteration of self-image becomes a necessary prerequisite for the ability to tolerate the increasing in-

---

* By *copping syndrome* we mean those activities related to the daily routine of making the contact for the drugs, obtaining the drugs, finding a place to "take off," all of which involve techniques of drug procurement as well as drug use.

volvement in the world of addiction. Movement back and forth through the early stages of Phase I is almost always seen in case studies of addicts. Resistance to further involvement with the addiction system, or the resistance to the increasing tolerance for addiction, reflects the unwillingness of the addict to accept the external reality factors of increasing criminal behavior and alienation from his earlier primary identifications and contacts.

What essentially characterizes the first transitional phase is movement based upon unwillingness to accept the final self-image in the system, that of the "junkie." The addict will at this time vacillate between acceptance of the addiction system and avoidance of it, i.e., attempts at "cure." One might say that the vacillation results from the struggle between his former self-image and the newer one he is developing in his increasing tolerance for addiction.

The type of detoxification or attempt to withdraw from drugs seen at this phase is the "avoidance detoxification." A second type which occurs after full entry into Phase II is the "maintenance detoxification." By *avoidance detoxification,* we mean the addict's utilization of detoxification as a device to meet crises of a legal, economic, or psychological nature in order to minimize the strains of remaining within the addiction system and continuing to use drugs. Hospitalization is sought, therefore, primarily to reduce his habit to a manageable level.

Avoidance Detoxification

As an illustration of an avoidance detoxification, we may, for example, take the case in which an addict signs into a voluntary program at a municipal narcotics ward. When this action occurs during the first transitional phase, it may signify that the motivation for this detoxification is the desire on the part of the addict to remove himself from further involvement in the addiction system and resume a life more representative of his prior drug-free state. During this stage, such efforts are negated by the consequences of detoxification. Withdrawal from drugs achieves little more than bringing the addict back to the point of initial entry into the life cycle of addiction, where the presence of his addiction set exerts its influence once again. This assumes that other aspects of his environment have not changed. However, since the addict has already built up his social-psychological tolerance for addiction to some degree, it becomes so much easier to be readdicted, especially since the hospitalization has reinforced his growing self-image as an addict by treating him as one.

Hence, we usually see the detoxified addict going through the same cycle of stages which characterize Phase I, until he is again in Phase II. After repetitions of this cycle, the addict builds up, through reinforcement, his tolerance of addiction; and his self-image will no longer be in contradiction to the addiction system. We then characterize him as being fully involved in Phase II rather than still in the transitional phase. It is conceivable that an addict can bypass the transitional phase by becoming fully enmeshed in the addiction system without having gone through any kind of detoxification. The probability of this is difficult to determine from the present evidence, and the likelihood of its occurring seems slight for the following reason: Until the user manifests withdrawal symptoms as a consequence of voluntary or involuntary deprivation of drug use, he probably will not know that he is addicted and may thus be able to avoid full identification with the community of addicts.[49]

Maintenance Detoxification

A second kind of detoxification which may occur during the first transitional phase, but more often occurs after the addict has moved into Phase II, or the addiction system, are those detoxifications which serve to help him function more adequately within that system. These detoxifications are termed *maintenance detoxifications*. They function to maintain the addict's way of life within the addiction system since they are mechanisms enabling him to resolve conflicts arising from crises within this system. Hence, when the addict's physiological need for drugs reaches a point where the cost is so high that he can no longer obtain enough money, legally or illegally, he must either cut down on his habit or else withdraw from drug use completely, i.e., be detoxified. These detoxifications are entered into even though the addict knows he will begin using drugs almost immediately afterward. The paradox presented here is that the "competent" * addict has learned how to use detoxification in order to con-

---

* The obvious fact that some addicts are more competent than others in the execution of the social roles associated with maintaining themselves as addicts has not been appreciated. It should be noted that some addicts are more skillful in obtaining money illegally and in exposing themselves minimally to risk. Other factors such as the use of drug paraphernalia without physical risk, either through infection or overdose, are also indicative of more competent behavior in using drugs. Some addicts are more skillful than others in finding better sources of supply and determining the purity of the drug. Still others may be more competent

tinue to use drugs. Further, his return will be associated with a revival of the hedonistic value of the drug for him. He will once again be able to experience a satisfactory "high" from the drug.

Most addicts seen on hospital wards are there for detoxifications which will permit their habits to be made manageable, rather than for the kinds of detoxification we have designated as "avoidance."[50] In other words, during Phase II, detoxification does not usually serve to bring the addict back to Phase I, but generally enables the addict to remain an addict by reducing strain.

PHASE II: TOLERANCE OF THE ADDICTION SYSTEM

This phase is characterized by the addict's full incorporation of the individual and sociocultural values as well as the knowledge of the mechanisms that have come to be associated with narcotics use in our society. These values have been elaborated by Becker[51] and Finestone[52] in their studies of various drug abusers and deviant groups. They include a rationale for the unique values of an addiction adaptation, the myths, argot, and development of a self-image which places the addict above the "square" in society. The addiction system also includes the numerous status relationships and role-sets involving the addict, pusher, dealer, cop, psychiatrist, hospital worker, lawyer, and others.

Two of the main functions of these aspects of the addiction system are: (1) to provide an alternative type of status achievement within the deviant population; and (2) to place positive values upon a way of life generally condemned by societal norms. In other words, the addict may be a "junkie," but he is "hip" and therefore not a "square" who rides a crowded subway train to an unsatisfying job. These values offer essential props for the addict way of life in providing a rationalization for the wide range of deviant activities which support the procurement and use of drugs. They are not acquired suddenly, but are the result of the socialization process which occurs

---

in masking their identity as addicts and thereby avoiding detection. These and other indicators of competence in dealing with the requirements of the addiction system appear to us to be indices of certain kinds of social strengths, albeit relative to a deviant social system. The significance of this should be explored, particularly for its rehabilitation implications.

as the user builds up his tolerance for potential addiction. Even prior to full entry into the addiction system, the addict has responded to the social structures of the community by having to engage in illicit activity in order to support his addiction. His commitment to addiction as a way of life may originally have been minimal but repeated reinforcement of condemned behavior inevitably leaves its mark on his developing self-image.

When a person is officially designated an addict via arrest or narcotics-hospital detoxification, or civil commitment, a self-image with elements linked to the identity of the stereotyped addict, i.e., the junkie, becomes difficult to avoid. This confrontation with an undesirable self-image may be more significant than physiological addiction for full admission to the addiction system.

The addiction system contains numerous elements, primarily negative and punitive, which the addict must tolerate or endure in order to remain within the system. Rejection by relatives and friends, surveillance, and possible harassment by police become part of the addict's way of life. It is again the addiction set, this time meshing with the social satisfactions of the addiction system, which permits him to tolerate those changes.

In short, the addict has, as a result of the previous stages of progressive involvement with drug use and its associated way of life, been socialized into the addiction system. He has learned more efficient techniques for using and acquiring drugs. In this system, the addict is required to be identified with and absorb the skills of a parallel criminal system. Involvement in the addiction system relies on the development of skills in the distribution and sale of drugs, shoplifting and other thefts of all kinds, pimping, and prostitution, as well as specific skills and sophistication in the use of drug rituals and detoxification.

In addition, the fixation upon narcotics use leads to the constriction of the addict's field of social and psychological involvement to the special relationships within the addiction system. This serves to reinforce his self-image as an addict. In a sense, the addiction system has become the "generalized other" and therefore part of the addict's self from which future responses to the social world will be drawn.

The state achieved in Phase II is relatively stable as a form of social homeostasis. It now becomes the addict's normal adaptation to a condition defined by society as pathological, but which has become tolerable to him. He operates in a system of social and psychological values which are rationalized in a way of life having strong group supports.

Because of the extent of involvement—physical, psychological, and social—of the addict within the addiction system, to drop out becomes a much more difficult task. By and large, we cannot talk of any dramatically successful means of treatment which directly achieves the usually accepted goals of rehabilitation for a significantly large number of addicts. Whatever limited success there has been (see Chapter 1) may perhaps be strengthened in the future should agencies take cognizance of and act upon the conditions (which we have called Phase III, Tolerance for Potential Abstinence) set forth in Table 1.

With the exception of those who do manage to respond to traditional, abstinence-oriented treatment, alternative ways of dropping out at this point include death by overdose or disease due to the by-products of heroin use, maturing-out or the spontaneous cessation of drug use among older addicts, as well as long-term involvement in an isolated total institution such as Synanon and Daytop. The latter agencies, however, do not fully bring the addict out of the addiction system since this type of agency is fully immersed in and oriented toward the addiction system. Because it is the dominant goal of rehabilitation at such places to create a "professional addict," who in turn becomes a therapeutic agent for other addicts, their survival depends upon a continuous supply of addicts so that their graduates will have a role to play. In this sense, we cannot regard this method, as long as it does not seek to move its members completely out of the addiction system or drug subculture, as a meaningful form of completed rehabilitation.

TRANSITION TO ABSTINENCE: TRANSITIONAL PHASE II

In the second transitional phase, we see a similar circular movement of addiction, withdrawal, and readdiction; but the meaning of this to the addict is different from that of the first transitional phase. Whereas in the first phase the purpose was the avoidance of identity as an addict, in the second, he now wishes to alter this self-image and develop a new one after he has already grown accustomed to his addict self-image. This poses an especially difficult problem in his rehabilitation. Should rehabilitation have been attempted during the first transitional phase, it would have been prior to the addict's having built up his tolerance of addiction. In the second transitional phase, he has not only learned to tolerate the addiction system, but his self-image is primarily related to that system. Alternatives to this self-image must be present in order to build an effective tolerance for abstinence. We classify this third type of detoxification as the rehabilitative type.

The distinctive characteristic of the rehabilitative type of detoxification is its determination and control, not by the addict but by the rehabilitation agent, which is not usually the case with avoidance and maintenance detoxifications. The addict, because he has built up his tolerance of addiction, may be assumed to find the addiction state of Phase II more familiar and less threatening than the abstinence state. We base this on the premise implicit in our model that a Phase II addict has adapted to the addiction system and tolerates the system so well that his patterns of social behavior and self-image are centered mainly within the addiction system. In other words, this has become his social world and way of life. As stated earlier, just as the addict must go from a world without drugs to the world of addiction via development of a tolerance for addiction, so must he now build up a tolerance for another state, the "square" world of abstinence, which is alien to his current way of life.

Treatment programs based upon the concept of transforming an addict into a nonaddict by the process of detoxification, even when it is coupled with lengthy aftercare, often confuse being drug-free with being abstinent. Just as the nonuser is not an addict because he begins to use drugs, so an addict is not necessarily fully abstinent when he is merely physically free of drugs. Both addiction and abstinence in our society represent more than physiological conditions since they both have psychological and social components as well.

The individual who uses drugs illegally and without a protected status necessarily becomes involved in human interactions that become an integral part of the addiction process and system. To look at an addict only in physiological terms is tantamount to viewing him in a vacuum. One builds not only a physiological tolerance while becoming addicted, but also a social and emotional tolerance. In our conceptualization, the emotional and self-image components are a necessary part of the definition of addiction when we are dealing with a Phase II type, i.e., one who is part of the addiction system. For the person who has adapted to this particular way of life, the physiological, social, and psychological components are interrelated. The removal of one element, i.e., drugs, from this functioning system, does not alter the state to its polar opposite, abstinence, but only causes strains and tensions to emerge more strongly in the remaining components which have not been touched. This reaction would characterize the operation of any system from which an essential part was withdrawn.

PHASE III: TOLERANCE FOR POTENTIAL ABSTINENCE

While the addict is functioning within the addiction system, the fact of involvement with its values, norms, and attitudes constitutes a normative adaptation or modus vivendi for him. To achieve a new adaptation which does not contain the elements of the addiction system, it now becomes necessary for him to develop a tolerance for abstinence.

Experimentation Stage: Recidivism

Experience in rehabilitation efforts with addicts suggests that the majority of addicts who are withdrawn from drugs eventually become recidivists. This cyclical pattern of detoxification, return to drugs, readdiction, and further detoxification is repeated so often for the individual addict that hospitals for detoxification are said to have a revolving-door orientation. The frequency with which the professional worker sees his patients return to drugs has led to feelings of frustration and inadequacy in dealing with them.

In the conceptualizations in this model, return to drugs following detoxification of those persons who have a highly developed tolerance for addiction does not necessarily represent failure. If one looks at total abstinence from the perspective of an addict who has adapted to the addiction system, any movement toward the abstinence system is of great importance. The tendency for human beings to gravitate toward the adaptational system with which they are most familiar or most comfortable is well known to the psychotherapist. Ideally, movement toward abstinence should be straight and unswerving with no relapse; but experience with other illnesses, both physical and emotional, indicates that relapse is often an integral part of the rehabilitation process. We therefore need to redefine our expectations in this stage of rehabilitation.

The model suggests that the building of tolerance for abstinence is heralded by a stage in which the addict attempts to break away from the addiction system and develop socially acceptable work patterns, new friends, etc. He fails and returns to the drug system which is more comfortable for him. His recidivism then consists, in our framework, not so much in a return to an abnormal system of drug use, but actually in a failure to adapt to a new system which would require an alteration of his self-image. In a sense, it is the new system which is abnormal for him.

If an individual is to be held in a continuous, ongoing treatment effort, we must begin to be aware of the forces which must be activated to resolve his identification with the addiction system and move it toward the abstinence system. Before he becomes fully committed to the addiction system as described in this paper, the user needs to develop skills, associations, and values supportive of the system. In much the same way, an effort to help the addict enter into, and maintain himself in, the abstinence system must be preceded by the development of skills, associations, and values which will support the new system. In many respects, the total institution and self-help orientations of the Synanon and Daytop Village programs attempt to accomplish these goals.[53]

This stage of experimentation is characterized, therefore, not only by experimentation with the absence of drugs, but probably even more importantly by involvement in the various sociocultural aspects of the abstinence system, i.e., the skills and norms of the larger society. It is success with these elements, however limited, which enables the tolerance of abstinence to be developed.

Adaptational Stage: Chemotherapy or Drug Substitution

Much as the addict continued to develop a tolerance for the addiction state, so must he now continue to develop a tolerance for abstinence. Under certain conditions, the addict may be regarded as needing a period of adaptation while using drugs, under a therapeutic regime, before sufficient tolerance can be built. It is felt that various chemotherapy supports are possible and may be desirable. Some success has been observed in the support given by tranquilizers. If such substances are provided, they may make it somewhat easier to bear the condition of abstinence from illicit drugs as well as the very severe problems of relating to the square world. This approach may not be indicated for all because of the dangers of alternative addictions.*

In the early stages of the life cycle of addiction, irregular use of heroin is tried by many potential addicts, and it appears that a number of these do not go on to addiction. Since the risk of irregular use leading to regular use is so great, heroin is not a desirable drug to be used at this stage. It is acknowledged, however, that the rejection of heroin as a chemotherapeutic tool is undoubtedly a function of social attitudes toward it, since methadone, a similar drug, is increasingly being accepted in experimental maintenance programs. It is important to note that use of chemotherapy during this stage is still a function of the interaction between the original addiction set of the addict and his present sociocultural milieu. The adaptational stage of the tolerance for abstinence, perhaps more than any other, requires the individualization of treatment techniques.

Physiological Stage: Drug-Free with Support

Those addicts who reach the final phase of the tolerance for abstinence may spend considerable time at the stage we call the physiological stage. By this, we mean the time period during which they receive support from a caseworker, therapist, group, or other intervention agent which enables them to continue building their tolerance for abstinence while they abstain from use of drugs or drug substitutes.

PHASE IV: TOLERANCE OF ABSTINENCE

Finally, only after the addict has built considerable tolerance for the abstinence system during Phase III, so that he is emotionally and socially prepared to enter the more normative community as customarily defined by the system of authority in the society, can he move

---

* There may be some addicts who are capable of making the transition from a state of physiological addiction to that of total abstinence without going through a stage of treatment which includes chemotherapy or drug therapy. At present, there does not appear to be any a priori means of determining who these are. Research and evaluation attempts are called for in this area.

into a complex psychosocial system of abstinence and function normally. It is only when an addict has reached this stage that we can talk about cure. It is obvious, however, that not many addicts reach this stage.

Implications for Intervention

The implications of the life-cycle-of-addiction concept for rehabilitation and intervention are readily apparent. Before rendering treatment to a drug abuser, it is essential to know the point he has reached in his life cycle since this will also indicate the intensity of his involvement with the addiction system. For instance, to place a young, physiologically addicted person who has not become fully involved in the addiction system into a segregated addict treatment facility might well expedite his entry into the addiction system.

To expect an addict whose life interests are controlled by long involvement with the addiction system suddenly to become abstinent would be equally unrealistic. Such an individual may require extensive long-term chemotherapeutic support before he ultimately moves into a more stable state of tolerance of abstinence.

The tendency in the addiction rehabilitation field today is for the advocates of particular treatment modalities to assume omnipotence for their approach and to believe that their treatment failures are either "not ready for treatment" or "untreatable." Yet a wide range of treatment modalities already has been developed [54] which show greater success for different types and classes of addicts. Rehabilitation personnel should become better oriented to the need for differential diagnosis of the addict's condition and be prepared to use the different approaches available by "partializing" services or by referring patients to other facilities when they recognize that their own is inappropriate for a particular patient. A life-cycle orientation may help them in their decision-making.

It must also be emphasized that the preceding descriptive model is constructed out of our knowledge of one particular population of drug-dependent individuals: the predominantly lower-class, urban users who are brought to the attention of correctional and treatment personnel and thereby become available for intensive study. We do have knowledge about other groups such as physician-, nurse-, and pharmacist-addicts for whom other models might be constructed and different pathways traced. The affluent middle-class and upper-class "hidden" addict represents still another type. It is our feeling that the concept of the life cycle of addiction, in its broader dimensions, can be applied with adaptations to these groups as well.

A RATIONAL APPROACH TO DIAGNOSIS AND TREATMENT

The implications of our life-cycle concept for diagnosis and treatment intervention will by this time be apparent: before instituting treatment in future, we shall first need to know (1) the point the addict has reached in the life cycle, since this will reveal the extent of his involvement with the addiction system; and (2) the degree to which he developed personal and social strengths prior to his addiction. It seems logical to assume that the greater the involvement with drugs and the weaker the previous ego and social balance, the greater the need for more forceful treatment intervention such as removal from the community to an institutional setting or therapeutic environment for a period of perhaps years. The converse of this would be to leave the addict in the community if he is functioning productively and has constructive social ties which have been a continuing source of stability and should therefore not be disrupted, but rather reinforced.

We also need to be more clear about the question of goals, which has been grossly misunderstood and has confounded our treatment efforts. At the Washington Heights Rehabilitation Center, we found the first signs of improvement reflected not so much in total immediate abstinence as we have demanded hitherto, but rather in other areas such as improvement in social functioning and interpersonal relations, reduction of criminality, and, gradually, decrease in drug use. If we reverse the early stages of our life-cycle model, we realize that rehabilitation will be a slow and painstaking process; for, the addict must now build a tolerance for abstinence in order to adapt to the abstinence system and conventional world. By misinterpreting what constitutes realistic goals, we previously made patients who slipped feel they were failures, discontinued our treatment, and thus helped root them more firmly in the addiction system.

To accomplish our goal of rational diagnosis and treatment, we would therefore need to avoid the mistake being made in various parts of the country today of leaning too exclusively on a uniform diagnosis and single treatment approach or model, and offer instead a comprehensive program comprising the full spectrum of treatment modalities, including residential centers such as Daytop Village and Phoenix House; the use of rational authority based on probationary control as practiced at the Washington Heights Rehabilitation Center; chemotherapy, including methadone maintenance and the narcotics antagonist cyclazocine; religious approaches such as Teen Challenge and the Damascus Church; and any other method which offers hope of success. The rationale for this proposal derives from the belief stressed repeatedly in this book that there is no universal "addict," but rather a variety of addicts who will respond only to different treatment approaches. Thus, Synanon will work for a certain number of addicts, not for all. This does not mean that Synanon is to be condemned but, rather, that we need to learn for whom it is effective; and this will be true of other approaches as well.

An advantage of this rationale is that no patient need be lost if he fails to make it in a particular modality. He can be moved to others, until he finds the one appropriate for him. In our experience at the Albert Einstein College of Medicine, a number of patients shifted back and forth between cyclazocine and methadone, finally remaining with the one with which they felt most comfortable. We shall undoubtedly also need to be eclectic at times, combining elements of different modalities to reinforce each other, as in our use of rational authority in the chemotherapy programs, or combining methadone maintenance with residential center treatment, or possibly using different treatment approaches or techniques for different phases of treatment.

It will be evident that our prospectus presupposes the existence of a central organizing agency in each city and state with a rationale such as ours, which could oversee the establishment of the wide-ranging program described. This agency would need to foster a far more consistent sharing of information and coordination of research and evaluation than have existed hitherto, and provide for epidemiological and longitudinal studies to learn more about how individuals become addicts. We could thus enter into the essential areas of prediction and primary prevention. To accomplish this, it will be necessary to standardize our instruments and integrate our evaluation of the many treatment facilities included, allowing also for replication of studies to eliminate the factor of charismatic influence. Only with such an approach, it seems, can we hope to overcome the prevailing chaotic situation and achieve a rational management of the addiction problem.

REFERENCES

1. Brill, L. Drug abuse as a social problem. *International Journal of the Addictions* 1:2, 1966.
2. Chein, I., Gerard, D., and Rosenfeld, I. *The Road to H.* New York: Behavioral Sciences Book Club, 1964, pp. 12–13.
3. Becker, H. Becoming a marijuana user. *American Journal of Sociology* 59:235–242, 1953.
4. Lasagna, L., Van Felsinger, J. M., and Beecher, H. R. Drug-induced mood changes in man. *Journal of the American Medical Association* 157:1006–1113, 1955.
5. *Ibid.*, p. 1113.
6. Chein, I. et al. *Op. cit.*, pp. 241 ff.
7. Simmel, E. Quoted in Fenichel, C. *The Psychoanalytic Theory of Neurosis.* New York: W. W. Norton, 1945, p. 377.
8. Escalona, S. K. Some Determinants of Individual Difference. *Transactions of the New York Academy of Science,* Sec. 11, Vol. 27, No. 7, May 1963.
9. Ackerman, N. W. *The Psychodynamics of Family Life.* New York: Basic Books, 1958.
10. Boszormenyi-Nagy, and Framo, J. L. *Intensive Family Therapy.* New York: Harper & Row, 1965.
11. Bowen, M. The Family of the Schizophrenic. In D. Jackson (Ed.), *Etiology of Schizophrenia.* New York: Basic Books, 1960.
12. Chein, I. et al. *Op. cit.*, pp. 251 ff.
13. Bowen, M. *Op. cit.*, pp. 346 ff.
14. Kolb, L. Cited in Ausubel, D., ref. 15.
15. Ausubel, D. *Drug Addiction.* New York: Random House, 1958.
16. Chein, I. et al. *Op. cit.*, pp. 195 ff.
17. Rado, S. The psychoanalysis of pharmacothymia. *Psychoanalytic Quarterly* 2:23, 1933.
18. Chein, I. et al. *Op. cit.*, pp. 27 ff.
19. Brotman, R., Meyer, A. S., Freedman, A., and Lieberman, L. Preliminary Report on Social Types of Addicts. Paper presented before National Research Council, NSF, Ann Arbor, Michigan, February 1963, pp. 94 ff.
20. Cloward, R. Illegitimate means, anomie and deviant behavior. *American Sociological Review* 24:164–176, 1959.
21. Cloward, R., and Ohlin, L. *Delinquency and Opportunity.* Glencoe, Ill.: Free Press, 1963.
22. Clausen, J. A. Social and psychological factors in narcotics addiction. *Law and Contemporary Problems* 22:34–51, 1957.
23. Volkman, C., and Cressy, D. R. Differential association and the rehabilitation of drug addicts. *American Journal of Sociology* 69:129–142, 1963.
24. Lindesmith, A. R. *Opiate Addiction.* Bloomington: Indiana University Press, 1947.
25. Lindesmith, A. R. Problems in the Social Psychology of Addiction. In D. M. Wilner and G. G. Kassebaum (Eds.), *Narcotics Addiction.* New York: McGraw-Hill, 1965.

26. Wikler, A. Conditioning Factors in Opiate Addiction. In D. M. Wilner and G. G. Kassebaum (Eds.). *Op. cit.* pp. 85–100.
27. Blum, R. H. Mind-Altering Drugs and Dangerous Behavior: Narcotics. In *Task Force Report: Narcotics and Drug Abuse*. The President's Commission on Law Enforcement and Administration of Justice. Washington, D.C.: U. S. Government Printing Office, 1967, p. 52.
28. Winick, C. The Life Cycle of the Narcotic Addict and of Addiction. *U.N. Bulletin on Narcotics* 16:22–32, 1964.
29. Chein, I. et al. *Op cit.*
30. Alksne, H., Trussell, R. E., and Elinson, J. *A Follow-up Study of Treated Adolescent Narcotic Users*. Report of the Columbia University School of Public Health and Administrative Medicine, 1959.
30a. Duvall, H. J., Locke, B. Z., and Brill, L. Follow-up study of narcotic drug addicts five years after hospitalization. *Public Health Reports* 78:185–193, 1963.
30b. O'Donnell, J. A follow-up of narcotic addicts. *American Journal of Orthopsychiatry* 34:948–954, 1964.
30c. Pescor, M. J. Follow-up study of treated narcotic drug addicts. *Public Health Reports*, Supplement No. 170, 1943.
31. *Taber's Cyclopedic Medical Dictionary* (9th ed.). Philadelphia: F. A. Davis Co., 1962.
32. Chein, I. et al. *Op. cit.*, pp. 152 ff.
33. Rado, S. The psychoanalysis of pharmacothymia (drug addiction). *Psychoanalytic Quarterly* 2:1–23, 1933.
34. Ehrenwald, J. *Neurosis in the Family and Patterns of Psychological Defense: A Study of Psychiatric Epidemiology*. New York: Harper & Row, 1963.
35. Kaufman, I., and Reiner, B. S. *Character Disorders in Parents of Delinquents*. New York: Family Service Association of America, 1959.
36. Johnson, A., and Szurek, T. Genesis of antisocial acting-out in children and adults. *Psychoanalytic Quarterly* 21:323–343, 1952.
37. Brill, L. Community approaches to the narcotic addict. *Canadian Journal of Corrections* vol. 6, 1963.
38. Merton, R. K. *Social Theory and Social Structure*. Glencoe, Ill.: Free Press, 1949.
39. Cloward, R., and Ohlin, L. *Delinquency and Opportunity*. Glencoe, Ill.: Free Press, 1963.
40. Brill, L. Drug abuse as a social problem. *International Journal of the Addictions* 1:7–21, 1966.
41. Alksne, H. et al. *Op. cit.*
42. *Ibid.*
43. Sutherland, E. H., and Cressy, D. R. *Principles of Criminology* (6th ed.). Chicago: J. B. Lippincott, 1960.
44. Szasz, T. The role of the counterphobic mechanism in addiction. *Journal of the American Psychoanalytic Association* 6:309–325, 1958.
45. Becker, H. *Outsiders: Studies in the Sociology of Deviancy*. Glencoe, Ill.: Free Press, 1963.

46. Wikler, A. On the nature of addiction and habituation. *British Journal of Addiction* 57:73–79, 1961.
47. Lindesmith, A. R. Problems in the Social Psychology of Addiction. In D. M. Wilner and G. G. Kassebaum (Eds.), *Narcotics*. New York: McGraw-Hill, 1965.
48. Mead, G. H. *Mind, Self and Society*. Chicago: University of Chicago Press, 1934.
49. Lindesmith, A. R. *Op. cit.*
50. Gamso, R. Hospital Treatment. In W. C. Bier (Ed.), *Problems in Addiction*. New York: Fordham University Press (Pastoral Psychology Series, No. 2), 1962.
51. Becker. *Op. cit.*
52. Finestone, H. Cats, Kicks and Color. In H. S. Becker (Ed.), *The Other Side*. London: Free Press of Glencoe, Collier-Macmillan Limited, 1964.
53. Lieberman, L. Current trends in the rehabilitation of narcotics addicts. *Social Work* 12:53–59, 1967.
54. *Ibid.*

Appendix A
QUESTIONNAIRES AND FORMS

THESE FORMS are included to give the reader more insight into and examples of the workings of the Washington Heights Rehabilitation Center, and also to aid him in setting up his own forms for such a project. They may also be used as a base for future comparisons of data.

OFFICE OF PROBATION OF THE COURTS OF THE CITY OF NEW YORK
NARCOTICS SERVICE
INITIAL SCREENING

CLIENT'S LAST NAME	FIRST	ALIAS	
PROBATION OR PRESENT ADDRESS		LAST ADDRESS	
BIRTH DATE MO DAY YR	ETHNICITY (SEE LEGEND)	USUAL OCCUPATION	
MARITAL STATUS (SEE LEGEND)			

CHARACTER OF ADDICTION

1. FIRST USE OF DRUGS
   DATE _____ AGE _____ KIND _____ ROUTE (SEE LEGEND) _____

2. DOES CLIENT CONSIDER HIMSELF AN ADDICT? (PROBE FOR HIS DEFINITION OF ADDICTION AND HOW THIS FITS HIM)
   ☐ YES ☐ NO (IF YES) WHY? _____ EXPLAIN PATTERN IF NOT CLEAR

3. LONGEST PERIOD OF CONTINUOUS DAILY DRUG USE:
   HOW LONG? _____ DATE ENDED _____

4A. DRUG OF CHOICE _____ ROUTE _____ 4B. SEC'D DRUG USED MOST OFTEN _____ ROUTE _____

5A. BRIEF DESCRIPTION OF TYPE, FREQUENCY AND AMOUNT OF DRUG USE AT HIGHEST POINT DURING THE LAST YEAR IN COMMUNITY. (TYPE OF DRUG, NUMBER OF TIMES USED DURING DAY, COST OF HABIT PER DAY)

   B. HOW LONG DID PERIOD OF HIGHEST USE LAST? _____

6. ARE TRACKS VISIBLE? (SEE LEGEND) ☐ YES ☐ NO

7. HAS CLIENT EVER EXPERIENCED WITHDRAWAL SYMPTOMS? (SEE LEGEND) ☐ YES ☐ NO (IF YES) WHEN AND WHAT KIND?

TREATMENT EXPERIENCE

8. PREVIOUS TREATMENT FOR DRUG ADDICTION

NAME OF INSTITUTION OR COMMUNITY AGENCY	NO. OF TIMES	FIRST TIME WENT-DATE	LAST TIME WENT-DATE	TYPE OF TREATMENT

MINIMAL CRITERIA FOR CONSIDERATION FOR PROGRAM

9A. CLIENT MUST APPEAR TO BE A LIKELY CANDIDATE FOR PROBATION

B. HEROIN OR OTHER ACCEPTABLE DRUG IS DRUG OF CHOICE* ☐ YES ☐ NO

C. HAS USED HEROIN OR OTHER ACCEPTABLE DRUG IN DAILY CONTINUOUS USE FOR AT LEAST TWO WEEKS AT SOME POINT DURING LAST YEAR IN COMMUNITY ☐ YES ☐ NO

D. HAS EXPERIENCED WITHDRAWAL SYMPTOMS AT LEAST ONCE ☐ YES ☐ NO

(IF YES TO ALL THREE ITEMS, CLIENT IS ELIGIBLE FOR PROGRAM)

* ACCEPTABLE DRUG OF CHOICE

☐ HEROIN	☐ METHADON	☐ PAREGORIC	☐ DILAUDID
☐ MORPHINE	☐ DOLOPHINE	☐ HYCODAN	☐ CODEINE
☐ PANTOPON	☐ DEMEROL	☐ PERCODAN	☐ COCINOL
			☐ DICODID

DISPOSITION

10. ☐ GROUP 1   ☐ GROUP 2   ☐ GROUP 3   ☐ NOT ACCEPTED   ☐ COMMITTED

COURT IN WHICH APPEARED | BOROUGH | PART | DATE

SIGNATURE OF PROBATION OFFICER

(SEE LEGEND ON REVERSE SIDE)

LEGEND

ETHNICITY — To include birthplace and racial identity (e.g. Jamaican Negro; East European Jew etc.)

MARITAL STATUS — Even if the more conventional conditions of married, single, divorced, etc. are present make specific notes concerning the kind of cohabitation involved - For example: married, living with another woman; single, living with woman.

(Get Details)

ROUTE — The way in which drugs are taken - Examples: orally, sniffing, intramuscular injections, intravenous injections.

TRACKS — The marks left because of repeated injections of drugs. They may be visible as needle punctures of the skin or as scars visually on the arms.

WITHDRAWAL SYMPTOMS — Physiological reactions associated with cessation of use of drugs after physiological addiction, usually characterized by sneezing, stomach cramps, goose-pimples on skin, hot and cold flashes, watering of eyes, etc.

THE CITY OF NEW YORK—DEPARTMENT OF
and THE OFFICE OF PROBATION

RECORD OF

Patient's Name _____ Case No

Probation Officer's Name _____ Program

(CIRCLE DATES ON

	1	2	3	4	5	6	7	8	9	10
Substance										
(Post TLC)										
Drug Status										
(Post TLC)										
How Determined										
*TLC Administered (Check)										

SUBSTANCE

H — Heroin
O — Other Drug (Specify)
? — Probable Use
    (Substance Unknown)
- - Not known if patient is
    using drugs (not probed)
N — No Drugs (probed)

DRUG STATUS

1. Patient Claims Use
2. Patient Probably Using
3. Don't Know
4. Patient Denies Use
5. Patient Denies Use,
   But is Probably Using
6. Institutionalized (Specify)

HOW DETERMINED

V — Report of Probation Off
W — Probed
X — Not Probed
Y — Not Probed,
    Volunteered
Z — Not Probed — Appeared
O — Report of other person

* Put check in box for day T.L.C. administered. After results
are gotten, put a (+) in same box if test was positive, (—)
if test was negative, or (Q) if test was questionable.

If, upon questioning the patient admits to having used on previously recorded days, edit into bottom half of *Use* box, but leave original code in top half of box. Enter new drugs admitted to in second half of substance box.

...ALTH—WASHINGTON HEIGHTS REHABILITATION CENTER
...HE COURTS OF THE CITY OF NEW YORK   Rev. 2/19/65

...LY DRUG USE

_____   Worker's Name _____

_____   Date of Entry _____ Month _____ Year _____

... PATIENT WAS SEEN)

2	13	14	15	16	17	18	19	20	21	22	23	24	25	26	27	28	29	30	31

T.L.C.   **OTHER DRUG — NAME AND DATES USED**

+ Positive   _____

− Negative   _____

Q Questionable   _____

                              _____

                              _____

                              _____

                              _____

WASHINGTON HEIGH[TS]

CASE ACTIV[ITY]

NAME _____ CASE NO. _____

MONTH _____ YEAR _____

DATE	ATTEMPTED ACTION WITH					INITIATED BY		RESULT OF JOINT MGMT DECISION			TYPE OF APPT.		TYPE AND LOCA[TION] OF ACTION				
	Pt.	P.O.	F.	W.	Other (Specify)	W.	Other (Specify)	Yes	No	X	S.	U.	O.	T.C.	H.V.	A.V.	L.
TOTAL																	

LEGEND: A.V. — Agency Visit
F. — Family
H.V. — Home Visit
L. — Letter (Sent or Received)
O. — Office

P.O. — Probation Officer
Pt. — Patient
S. — Scheduled
T.C. — Telephone Call
U. — Unscheduled

...BILITATION CENTER
...YSIS FORM

...KER'S NAME _____ S.W. _____ P.H.N. _____ OTHER _____

...E ENTERED PROGRAM _____ PROGRAM MONTH _____

ACTION COMPL.		PURPOSE OF ACTION	RESULTS OF ACTION INCLUDING FUTURE DISPOSITION
No	Y		

W. — Worker
X. — Result of Cooperative Decision with Other Agency Excluding Probation Office
Y. — Action Completed with Person Other than Originally Intended.

PROBATION
I.D. NO.

Q. I.D. NO.

WASHINGTON HEIGHTS REHABILITATION CENTER
Evaluation Program
Intake Questionnaire

Interviewer _____

Open with a Description of Evaluation-Research Role and Activity

1. Name _____ Date of Interview _____
2. What is your nickname or what are you usually called in the street? _____
3. Address _____ Apartment number _____
4. Phone number _____ a) Where is this?
5. Is there any other place we can reach you if you are not at (Q. 3)? Yes _____
   (*If yes*) No _____
   Address _____ Apartment number _____
   _____ a) Phone number _____
6. Where are some of the places you might hang out in case we want to see you again?

7. How old are you? _____   8. Date of birth _____
9. Place of birth _____ 10. Where raised _____
11. Time in N.Y.C. _____ 12. Time in U.S.A. _____
13. Mother's birthplace _____ 14. Father's birthplace _____
15. Last school year completed? (*Circle below*)

   Elementary School   High School   College
   1 2 3 4 5 6 7 8   9 10 11 12   13 14 15 16

16. Age left school _____

17. Other schools (*Specify*)   None _____
    Kind of School   Time Spent There
    _____   _____
    _____   _____

18. Was your father (*or father surrogate*) at home when you grew up (*until about age 16*)?   Yes _____
    No _____
    (*If yes*)
    a) What kind of work did he usually do? (*Occupation and industry*)

       1) How much money did he usually make? _____ per week
       2) About what year would you say that was? _____

b) How far did he get in school? No schooling _____
(*Elementary school goes through* Elem. Inc. _____
the 8th grade. High school be- Elem. Grad. _____
gins with the 9th grade.) H.S. Inc. _____
    H.S. Grad. _____
    College Inc. _____
    College Grad.
    or more _____

    1) Other kind of school (*Specify*) _____

(*If No to Q. 18*)

19. Who made the money to take care of your family when you were growing up? _____
    a) Who raised you? (*Relationship*) _____
    (*If a person rather than an agency, but not father*)
    b) What kind of work did he/she usually do?

    c) How much money did he/she usually make? _____ per week
    d) How far did he/she get in school? _____

20. Ethnicity of respondent White _____ If Puerto Rican, skin
        Negro _____ color and racial fea-
        Puerto Rican _____ tures:
        Other (*Specify*) _____ White _____
        Negro _____
        Trigueno _____
        (mixed)

21. Religion in which raised _____ *Denomination:* _____
    a) Present religion _____ *Denomination:* _____
       (*If different*)
       1) Did you convert? Yes_____ No_____

22. Branch of Service _____ Non-vet _____ Wartime Merchant Marine _____
    a) Length of service _____
    b) Highest rank _____
    c) Type of discharge _____

23. During the last 12 months (*in the community*) how many months were you working? _____
    a) How many jobs did you have during this time? _____

24. What was the highest job you ever held? _____
    a) How long ago did you have that job? _____
    b) How long did it last? _____

25. What was the most money you ever made on any job? _____ per week

26. How many jobs have you held since you left school? _____

27. Did you like any of the jobs you ever held? Yes_____
        No_____

    (*If liked any job*)
    a) Which one of those you liked did you like the most? _____
       1) Why did you like this job?

INTAKE QUESTIONNAIRE

28. What kind of job would you most like to have some day?

29. What would it take to be able to get a job like that? (*Probe for type of training needed if not originally indicated*)

30. Do you think you would be able to do that type of learning? Yes_____ No_____
31. Do you have any special skills or training in any types of jobs? Yes_____ No_____
    (*If yes*)
    a) What are they?

    b) Which ones did you learn during the past year?
    (*If none check here*)_____

32. Do you know what the New York State Employment Service is? Yes_____ No_____
    (*If respondent never at N.Y.S.E.S.*)
    (*Ask of all*)
33. Are you now listed with the New York State Employment Service for a job? Yes_____ No_____
    (*If no*)
    a) Were you ever listed with the New York State Emment Service for a job? Yes_____ No_____
    (*If yes to 32 or 32a*)
    1) When were you last at the New York State Employment Service? _____
    2) During the last time you were out of work for three months or more, how many times did you go there? _____
34. Are you listed somewhere else for a job? Yes_____ No_____

    (*If yes*)
    a) Where?

    b) When was the last time you were there? _____
35. Where else have you ever gone to look for a job? (*Refers to employment agencies or similar places; newspapers, etc.*)

    (*Ask for each place mentioned*)
    a) When was this?

36. Where were you living just before you were arrested?
    (*Address*) _____
    _____

   a) Who else lived there with you?

   b) Roughly how many days a week did you live there? Every day_____
                                                        Other (*Specify*)——
      (*If not all week*)
      1) Where else did you live?
         (*Address*) _____
         _____

   c) Where do you plan to live now?   (*Same as* Q. 36) _____
      (*If different from* Q. 36)
      (*Address*) _____
      _____

37. Are you single, married, divorced, or what?   Single   _____
                                                  Married   _____
                                                  Common-law   _____
                                                  Divorced   _____
                                                  Separated   _____
                                                  Widowed   _____
                                                  Other (*Specify*) _____
   (*If single, divorced, separated, or widowed*):
   a) Were you living with a girl at the time of your   Yes_____
      arrest?   No_____
   (*If no*)
   b) Did you have a girl you were seeing a lot of at   Yes_____
      the time of your arrest?   No_____
38. Do you have any children?   Yes_____
                                                           No_____
   (*If yes*)
   a) How many?   _____
   b) Are these from your present wife (or the girl you're Yes_____
      living with)?   No_____
   (*If no, get details of circumstances*)
   c) Do you support and take care of these children? (*Get details*)
                                           Yes, both   _____
                                           Yes, support only   _____
                                           Yes, take care only   _____
                                           No, did but not now   _____
                                           No, never   _____
39. *Ascertain which of following was situation for respondent at time of arrest.*
    Married and living with wife   _____
    Married, but has another steady girlfriend   _____
    Married, not living with wife but no steady girlfriend   _____
    Living common-law   _____
    Has steady girlfriend but is not living with her   _____

INTAKE QUESTIONNAIRE

Sees girls only on intermittent basis _____
Sees no girls at all _____
Other (*Describe*) _____ _____
a) What is the situation now? Same _____
                                           Different _____
(*If present situation differs, describe how and state which of the above now applies.*)

40. *For appropriate situation at present as defined above, get information concerning the following areas. If two relationships, e.g.,* married *and* steady girlfriend, *repeat questions for each.*

    Reasons for Summary Rating   Summary

a) Present satisfactions with relationship(s) in general
                                          Apparently satisfied _____
                                          Some dissatisfaction _____
                                          Highly dissatisfied _____
                                          Can't determine _____

b) Present sexual satisfactions (frequency and quality)

Frequency per week		Quality	
None	_____	Very satisfactory	_____
Less than 1 per month	_____	Somewhat satisfactory	_____
Less than 1 per week	_____	Little enjoyment	_____
1	_____	Indifferent	_____
2	_____	Dislikes	_____
3	_____		
4	_____		
5	_____		
6+	_____		

c) Present difficulties with the relationship(s)
                                          Great deal of difficulty _____
                                          Some difficulty _____
                                          Get along well _____
                                          Can't determine _____

d) Plans for continuation of relationship(s)
    Intermittent: Plans to continue relationship(s) _____
    Permanent: Will definitely stay together _____
                   Doubts about staying together _____

e) Does she go out with other men?   Yes _____
                                        No _____
                                        Can't determine _____

f) Does he go out with other women?   Yes _____
                                        No _____
                                        Can't determine _____

g) Present and recent homosexuality   Yes   _____
                                                                          No   _____
                                                                          Respondent refuses
                                                                                  to answer   _____

41. We would like to learn a little about the early home life that you had. Were both of your parents always around up to the time you were 16 years old?   Yes_____ No_____

(*If no*)

  a) Which parent was not there?   Father _____ Mother _____ Both _____

  b) What happened to your father (mother)?

Missing Because of	Mother	Father
Death	_____	_____
Desertion	_____	_____
Divorce	_____	_____
Separation	_____	_____
Other (*Specify*)	_____	_____
D.N.A. (*Present*)	_____	_____

  c) How old were you when that happened?   Mother _____ Father _____
     (*Enter age of respondent at time parent left or died*)

  d) *If either parent gone, ask if other parent has remarried and still lives with new spouse.*
     Parent did not remarry   _____
     Parent remarried; still with new spouse   _____
     Parent remarried; no longer with new spouse   _____

42. How many brothers and sisters do you have?   Brothers _____ Sisters _____
(*Include step-siblings*)

43. Who else lives at the place you live in now?   No one _____

Name	Relationship to Respondent	Age	Sex	How Often Seen by Respondent

  a) Whose apartment is this? _____
  b) What is the rent? _____
  c) Do you pay any of this?   Yes_____ No_____

    (*If yes*)
    How much? _____

  d) Do you give any (other) money to the house? (*Get details*)

INTAKE QUESTIONNAIRE

44. Is any member of your family presently receiving welfare assistance? Yes_____ No_____
    (If yes)
    a) Who? _____

45. Who do you usually eat your meals with?

	Weekdays	Where	Weekends	Where	Skips This Meal
Breakfast					
Lunch					
Dinner/Supper					

46. Would you like to get away from your family completely? Yes_____ No_____
    (D.N.A. to spouse)
    a) *(If yes)* Why? *(Probe deeply)*

    b) *(If no)* Why not? *(Probe deeply)*

47. Do you do things together now with your family? Yes_____ No_____
    (D.N.A. to spouse or children)
    (If yes, probe for five items)

a) What things?	b) How often?	c) Last time
1.		
2.		
3.		
4.		
5.		

    d) Which one of these things do you most enjoy doing? #_____

48. Is there any one person in your family that you really want to be like? Yes_____
    (D.N.A. to spouse or children) No_____ *(specifies there is no one he wants to be like)*
    Be like all of them *(specifies he cannot choose among them: likes all of them)*

    (If yes)
    a) Who?

b) Why?

49. Is there any one person outside of your family that you really want to be like?   Yes_____ No_____
    (If yes)
    a) Who?

    b) Why?

50. Does any other person in your family use drugs?   Yes_____ No_____

    Did any other person in your family use drugs in the past?   Yes_____ No_____

    (D.N.A. to spouse or children)
    (If yes to either, repeat series of questions for each person using drugs)
    a) Who?

    b) What drugs?

    c) How long?

    d) How much? (average quantity and cost per day)?

    e) Ever addicted?

    f) Present drug status?

    (If not now using)
    a) When did he/she stop using?

    b) How was he/she able to stop using (kind of treatment, etc.)?

c) What is he/she doing now (i.e. modal activity, working, criminality, etc.)?

51. Is there anyone in your family that has any kind of problem with too much drinking? (*Family of orientation or family of procreation*) Yes_____ No_____
    (*If yes*)
    a) Who?

52. Does anyone in your family have any other kind of problem he may need some help with? (*Family of orientation or family of procreation*) Yes_____ No_____ DK_____

    (*If yes*)
    a) Who?

    b) What kind of problem?

(*Ask the following questions if married, including common-law, and living with spouse: Q. 53–56*)
53. How well do you get along with your wife? (*Probe deeply*)

54. Would you like to break up with your wife? Yes_____ No_____

    (*If yes*)
    a) Why? (*Probe deeply*)

    (*If no*)
    b) Why not? (*Probe deeply*)

55. Do you ever do things together with your wife? Yes_____ No_____

    (*If yes, probe for five items*)

a)	b)	c)
What things?	How often?	Last time
1.		
2.		
3.		
4.		
5.		

d) Which one of these things do you most enjoy doing? #_____

56. Did your wife or children ever use drugs? Yes_____ No_____

(*If yes, specify who and get details of*)
a) What drugs?

b) How long?

c) How much (average quantity and cost per day)?

d) Ever addicted?

e) Present drug status?

(*If not now using*)
a) When did he/she stop?

b) How was he/she able to stop (kind of treatment, etc.)?

c) What does he/she do now (i.e., modal activity: works, prostitutes, housewife, etc.)?

57. Just before you were arrested, what did you do in your spare time?
(*Probe for at least five items. Do not accept "nothing," "hustling," or "drugs" as an answer.*)

a)	b)	c)
What things?	How often?	Last time
1.		
2.		
3.		
4.		
5.		

INTAKE QUESTIONNAIRE

d) Was this when you were on drugs or off drugs? On drugs _____
  Off drugs _____
e) Which of these things did you most enjoy doing? # _____
f) How many of these things do you *really* enjoy doing? _____
  (*If any*)
  1) Which ones are they? #'s _____ _____ _____ _____ _____

58. Just before you were arrested, what did you do in your spare time when you were _____ drugs?

(*Ask for opposite drug status of response to 57d*)

a) What things?	b) How often?	c) Last time
1. _____	_____	_____
2. _____	_____	_____
3. _____	_____	_____
4. _____	_____	_____
5. _____	_____	_____

  d) Which of these things did you most enjoy doing? # _____
  e) How many of these things do you really enjoy doing? _____
    (*If any*)
    1) Which ones are they? #'s _____ _____ _____ _____ _____

59. What would you most like to do if you had the money and time?
  1st Response Use drugs _____
  Nothing _____

(*If "drugs" or "nothing," record and probe more deeply for alternate responses*)

60. In the last continuous month in the community did you:

	Yes	No
Go to any parties or dances	_____	_____
Have a few drinks with friends	_____	_____
Visit a friend who does *not* use drugs	_____	_____
Go to church	_____	_____
Do any gambling	_____	_____
Watch TV all day long	_____	_____
Read a book	_____	_____
Play some sport	_____	_____
Go out on a date with a girl	_____	_____

61. Outside of your relatives, about how many people do you go around with at least once in a while? Number on: _____ off: _____

	On	Off
a) How many of these are drug users?	_____	_____
b) How many of these drug users are your *real close* friends?	_____	_____

248   APPENDIX A

    c) How many of these drug users are men? _____ _____
    d) How many of these drug users are women? _____ _____
    e) How many of these people do not use drugs? _____ _____
    f) How many of these non-drug users are your
        real close friends? _____ _____
    g) How many of the non-drug users are men? _____ _____
    h) How many of the non-drug users are women? _____ _____
62. Where do you go to find new friends?

    a) Anywhere else?

63. Drugs (*Read as is*)
    We'd like to get a picture, now, of what happened when you first used drugs. Let's start with the first time you used any kind of drug—narcotics, or pot or glue, or anything.
    (*Interviewer should get from the respondent a complete chronological description of his initial drug use up until his first addiction. All relevant material such as age, types of drugs, frequency of use, amounts used, costs, routes, and methods of support of habit should be included. When respondent has completed his description, interviewer should ask "How did you know that you were addicted?" This checklist should be used only as a reminder, to the interviewer, of the kinds of data we wish to collect.*)

    Type of drugs   Routes
    Age used   Means of support of drug use
    Frequency of use (times per day, per   Simultaneous drugs used
       week)
    Amount used (in quantity and cost per
       day)

64. What drugs were you using during the week before your arrest? (*First ask and then circle drug used most often at this time*)

Drug	Route	Amount	Frequency	Usual Times of Day
1.				
2.				
3.				

        a) During the last six months (in the community)   Yes_____
            did you use any other drugs?   No_____
            (*If yes*) Which ones?

INTAKE QUESTIONNAIRE

Drug	Route	Amount	Frequency	Usual Times of Day
1.				
2.				
3.				

b) Since you've been addicted did you use any drugs other than those already mentioned? (*If yes*) Which ones?

Yes _____
No _____

Drug	Route	Amount	Frequency	Usual Times of Day	When Used	Why Did You Stop Using This Drug?
1.						
2.						
3.						

c) Did you ever use any kind of drug or pill a few times and then stop using it? (*If yes*)

Yes _____
No _____

Drug	Route	Amount	Frequency	Usual Times of Day	When Used	Why Did You Stop Using This Drug?
1.						
2.						
3.						

d) Did you ever use any drugs to help cut down on your heroin use by yourself? (*If yes*)

Yes _____
No _____

Drug	Route	Amount	Frequency	Usual Times of Day	When Used	Why Did You Stop Using This Drug?
1.						
2.						
3.						

65. How were you supporting your habit at the time of your arrest? (*If pawning, where were goods obtained? May include work, if volunteered*)

Method	Frequency
1.	
2.	

3. _____

a) During the last six months (in the community) did you support your habit in any other way? Yes____ No____
(*If pawning, where were goods obtained?*
May include work if volunteered)
(*If yes*) Which ways?

	Method	Frequency
1.		
2.		
3.		

b) Since you've been addicted have you ever supported your habit in any other ways? Yes____ No____
(*If pawning, where were goods obtained?*
May include work if volunteered)
(*If yes*) Which ways?

	Method	Frequency
1.		
2.		
3.		

c) Have you ever done any of these *other* things to support your habit? (*Read only those not already mentioned but check ones previously mentioned as well as new ones*)

1. Gambling _____   7. Loaning works _____
2. Begging _____   8. Copping for someone else _____
3. Running numbers _____   9. Selling drugs _____
4. Sex with men _____   10. Mugging _____
5. Conning (*Describe*)_____   11. Breaking and entering _____
_____   12. Shoplifting _____
6. Pimping _____   13. Other (*Specify*) _____

(*Ascertain and circle which of these done last year in community*)

a) Which of all these things have you done most often to support your habit? #_____
b) Did you ever do any of these things for reasons other than to support your habit? Yes____ No____
(*If yes*) Which ones? #____ #____ #____

66. (*Interviewer should ask respondent to think back to and describe his most intensive period of drug use. All relevant material such as age, length of intensive period, types of drugs used, frequency of use, amounts used, costs, routes, and methods of support of habit should be included. Question to be interpreted as period in which largest amount of drugs used in one day and one week. This checklist should be used only as a reminder, to the interviewer, of the kinds of data we wish to collect.*)

Types of drugs
Age of most intense period
Length of most intense period
Frequency of use (times per day, per week)

Routes
Means of support of drug use
Simultaneous drugs used

INTAKE QUESTIONNAIRE

Amount used (in quantities and cost per day)   Reason for termination of intensive drug use

67. When did you last get detoxified from drugs?_____
    a) Where was this?   Jail_____   Hospital_____   Street_____
    (*If not jail*)
        1) Was this voluntary or not?   Voluntary_____   Not voluntary_____
    b) How long did it take?_____
    c) How were you detoxified?   Cold, no medication   _____
                                            Methadone, alone   _____
                                            Methadone plus other drugs
                                                 (*Specify*)   _____
                                            Other drugs alone (*Specify*)   _____
    d) When you left the (hospital) (jail)
    (or finished kicking on your own) did
    you think you were physically clean of   Yes_____
    drugs?   No_____
    (*If yes*)
    1) Why?

    (*If no*)
    2) Why not?

    e) When you left the (hospital) (jail)
    (or finished kicking on your own) did
    you think you were mentally clean of   Yes_____
    drugs?   No_____
    (*If yes*)
    1) Why?

    (*If no*)
    2) Why not?

68. After you were detoxified how long was it before you first used drugs again?

    (*If now abstinent repeat Q. 67 and Q. 68 for last previous detoxification*)
    a) (Determine how much time there was between last two hospital detoxi-

APPENDIX A

fications, providing there was no imprisonment or other institutionalization in between)

69. (*Interviewer should ask respondent to give a description of his use of drugs from his first use after his last detoxification until he was fully readdicted. All relevant information such as dates, types of drugs used, amounts, frequencies, costs, and methods of support of habit should be included. This applies to the last time respondent was addicted after a detoxification. This checklist should be used only as a reminder, to the interviewer, of the kinds of data we wish to collect.*)

Type of drugs   Routes
Frequency of use (times per day, per week) Means of support of drug
                                            use
Amounts used (in quantity and cost per day) Simultaneous drugs used

70. (*Interviewer should ask respondent to think back over his last year in the community. Interviewer should get a complete chronological description by month of that year. This description should include respondent's actions in the following areas: hospital involvement, jail involvement, arrests, other institutions, agencies of any kind, work, and periods of abstinence. Names of agencies, hospitals, etc., and kind of work done on jobs are necessary. Drug activity includes types of drugs, amounts used, frequency of use, routes, and methods of support of habit. Indicate under "work" whether respondent worked full month [F], most of month, over half [M]; part of month, less than half [P], or not at all [—].*)

Month, Year	If in Community		Arrests, Charges, Jail Involvement	Hospital and Other Institutional Involvement	In N.Y.C.	Outside N.Y.C. (*Specify*)
	Work	Drugs				

71. Which hospitals have you kicked at? (*If any, ask for each*) How many times have you kicked there? Was it voluntary or not?

   Hospital   Number of Times Kicked   Voluntary
1. _____   _____   _____
2. _____   _____   _____
3. _____   _____   _____

a) Which of these have you gone to during the past year? (*If any, ask for*

INTAKE QUESTIONNAIRE

each) How many times have you kicked there during the past year? Was it voluntary or not?

Hospital	Number of Times Kicked	Voluntary
1. _____	_____	_____
2. _____	_____	_____
3. _____	_____	_____

(*Estimate total number of weeks spent in hospital for detoxification during past year and enter here*)_____

(*Interviewer should specify if respondent has been to a hospital without kicking*)

72. About how many times have you kicked on your own? _____
    a) How many times have you kicked on your own during the past year? _____
    b) (*If ever kicked on own, get details on how and what used*)

    c) Did you ever *cut down* on your habit by yourself?   Yes_____
                                                              No_____

    (*If yes, get details*)

73. Did you ever kick anywhere else?   Yes_____
                                         No_____

    (*If yes*)

	a) Where	b) When	c) Voluntary or Involuntary
1.	_____	_____	_____
2.	_____	_____	_____
3.	_____	_____	_____

    d) Which of these were during the past year? #1_____ 2._____ 3._____

74. Did you ever get any other kind of help for your drug addiction problem?   Yes_____
                                                                                 No_____
    (*If yes*)
    a) Where was that? (*Anywhere else?*)

    b) When? (*Ask for each*)

c) What kind of help did you get there? (*Specify for each*)

75. Were you ever in a hospital for some reason Yes_____
    other than detoxification? No_____
    (*If yes*)
    a) What were you in there for?

    b) When?

    c) What hospital was that (hospitals were these?)

76. How often do you generally drink alcohol?
    a) When using?

    b) When not using?

77. How much do you generally drink at those times?
    a) When using?
                            (*Interviewer should estimate amount in ounces of whiskey per day*)
    b) When not using?

78. Have you ever gotten into any trouble with the law Yes_____
    because of your drinking? No_____
    (*If yes*)
    a) What kind of trouble?

    (*If no*)
    b) Why do you think you haven't gotten into trouble with the law because of your drinking?

79. Have you ever gotten into any other kind of trouble
    because of your drinking, such as health problems, Yes_____
    job problems, family problems, etc.? No_____

(If yes)
a) What kind of trouble?

(If no)
b) Why do you think you haven't gotten into this kind of trouble because of your drinking?

80. How many times have you been arrested in your life? Includes J.D., etc.   Number of arrests _____

a) Arrested for	b) When	c) Age	d) Disposition of Case (*Include agency to which referred and length of institutionalization*)
1. _____	_____	_____	_____
2. _____	_____	_____	_____
3. _____	_____	_____	_____

(*Circle any of the above that took place prior to drug use*)

81. Are there any other times that you've ever been in trouble with the law that you've been brought before the courts?   Yes _____   No _____

(If yes)

a) What for	b) When	c) Age	d) What Happened
1. _____	_____	_____	_____
2. _____	_____	_____	_____
3. _____	_____	_____	_____

(*Circle any of the above that took place prior to drug use*)

82. About how much time have you spent in prison? Years _____ Months _____
83. When were you first in prison? Year _____ Month _____
84. When was the last time you were in prison? Year _____ Month _____
85. How many times have you been sent away from home by the courts on a juvenile delinquency or youthful offender charge?   Number of times _____

(If ever sent)
a) What is the total amount of time you've been away because of that?   Years _____ Months _____
(*Probe to determine if this time included in Q. 82 and check here*)
   Yes _____   No _____
b) How old were you when you were first sent away?   Age _____
c) How old were you when you were last sent away?   Age _____

86. During the last year did you do anything illegal other than the things we

talked about before? (*Refers to acts for which a person may be incarcerated at some institution*)
(*If yes*)

	a) What did you do?	b) What month(s)?	c) How many times?
1.	_____	_____	_____
2.	_____	_____	_____
3.	_____	_____	_____

Just two more questions.

87. What have you heard about the program here?

88. Do you want any kind of help with anything at all?   Yes_____ No_____
(*If yes*)
a) What do you want help with?

	Q.	I.D.	NO.

WASHINGTON HEIGHTS REHABILITATION CENTER
Evaluation Program
Follow-up Questionnaire

Interviewer _____

1. Name _____ Date of Interview _____
2. Where are you living now?
   Address _____ Apartment Number _____
   _____
3. Phone number _____   a) Where is this?
4. Is there any other place we can   Yes _____
   reach you if you are not at Q. 2? No _____
   (If yes)
   Address _____ Apartment Number _____
   _____   a) Phone Number _____
5. Where are some of the places you might hang out in case we want to see you again?

6. How many places have you lived in during the past year?
                    Number of places _____
   a) Where are these places?
   (Get information in terms of area in borough, not specific address, e.g., East Harlem, Bedford-Stuyvesant, Pelham Bay, etc.)
   1. _____ 4. _____
   2. _____ 5. _____
   3. _____ 6. _____
   (Probe to be sure that all temporary residences such as rooming houses, friends' houses, Y.M.C.A., etc. are noted above. Indicate a "T" next to all temporary residences of less than one month. All information above should be listed in chronological order.)
7. Have you attended any kind of school since   Yes _____
   you've been in the program?   No _____

| | | Termination Certificate ||
Kind of School	Time Spent There	Yes	No
1. _____	_____	_____	_____
2. _____	_____	_____	_____
3. _____	_____	_____	_____

8. Since you've been in the program, how many
   months have you been working?   Months _____
   a) How many jobs did you have during this time? _____
9. Why did you leave that (those) job(s)? (Ask if respondent had at least one job during year at which he is not presently working)

Kind of Job	Why Left
1. _____	_____
2. _____	_____
3. _____	_____

10. Since you've been in the program, have you had at least one job which you consider to be better than any you had before? Yes_____ No_____

    (If yes)
    a) What job was that?

    b) When did you have it?

    c) How long did it last?

    d) In what ways was it better?

11. What was the most money you made on any job since you've been in the program?
    (Exclude one-day odd jobs)

12. What kind of job would you most like to have some day?

13. What would it take to be able to get a job like that? (Probe for type of training needed if not originally indicated)

14. Do you think you would be able to do that type of learning? Yes_____ No_____

15. Did you learn any skills or get training in any kinds of jobs since you came into the program? Yes_____ No_____
    (If yes)
    a) What skills (training)?

16. Are you now listed with the New York State Employment Service for a job? Yes_____ No_____
    (If no)
    a) Were you listed with the New York State Employment Service for a job at any time since you came into the program? Yes_____ No_____
    (If yes to 16 or 16a)

FOLLOW-UP QUESTIONNAIRE

    a) When were you last at the New York State Employment Service? _____

    b) During the last time you were out of work for three months or more, how many times did you go there? _____

17. Have you gone to any other kinds of places for a job since coming into the program?   Yes_____ No_____

    (If yes)

    a) Which ones?

        1. _____

        2. _____

        3. _____

18. *(Ascertain respondent's legal marital status)*

    _____ Married

    _____ Married, common-law

    _____ Divorced

    _____ Separated

    _____ Widowed

    _____ Single

    (If married)

    _____ Living with wife, no extramarital activities

    _____ Living with wife, some extramarital activities

    _____ Living with wife, has a steady girlfriend

    _____ Not living with wife, sees no girls

    _____ Not living with wife, sees girls intermittently

    _____ Not living with wife, seeing a girl steadily

    _____ Not living with wife, living with girl in relationship not considered common-law by respondent

    (If married, common-law)

    _____ Living with wife, no extramarital activities

    _____ Living with wife, some extramarital activities

    _____ Living with wife, has a steady girlfriend

    _____ Not living with wife, sees no girls

    _____ Not living with wife, sees girls intermittently

    _____ Not living with wife, seeing a girl steadily

    _____ Not living with wife, living with girl in relationship not considered common-law by respondent

    (If divorced)

    _____ Sees no girls

    _____ Sees girls intermittently

    _____ Seeing a girl steadily

    _____ Living with a girl in relationship not considered common-law by respondent

    (If legally separated)

    _____ Sees no girls

    _____ Sees girls intermittently

    _____ Seeing a girl steadily

    _____ Living with a girl in relationship not considered common-law by respondent

(*If widowed*)
_____ Sees no girls
_____ Sees girls intermittently
_____ Seeing a girl steadily
_____ Living with a girl in relationship not considered common-law by respondent

(*If single*)
_____ Sees no girls
_____ Sees girls intermittently
_____ Seeing a girl steadily
_____ Living with a girl in relationship not considered common-law by respondent

(*If married or living with a girl*)
a) Is this a different girl from the one you told us about a year ago?   Yes_____   No_____

19. Do you have any children?   Yes_____   No_____

(*If yes*)
a) How many? _____
b) Were any of these children born since you came into the program?   Yes_____   No_____
c) Do you support and take care of these children? (*Get details*)

   Yes, both   _____
   Yes, support only _____
   Yes, take care only _____
   No, did but not now _____
   No, never   _____

20. (*For appropriate situation at present as defined above, get information concerning the following areas. If two relationships, e.g., married and steady girlfriend, repeat questions for each.*)

    Reasons for summary rating   Summary

    a) Present satisfactions with the relationship(s) in general
       Apparently satisfied   _____
       Some dissatisfaction   _____
       Highly dissatisfied   _____
       Can't determine   _____

    b) Present sexual satisfactions (frequency and quality)

    Frequency per Week   Quality
    None   _____   Very satisfactory   _____
    Less than 1 per month _____   Somewhat satisfactory _____
    Less than 1 per week _____   Little enjoyment   _____
    1   _____   Indifferent   _____
    2   _____   Dislikes   _____
    3   _____
    4   _____
    5   _____
    6+   _____

    c) Present difficulties with the relationship(s)
       Great deal of difficulty   _____

FOLLOW-UP QUESTIONNAIRE

                  Some difficulty   _____
                  Get along well   _____
                  Can't determine   _____

d) Plans for continuation of relationship(s)
      Intermittent: Plans to continue relationship(s) _____
      Permanent: Will definitely stay together   _____
              Doubts about staying together   _____

e) Does she go out with other men?   Yes   _____
                                     No   _____
                                     Resp. doesn't know   _____
                                     Can't determine   _____

f) Does he go out with other women?   Yes   _____
                                         No   _____
                                       Can't determine   _____

g) Present and recent homosexuality   Yes   _____
                                         No   _____
                                     Respondent refuses
                                          to answer   _____

21. Who else lives at the place you live in now?   No one _____

Name	Relationship to Respondent	Age	Sex	How Often Seen by Respondent

a) Whose apartment is this? _____
b) What is the rent? _____
c) Do you pay any of this?   Yes_____
                                                   No_____

(If yes)
How much?
d) Do you give any (other) money to the house? (*Get details*)

22. Is any member of your family presently receiving   Yes_____
    Welfare assistance?   No_____
    (*If yes*)
    a) Who?

23. Who do you usually eat your meals with? What about breakfast during the week?

	Weekdays	Where	Weekends	Where	Skips This Meal
Breakfast					
Lunch					
Dinner/Supper					

24. Would you like to get away from your family   Yes_____
    completely?   No_____

a) *(If yes)*
   Why? *(Probe deeply)*

b) *(If no)*
   Why not? *(Probe deeply)*

25. Do you do things together now with your family?   Yes_____
    (D.N.A. to spouse or children)   No_____
    (If yes, probe for five items)

a) What time?	b) How often?	c) Last time
1. _____	_____	_____
2. _____	_____	_____
3. _____	_____	_____
4. _____	_____	_____
5. _____	_____	_____

    d) Which one of these things do you most enjoy doing? #_____

26. Does any other person in your family use drugs?   Yes_____
                                                            No_____
    Did any other person in your family use drugs in the past? Yes_____
    (D.N.A. to spouse or children)   No_____
    (If yes to either, repeat series of questions for each person using drugs)
    a) Who?

    b) What drugs?

    c) How long?

    d) How much (average quantity and cost per day)?

    e) Ever addicted?

    f) Present drug status?

    (If not using now)
    a) When did he/she stop using?

b) How was he/she able to stop using (kind of treatment, etc.)?

c) What is he/she doing now (i.e., modal activity, working, criminality, etc.)?

27. Does anyone in your family have any kind of problem he may need some help with? (*Family of orientation or family of procreation*)

                          Yes   _____
                          No   _____
                          Doesn't know _____

(*If yes*)
a) Who?

b) What kind of problem?

(*Ask the following questions if married, including common-law, and living with spouse:* Q. 28–31)

28. How well do you get along with your wife? (*Probe deeply*)

29. Would you like to break up with your wife?   Yes_____
                                                           No_____

(*If yes*)
a) Why? (*Probe deeply*)

(*If no*)
b) Why not? (*Probe deeply*)

30. Do you ever do things together with your wife?   Yes_____
                                                                No_____

(*If yes, probe for five items*)

	a) What things?	b) How often?	c) Last time
1.	_____	_____	_____
2.	_____	_____	_____
3.	_____	_____	_____
4.	_____	_____	_____
5.	_____	_____	_____

d) Which one of these things do you most enjoy doing? #_____

31. Did your wife or children ever use drugs? Yes_____
    No_____

(*If yes, specify who and get details of*)

a) What drugs?

b) How long?

c) How much (average quantity and cost per day)?

d) Ever addicted?

e) Present drug status?

(*If not now using*)
a) When did he/she stop?

b) How was he/she able to stop (kind of treatment, etc.)?

c) What does he/she do now (i.e., modal activity, works, prostitutes, is housewife, etc.)?

32. During the past week what have you been doing in your spare time?
    (*Probe for at least five items. Do not accept "nothing," "hustling," or "drugs" as an answer*)

	a) What things?	b) How often?	c) Last time
1.	_____	_____	_____
2.	_____	_____	_____
3.	_____	_____	_____
4.	_____	_____	_____
5.	_____	_____	_____

d) During this time were you on drugs or off drugs? On drugs _____
   Off drugs _____
e) Which of these things did you most enjoy doing?   # _____
f) How many of these things do you really enjoy doing?   _____
   (*If any*)
   1) Which ones are they?   #'s ___ ___ ___ ___ ___

33. When you were last _____ drugs, what did you do in your spare time?
    (*Ask for opposite of response to Q. 32d*)

a) What things?	b) How often?	c) Last time
1. _____	_____	_____
2. _____	_____	_____
3. _____	_____	_____
4. _____	_____	_____
5. _____	_____	_____

    d) Which one of these things do you most enjoy doing? # _____
    e) How many of these things do you really enjoy
       doing?   _____
       (*If any*)
       1) Which ones are they?   #'s ___ ___ ___ ___ ___

34. What would you most like to do if you had the money and time?
    (*If drugs or nothing, record and probe more deeply for alternate responses*)
                                   First Response: Use drugs _____
                                                   Nothing _____
                                           Other (*Specify*) _____

35. In the last continuous month in the community did you:

	Yes	No
Go to any parties or dances	___	___
Have a few drinks with friends	___	___
Visit a friend who does *not* use drugs	___	___
Go to church	___	___
Do any gambling	___	___
Watch TV all day long	___	___
Read a book	___	___
Play some sport	___	___
Go out on a date with a girl	___	___

36. Outside of your relatives, about how many people
    did you go around with at least once in a while
    since you came into the program?
                              Number on: _____
                              Number off: _____
                                    On   Off
    a) How many of these are drug users?   ___   ___
    b) How many of these drug users are your
       real close friends?   ___   ___

APPENDIX A

c) How many of these drug users are men? _____ _____
d) How many of these drug users are women? _____ _____
e) How many of these people do not use drugs? _____ _____
f) How many of these non-drug users are your
real close friends? _____ _____
g) How many of the non-drug users are men? _____ _____
h) How many of the non-drug users are women? _____ _____

37. Where do you go to find new friends?

a) Anywhere else?

38. How long after coming into this program did you
continue to use any drug of any kind? _____
(*If not heroin or other opiate*)
a) How long after coming into this program did
you continue to use heroin or other opiate? _____
b) What drugs were you using during the past month?
(*First ask and then circle drug used most often
at this time*) None_____

Drug	Route	Amount	Frequency	Usual Times of Day
1.				
2.				
3.				

c) During the last six months (in the community) Yes_____
did you use any other drugs? No_____
(*If yes*) Which ones?

Drug	Route	Amount	Frequency	Usual Times of Day
1.				
2.				
3.				

d) Since you've been in the program did you use any Yes_____
drugs other than those already mentioned? No_____

Q. 38(c) During the last six months (in the community)
did you use any of the drugs that you used during
the past month? (*Interviewer should read aloud to* Yes_____
the respondent those drugs mentioned in Q. 38b) No_____
(*If yes*) Which ones?

	Drug	Route	Amount	Frequency	Usual Times of Day
1.					
2.					
3.					

Q. 38(d) During the time you've been in the program prior to six months ago did you use any of the drugs that you have used in the past six months? (*Interviewer should read aloud to the respondent those drugs mentioned in* Q. 38b *and* 38c) Yes____ No____
    (*If yes*) Which ones?

	Drug	Route	Amount	Frequency	Usual Times of Day	When Used	Why Did You Stop Using This Drug?
1.							
2.							
3.							

    (*If yes*) Which ones?
e) Since you've been in the program, did you use any kind of drug or pill a few times and then stop using it? Yes____ No____
    (*If yes*)

	Drug	Route	Amount	Frequency	Usual Times of Day	When Used	Why Did You Stop Using This Drug?
1.							
2.							
3.							

f) During the time that you've been in the program did you ever use any drugs to help cut down on your heroin use by yourself? Yes____ No____
    (*If yes*)

	Drug	Route	Amount	Frequency	Usual Times of Day	When Used	Why Did You Stop Using This Drug?
1.							
2.							
3.							

39. How were you supporting your habit during the past month? (*If pawning, where were goods obtained? May include work, if volunteered*)
                      D.N.A. (*No drug use*)____

APPENDIX A

              Method   Frequency

1. _____
2. _____
3. _____

a) During the last six months (in the community) did you support your habit in any other way?
   (*If pawning, where were goods obtained?*   Yes_____
   May include work if volunteered)   No_____
                               D.N.A. (*No drug use*)_____

   (*If yes*) Which ways?

              Method   Frequency

1. _____
2. _____
3. _____

b) Since you've been in the program have you supported your habit in any other ways?
   (*If pawning, where were goods obtained?*   Yes_____
   May include work if volunteered)   No_____
                               D.N.A. (*No drug use*)_____

   (*If yes*) Which ways?

              Method   Frequency

1. _____
2. _____
3. _____

Q. 39(a) During the last six months (in the community) did you support your habit in any of the ways you mentioned for the past month? (*Interviewer should read aloud to the respondent those methods mentioned in Q. 39*)   Yes_____
                                           No_____

   (*If yes*) Which ways?

              Method   Frequency

1. _____
2. _____
3. _____

Q. 39(b) During the time you've been in the program prior to six months ago did you support your habit by any of the methods that you mentioned for the past six months? (*Interviewer should read aloud to the respondent those methods mentioned in Q. 39 and 39a*)   Yes_____
                                           No_____

   (*If yes*) Which ways?

              Method   Frequency

1. _____
2. _____
3. _____

c) Have you done any of these other things to support your habit since you came into the program? (*Read only those not already mentioned but check ones previously mentioned as well as new ones*)

D.N.A. (*No drug use*)_____

1. Gambling _____
2. Begging _____
3. Running numbers _____
4. Sex with men _____
5. Conning (*Describe*) _____
   _____
6. Pimping _____
7. Loaning works _____
8. Copping for someone else _____
9. Selling drugs _____
10. Mugging _____
11. Breaking and entering _____
12. Shoplifting _____
13. Other _____

1) Which of all of these things have you done most often to support your habit since you came into the program? _____
2) Did you do any of these things for reasons other than to support your habit since you came into the program? Yes_____ No_____
   (*If yes*) Which ones? _____ _____ _____

40. *If respondent used drugs during past year*
    When did you last get detoxified from drugs? _____
    (*If the above date is since the respondent is in the program, ask Q. 40a–42*)
    a) Where was this? Jail_____ Hospital_____ Street_____
       (*If not jail*)
       1) Was this voluntary or not? Voluntary_____ Not voluntary_____
    b) How long did it take? _____
    c) How were you detoxified? Cold, no medication _____
       Methadone, alone _____
       Methadone plus other drugs (*Specify*)_____
       Other drugs alone (*Specify*) _____
    d) When you left the (hospital) (jail) (or finished kicking on your own) did you think you were physically clean of drugs? Yes_____ No_____
       (*If yes*)
       1) Why?

       (*If no*)
       2) Why not?

    e) When you left the (hospital) (jail) (or finished kicking on your own) did you think you were mentally clean of drugs? Yes_____ No_____
       (*If yes*)
       1) Why?

(*If no*)
2) Why not?

41. After you were detoxified how long was it before you first used drugs again? _____
42. (*Interviewer should ask respondent to give a description of his use of drugs from his first use after his last detoxification since he came into the program until he was fully readdicted. All relevant information such as dates, types of drugs used, amounts, frequencies, costs, and methods of support of habit should be included. This applies to the last time respondent was addicted after a detoxification. If the last time respondent was addicted after a detoxification was before he entered the program, do not ask this question. This checklist should be used only as a reminder, to the interviewer, of the kinds of data we wish to collect.*)

   Type of drugs
   Frequency of use (times per day, per week)
   Amounts used (in quantity and cost per day)
   Routes

   Means of support of drug use
   Simultaneous drugs used

43. (*Interviewer should ask respondent to think back over his last year* in the community. *Interviewer should get a complete chronological description by month of that year. This description should include respondent's actions in the following areas: hospital involvement, jail involvement, arrests, other institutions, agencies of any kind, work, and periods of abstinence. Names of agencies, hospitals, etc., and kind of work done on jobs are necessary. Drug activity includes types of drugs, amounts used, frequency of use, routes, and methods of support of habit. Indicate under "work" whether respondent worked full month* [F]; *most of the month, over half* [M]; *part of month, less than half* [P]; *or not at all* [—].)

Month, Year	If in Community		Arrests, Charges, Jail Involvement	Hospital and Other Institutional Involvement	In N.Y.C.	Outside N.Y.C. (*Specify*)
	Work	Drugs				

44. Which hospitals have you kicked at since coming into the program? (*If any, ask for each*) How many times have you kicked there? Was it voluntary or not?

FOLLOW-UP QUESTIONNAIRE

	a) Hospital	b) Number of Times Kicked	c) Voluntary
1.	_____	_____	_____
2.	_____	_____	_____
3.	_____	_____	_____

45. About how many times did you kick on your own since coming into the program? _____

   a) Did you cut down on your habit by yourself since you came into the program?   Yes_____ No_____
   (If yes, get details)

46. Did you ever kick anywhere else since you came into the program?   Yes_____ No_____
   (If yes)

	a) Where	b) When	c) Voluntary or Involuntary
1.	_____	_____	_____
2.	_____	_____	_____
3.	_____	_____	_____

47. Did you get any other kind of help for your drug addiction problems besides the W.H.R.C. or Probation Program since you came into the program?   Yes_____ No_____
   (If yes)
   a) Where was that? *(Anywhere else)*?

   b) When? *(Ask for each)*

   c) How long were you there? *(Specify for each)*

   d) What kind of help did you get there? *(Specify for each)*

   e) Have you used any drugs or tranquilizers under a doctor's care since coming into the program?   Yes_____ No_____

48. Were you in a hospital for some reason *other* than detoxification since coming into the program?   Yes_____ No_____
   (If yes)
   a) What were you in there for?

b) When?

c) What hospital was that (hospitals were these)?

49. How often did you usually drink alcohol since you came into the program?
   a) When using drugs?

   b) When not using drugs?

50. How much do you generally drink at those times?
   a) When using drugs?
                           (*Interviewer should estimate amount in ounces of whiskey per day*)
   b) When not using drugs?

51. Have you gotten into any trouble with the law because of your drinking since coming into the program?   Yes_____ No_____
   (*If yes*)
   a) What kind of trouble?

52. Have you had any kind of problems with your health, your job, your family, or anything because of your drinking since coming into the program?   Yes_____ No_____
   (*If yes*)
   a) What kind of trouble?

53. How many times have you been arrested since you came into the program?   _____
   (*If arrested*)

a) Arrested for	b) When	c) Disposition of Case
1.		
2.		
3.		

54. Have you had any violations of probation other than arrests?   Yes_____ No_____
   (*If yes*)
   a) How many? _____

	b) Type of Violation	c) Action Taken
1.	_____	_____
2.	_____	_____
3.	_____	_____

55. About how much time have you spent in jail since you came into the program? _____

56. Since coming into the program did you do anything illegal other than the things we talked about before? (*Refers to acts for which a person may be incarcerated at some institution*)
    (*If yes*)

	a) What did you do?	b) What month(s)?	c) How many times?
1.	_____	_____	_____
2.	_____	_____	_____
3.	_____	_____	_____

57. At present, do you want any other kind of help with anything at all from this or any other agency? Yes_____ No_____
    (*If yes*)
    a) What do you want help with?

58. Where was interview done? (*If done in more than one place please indicate all places*)

WASHINGTON HEIGHTS REHABILITATION CENTER

Center Worker's Initial Evaluation and Assessment of Patients

Month _____   Year _____

Patient's Name _____   Case No. ☐☐☐

Worker's Name _____   S.W. ___ P.H.N. ___ Other ___

Probation Officer's Name _____

Date of Entry _____

Program Month _____

I. DRUG USE

A. Rate on the following scale the degree to which the patient needs help in this area:

Needs no help   0 1 2 3 4 5 6 7 8 9 10   Needs intensive help, treatment, or guidance

1. State very briefly factors about the patient which enabled you to make the above evaluation:

   a) How sure are you of the validity of the evidence?

      I am fairly confident ____ 1
      I am somewhat doubtful ____ 2
      I am very doubtful ____ 3
      I can make no decision regarding the validity of the evidence ____ 4

B. Rate on the following scale the degree to which the patient manifests competence presently, in this area:

Very competent, usually reaches chosen goals   0 1 2 3 4 5 6 7 8 9 10   Very incompetent, unsuccessful at reaching chosen goals

1. State very briefly factors about the patient which enabled you to make the above evaluation:

The format and questions used to assess the patient's problems for the area of drug use (*I. DRUG USE*) was continued for the following areas, all of which together constituted the worker's initial evaluation.

    II. DELINQUENT OR ANTI-SOCIAL BEHAVIOR
       (Criminality, violation of probation, fighting, or other anti-social acts)
   III. WORK
   IV. FAMILY
    V. GENERAL INTERPERSONAL RELATIONSHIPS
       (Excluding family, but including sexual relationships and adjustments)
   VI. LEISURE-TIME AND RECREATIONAL ACTIVITIES
       (Includes friendship relationships)
  VII. HEALTH
       (Physical)
 VIII. EXTENT TO WHICH RELATIONSHIP (WITH WORKER) HAS BEEN BUILT
       (Omit Part B)

In addition, two general items were added at the end.

   IX. MANNER AND AREAS IN WHICH COERCION (OR OTHER ASPECT OF AUTHORITY) SHOULD BE EMPLOYED
    X. MANNER AND AREAS IN WHICH REACHING-OUT TECHNIQUES SHOULD BE EMPLOYED

WASHINGTON HEIGHTS REHABILITATION CENTER

Center Worker's Monthly Evaluation and Assessment of Patients

Month _____ Year _____
Patient's Name _____ Case No. [| |]
Worker's Name _____ S.W. ___ P.H.N. ___ Other ___
Probation Officer's Name _____
Date of Entry _____
Program Month _____

I. DRUG USE

A. During the last month, has there been any movement or satisfactory progress, *from your point of view?*

Great deal of progress	___1
Some progress	___2
No change	___3
Some deterioration	___4
Great deal of deterioration	___5
Can't determine	___6

    1. What evidence can you cite for this?

        a) How sure are you of the validity of the evidence?

I am fairly confident	___1
I am somewhat doubtful	___2
I am very doubtful	___3
I can make no decision regarding the validity of the evidence	___4

B. Where would you rate this patient this month on the following scale?

Needs no help at this time 0 1 2 3 4 5 6 7 8 9 10 Needs intensive help, treatment, or guidance

    1. State evidence concerning the patient which enabled you to rate him:

        a) How sure are you of the validity of the evidence?

I am fairly confident	___1
I am somewhat doubtful	___2
I am very doubtful	___3

I can make no decision regarding
the validity of the evidence ____4

C. During the last month, has there been any change in the competence of the patient in his handling of this area?

+ Great deal of change ____1
+ Some change ____2
No change ____3
− Some change ____4
− Great deal of change ____5
Can't determine ____6

1. What evidence can you cite for this?

———————————————

The format and questions used to evaluate change during the preceding months for the area of drug use (*I. DRUG USE*) was continued for the following areas, all of which together constituted the worker's monthly evaluation.

    II. DELINQUENT OR ANTI-SOCIAL BEHAVIOR
        (Criminality, violation of probation, fighting, or other anti-social acts)
    III. WORK
    IV. FAMILY
    V. GENERAL INTERPERSONAL RELATIONSHIPS
        (Excluding family, but including sexual relationships and adjustments)
    VI. LEISURE-TIME AND RECREATIONAL ACTIVITIES
        (Includes friendship relationships)
    VII. HEALTH
        (Physical)
    VIII. EXTENT TO WHICH RELATIONSHIP (WITH WORKER) HAS BEEN BUILT
        (Omit Part C)

In addition, two general items were added at the end.

    IX. MANNER AND AREAS IN WHICH COERCION (OR OTHER ASPECT OF AUTHORITY) SHOULD BE EMPLOYED
    X. MANNER AND AREAS IN WHICH REACHING-OUT TECHNIQUES USED DURING PAST MONTH

WASHINGTON HEIGHTS REHABILITATION CENTER

Worker's and Probation Officer's Final Evaluation and Assessment of Patients

Months in Program _____   Date of Report _____

Patient's Name _____   P.O. or Center Case No. [   ]

Workers' Names _____   S.W. _____   P.H.N. _____

Probation Officers' Names _____

Is patient being terminated from probation at present?   Yes _____
                                                          No _____

When was patient last seen?   Date _____

I. DRUG USE

A. During the program, has there been any movement or satisfactory progress, *from your point of view?*

Great deal of progress _____1
Some progress _____2
No change _____3
Some deterioration _____4
Great deal of deterioration _____5
Can't determine _____6

    1. What evidence can you cite for this?

        a) How sure are you of the validity of the evidence?

I am fairly confident _____1
I am somewhat doubtful _____2
I am very doubtful _____3
I can make no decision regarding the validity of the evidence _____4

B. Where would you rate this patient at present on the following scale?

Needs no help at this time 0 1 2 3 4 5 6 7 8 9 10 Needs intensive help, treatment, or guidance

    1. State evidence concerning the patient which enabled you to rate him:

        a) How sure are you of the validity of the evidence?

I am fairly confident _____1
I am somewhat doubtful _____2
I am very doubtful _____3
I can make no decision regarding the validity of the evidence _____4

The format and questions used by workers and the probation officers to evaluate each patient at the end of the program for the area of drug use (*I. DRUG USE*) was continued for the following areas, all of which together constituted the workers' and probation officers' final evaluation and assessment of patients.

    II. *DELINQUENT OR ANTI-SOCIAL BEHAVIOR*
        (Criminality, violation of probation, fighting, or other anti-social acts)
    III. *WORK*
    IV. *FAMILY*
    V. *GENERAL INTERPERSONAL RELATIONSHIPS*
        (Excluding family, but including sexual relationships and adjustments)
    VI. *LEISURE-TIME AND RECREATIONAL ACTIVITIES*
        (Includes friendship relationships)
    VII. *HEALTH*
        (Physical)
    VIII. *EXTENT TO WHICH RELATIONSHIP (WITH WORKER AND PROBATION OFFICER) HAS BEEN BUILT*
        (Omit Part B)

In addition, three general items were added at the end.

    IX. *MANNER AND AREAS IN WHICH COERCION (OR OTHER ASPECT OF AUTHORITY) WAS USED DURING THE PERIOD OF EXPOSURE TO THE PROGRAM*
    X. *MANNER AND AREAS OF REACHING-OUT TECHNIQUES USED DURING THE PERIOD OF EXPOSURE TO THE PROGRAM*
    XI. *MANNER IN WHICH JOINT MANAGEMENT WAS USED DURING THE PERIOD OF EXPOSURE TO THE PROGRAM*

WASHINGTON HEIGHTS REHABILITATION CENTER

Center Worker's Evaluation and Assessment of Family

Month _____ Year _____

Patient's Name _____ Case No. [| |]

Worker's Name _____ S.W. ____ P.H.N. ____ Other ____

Family of Orientation: Primary_____ Secondary_____
Family of Procreation: Primary_____ Secondary_____

I. MEMBERS OF FAMILY BEING EVALUATED (include non-family members who are living in household)

Name	Relationship to Client	Sex	Age	Marital Status	Ethnicity	Level of Education	Occupation	Religious Denomination

II. *PHYSICAL CHARACTERISTICS OF HOUSEHOLD*

A. Describe physical facilities, housekeeping standards, furniture, and any other information relevant to the physical setup of the home. Include description of the building and the neighborhood.

B. Degree to which the physical setup of the household is a problem for the family.

```
0  1  2  3  4  5  6  7  8  9  10
Not a                    A major
problem                  problem
```

1. Upon what evidence do you base this decision?

    a) How sure are you of the   I am fairly confident ____1
        validity of the evidence?   I am somewhat doubtful ____2

                                               I am very doubtful _____3
                        I can make no decision regarding
                               the validity of the evidence _____4

C. What steps, if any, do you feel should be taken in order to modify any problems that exist in this area at present?

III. ECONOMIC SITUATION OF FAMILY

A. Describe family's sources of income, job situations, uses of money, financial problems, and any other information relevant to the family's economic situation.

B. Degree to which the economic situation is a problem for the family.

   0 1 2 3 4 5 6 7 8 9 10
Not a   A major
problem   problem

    1. Upon what evidence do you base this decision?

        a) How sure are you of the   I am fairly confident _____1
            validity of the evidence?   I am somewhat doubtful _____2
                                                      I am very doubtful _____3
                        I can make no decision regarding
                               the validity of the evidence _____4

C. What steps, if any, do you feel should be taken in order to modify any problems that exist in this area at present?

IV. HEALTH CONDITIONS AND PRACTICES OF FAMILY

A. Describe the health conditions and practices of the family, including all existent diseases and their treatment and any other information relevant to this area.

B. Degree to which the situation concerning health conditions and practices is a problem for the family.

   0 1 2 3 4 5 6 7 8 9 10
Not a   A major
problem   problem

1. Upon what evidence do you base this decision?

    a) How sure are you of the validity of the evidence?

I am fairly confident _____1
I am somewhat doubtful _____2
I am very doubtful _____3
I can make no decision regarding the validity of the evidence _____4

C. What steps, if any, do you feel should be taken in order to modify any problems that exist in this area at present?

V. USE OF COMMUNITY RESOURCES

A. Describe the family's use of community resources (or lack thereof) in the areas of school, church, and health resources, as well as social and recreational agencies and include any other information regarding the use of any resource that you feel is relevant to this area.

B. Degree to which family's use (or lack thereof) of community resources is a problem:

0 1 2 3 4 5 6 7 8 9 10
Not a   A major
problem   problem

1. Upon what evidence do you base this decision?

    a) How sure are you of the   I am fairly confident ____ 1
        validity of the evidence?   I am somewhat doubtful ____ 2
                                                 I am very doubtful ____ 3
                              I can make no decision regarding
                                    the validity of the evidence ____ 4

C. What steps, if any, do you feel should be taken in order to modify any problems that exist in this area at present?

VI. LEISURE-TIME ACTIVITIES

A. Describe the family's (individually and as a whole) participation (or lack thereof) in any types of leisure-time activities.

B. Do you feel that any changes should be   Yes_____
    made in this area?   No_____
    1. *(If yes)*
       What would you suggest?

VII. MARITAL RELATIONSHIP

A. Describe the marital relationship including what you see as problem areas and areas of strength. Any other information that you feel is relevant to the marital situation may be included.

B. Degree to which the marital relationship is a problem for the family.

```
0   1   2   3   4   5   6   7   8   9   10
Not a                       A major
problem                     problem
```

1. Upon what evidence do you base this decision?

   a) How sure are you of the validity of the evidence?

   I am fairly confident _____1
   I am somewhat doubtful_____2
   I am very doubtful _____3
   I can make no decision regarding the validity of the evidence _____4

C. What steps, if any, do you feel should be taken in order to modify any problems that exist in this area at present? If you feel that the present situation should be sustained rather than modified, please say so and explain why.

VIII. BEHAVIORAL AND ADJUSTMENT PROBLEMS

A. Describe behavior and adjustment of family members in such areas as sexual problems, drinking and/or drug problems, physical and/or mental problems, and delinquent and/or anti-social behavior problems. Include any other information that you feel is relevant to any individual family member's behavior and adjustment.

B. Degree to which any problems within the area of behavior and adjustment are a family problem.

```
0  1  2  3  4  5  6  7  8  9  10
Not a                    A major
problem                  problem
```

1. Upon what evidence do you base this decision?

    a) How sure are you of the validity of the evidence?

        I am fairly confident _____1
        I am somewhat doubtful _____2
        I am very doubtful _____3
        I can make no decision regarding the validity of the evidence _____4

C. What steps, if any, do you feel should be taken in order to modify any problems?

IX. WHAT KINDS OF RELATIONSHIPS WITHIN THE FAMILY DOES YOUR CLIENT HAVE?
(Include description of his interactions with other family members)

A. Degree to which relationship(s) between client and family present a problem for the family.

```
0  1  2  3  4  5  6  7  8  9  10
Not a                    A major
problem                  problem
```

1. Upon what evidence do you base this decision?

    a) How sure are you of the validity of the evidence?

        I am fairly confident _____1
        I am somewhat doubtful _____2
        I am very doubtful _____3
        I can make no decision regarding the validity of the evidence _____4

B. What steps, if any, do you feel should be taken in order to modify any problems that exist in this area at present?

X. IN WHAT WAY(S), IF ANY, DOES THE FAMILY HELP MAINTAIN YOUR CLIENT AS A DRUG USER?

A. What are the family attitudes toward addiction?

B. Degree to which your client's drug use is a problem for the family.

    0 1 2 3 4 5 6 7 8 9 10
  Not a   A major
  problem   problem

1. Upon what evidence do you base this decision?

    a) How sure are you of the validity of the evidence?

    I am fairly confident ____1
    I am somewhat doubtful ____2
    I am very doubtful ____3
    I can make no decision regarding the validity of the evidence ____4

C. What steps, if any, do you feel should be taken in order to modify any problems that exist in this area at present?

XI. DESCRIBE THE GOALS THE FAMILY HAS FOR YOUR CLIENT
(Areas such as dating, marriage, home life, school, job, drug-use, treatment for drug use, etc. can be covered here.)

    A. Do you feel that the goals the family has for your client are realistic?

                                                    Generally, yes_____

                                                    Generally, mixed_____

                                                        Generally, no_____

      1. Explain.

    B. What changes, if any, do you feel should be developed within the family in order to make their goals for your client more reasonable?

XIII. RELATIONSHIP TO CENTER WORKER
(This should include general statement regarding the character of the relationship between the family and the worker.)

    A. Describe the way(s) in which the family perceives this agency.

    B. With which family member(s) has the worker been most involved during the past six months?
(*If client, then mention family member next most involved with*)

1. Explain your reasons for this.

XIV. ARE THERE ANY STEPS NOT PREVIOUSLY MENTIONED THAT YOU FEEL SHOULD BE TAKEN IN ORDER TO ENABLE THE FAMILY TO COPE BETTER WITH THEIR PROBLEMS?

Yes_____
No_____

A. (If yes)
What are they?

XV. COMMENTS

Appendix B

SELECTED CHARACTERISTICS OF ADDICT POPULATION PLACED ON PROBATION DURING INTAKE PERIOD, GROUPS I AND II COMBINED

WE ARE INCLUDING these marginals taken from the Intake Questionnaire so that the reader may compare some of the characteristics of our population with those of others. Readers interested in other data from the questionnaires should contact the authors.

Age	No.	Percent
16 or under	8	4
17	22	12
18	31	17
19	25	14
20	12	7
21	16	9
22	16	9
23–25	22	12
26 or over	28	16
	180	100

Race	No.	Percent
White	55	31
Negro	60	33
Puerto Rican (white)	19	11
Puerto Rican (Negro)	6	3
Puerto Rican (*trigueño*, mixed)	39	22
Caribbean *trigueño* (other than Puerto Rican)	1	*
	180	100

Religion in which raised	No.	Percent
Catholic	110	61
Protestant	56	31
Jew	11	6
None	3	2
	180	100

Place of birth	No.	Percent
New York City	104	58
Southern United States	18	10
Other United States	8	5
Puerto Rico	45	25
Other Caribbean	1	*
Europe	3	2
Other	1	*
	180	100

Note: All asterisks found in the percent columns of the following tabulations indicate less than one-half of one percent (or less).

CHARACTERISTICS OF ADDICT POPULATION

Where raised	No.	Percent
New York City	150	83
New York State	1	*
Southern United States	7	5
Other United States	2	1
Puerto Rico	18	10
Other	2	1
	180	100

Address (Borough or area in which respondent lives)	No.	Percent
Washington Heights	8	5
Harlem (other than East Harlem and Washington Heights)	26	14
East Harlem	19	11
Other Manhattan	33	18
Bronx	45	25
Brooklyn	23	13
Queens	26	14
	180	100

Last school year completed	No.	Percent
Elementary, incomplete	6	3
Elementary, graduate	16	9
High school, incomplete	129	72
High school, graduate	21	12
College, incomplete	8	4
	180	100

Marital status	No.	Percent
Single	137	76
Married	26	14
Married, common-law	6	3
Divorced	3	2
Separated	8	4
	180	99

Situation re: wife, girlfriend, etc., at time of arrest	No.	Percent
Married and living with wife	23	13
Married, not living with wife, but no steady girlfriend	9	5
Living common-law[a]	13	7
Has steady girlfriend but is not living with her	71	39
Sees girls on intermittent basis	50	28
Sees no girls at all	13	7
Other	1	*
	180	99

[a] Seven of these cases do not consider these relationships as permanent enough to be classified above as married, common-law.

Children	No.	Percent
Yes	43	24
No	137	76
	180	100

"Do you support and take care of these children?"	No.	Percent of those who have children
Yes, both	15	35
Yes, support only	2	5
Yes, take care only	8	19
No, did but not now	14	33
No, never	3	7
Other situation	1	2
	43	101
Does not apply (do not have children)	137	

CHARACTERISTICS OF ADDICT POPULATION

"Did your wife ever use drugs?"	No.	Percent
Yes	4	11
No	33	89
	37	100
Does not apply (not married or not living with spouse)	143	

Were both parents[a] living at home until respondent was 16?	No.	Percent
Yes	89	49
No, father and mother missing	10	6
No, father missing	73	41
No, mother missing	8	4
	180	100

[a] Includes step-parents if a parent was replaced by marriage and was present for most of the years.

"How far did he (your father) get in school?"	No.	Percent
No schooling	4	4
Elementary, incomplete	26	24
Elementary, graduate	27	25
High school, incomplete	24	22
High school, graduate	12	11
College, incomplete	2	2
College, graduate or more	7	6
Don't know	8	7
	110	101
Does not apply (no father at home)	70	

"What kind of work did he (father) usually do?"	No.	Percent
Higher executives, proprietors of large concerns, and major professionals	2	2
Business managers, proprietors of medium-sized businesses, and lesser professionals	1	1
Administrative personnel, small independent businesses, and minor professionals	20	18
Clerical and sales workers, technicians, and owners of little businesses	3	3
Skilled manual employees	23	21
Machine operators and semiskilled employees	31	28
Unskilled employees	29	26
Not employed	1	1
	110	100
Does not apply (no father at home)	70	

Hollingshead scale rating of social position (based on two factors: education and occupation of father)	No.	Percent
Class I	2	1
Class II	7	4
Class III	12	8
Class IV	61	37
Class V	81	50
	163	100
Can't determine	17	

"Does any other person in your family use drugs? Did any other person in your family use drugs in the past?" (Family of orientation)	No.	Percent
Yes	43	24
No	137	76
	180	100

"Is there anyone in your family who has any kind of problem with too much drinking?" (Family of orientation)	No.	Percent
Yes	27	15
No	153	85
	180	100

"What was the highest job you ever held?"	No.	Percent
Administrative personnel, small independent businesses, and minor professionals	11	6
Clerical and sales workers, technicians, and owners of little businesses	29	16
Skilled manual employees	14	8
Machine operators and semiskilled employees	60	33
Unskilled employees	62	34
No highest job	1	*
Never worked	3	2
	180	99

"During the last 12 months (in the community) how many months were you working?"	No.	Percent
None	11	6
One or less	8	4
Over 1–3	27	15
Over 3–5	37	21
Over 5–7	44	24
Over 7–9	18	10
Over 9–11	11	6
Over 11–12 (1 year)	24	13
	180	99

"How many jobs did you have during this time?"	No.	Percent
One	62	37
Two	60	36
Three	27	16
Four	12	7
Five or more	8	5
	169	101
Does not apply (did not work during the last 12 months)	11	

Total months worked or in school during last year in the community	No.	Percent
None	13	7
1	9	5
2	12	7
3	13	7
4	13	7
5	16	9
6	13	7
7	15	8
8	15	8
9	13	7
10	12	7
11	8	4
12	28	16
	180	99

Veteran status	No.	Percent
None	152	84
Army	18	10
Navy	5	3
Air Force	3	2
Merchant Marine (wartime)	1	*
Coast Guard	1	*
	180	99

CHARACTERISTICS OF ADDICT POPULATION

Age at which first tried any drug	No.	Percent
14 or under	59	33
15	32	18
16	24	13
17	23	13
18	20	11
19	13	7
20, 21	5	3
22, 23	2	1
24, 25	—	—
26 or over	2	1
	180	100

First drug tried	No.	Percent
Marijuana	127	71
Heroin	23	13
Other opiate	8	4
Barbiturate (goofballs)	5	3
Amphetamine	1	1
Hypnotic	4	2
Cocaine	—	—
Glue, gasoline	10	6
Other	1	*
No information	1	*
	180	100

Total number of different drugs ever used	No.	Percent
1–2	45	25
3–5	85	47
6–9	33	18
10–12	13	7
13–15	3	2
16–20	1	*
	180	99

APPENDIX B

Total number of months used drugs during last year in the community	No.	Percent
None	1	*
1	1	*
2	1	*
3	3	2
4	12	7
5	4	2
6	8	4
7	12	7
8	10	6
9	18	10
10	28	16
11	30	17
12	52	29
	180	100

"How often do you generally drink alcohol (when using drugs)?"	No.	Percent
Daily	40	22
A few times per week	35	19
Once per week, on weekends	42	23
Every few weeks, couple of times per month	15	8
Occasionally, rarely, at infrequent parties, etc.	24	13
Never	23	13
No information	1	*
	180	98

"How often do you generally drink alcohol (when not using drugs)?"	No.	Percent
Daily	40	22
A few times per week	35	19
Once per week, on weekends	42	23
Every few weeks, couple of times per month	15	8
Occasionally, rarely, at infrequent parties, etc.	24	13
Never	23	13
No information	1	*
	180	98

CHARACTERISTICS OF ADDICT POPULATION

"How many times have you been arrested in your life?"	No.	Percent
1	38	21
2	42	23
3	34	19
4	22	12
5	25	14
6	7	4
7	4	2
8	3	2
9	1	*
10 or more	4	2
	180	99

"About how much time have you spent in prison?"	No.	Percent
None	35	19
Less than 15 days	48	27
Over 15 days–1 month	39	22
Over 1 month–3 months	29	16
Over 3 months–6 months	9	5
Over 6 months–9 months	5	3
Over 9 months–12 months	4	2
Over 12 months–18 months	2	1
Over 18 months–24 months	3	2
Over 24 months	6	3
	180	100

"First arrest—was it prior to drug use?"	No.	Percent
Yes	43	24
No	136	76
No information	1	*
	180	100

Various illicit ways of supporting habit	No.	Percent
Copping[a] for someone else	123	68
Loaning works	114	63
Conning	81	45
Gambling	66	37
Breaking and entering	63	35
Shoplifting	60	33
Selling drugs	58	32
Pimping	32	18
Begging	32	18
Mugging	29	16
Homosexual prostitution	20	11
Running numbers	10	6
Other illegal activities	12	7

[a] Purchasing drugs.

"If have ever supported habit by conning, what type of conning?"	No.	Percent
Get money from others to cop (purchase drugs) for them, then not show up	33	41
Get money from others for merchandise, not show up with merchandise	5	6
Door-to-door selling of phony items, fraud	8	10
Murphy game[a]	7	9
"Beat"[b] people for money other than the above methods	21	26
"Beat" addicts or pushers for drugs	2	2
Cheat at various forms of gambling	2	2
Other	3	4
	81	100

[a] Pretense at prostitution with partner pretending to be outraged boyfriend.
[b] Cheating as a means of taking something from someone.

"Do you want any kind of help with anything at all?"	No.	Percent
Yes	108	61
No	72	39
	180	100

Index

Index

Abrahamsen, D., criminal theory of, 144
Abstinence
  adaptational stage, 219–220
  as admission requirement, 119
  as approach to treatment, 1, 4, 19, 33
  confirmation of, 85–86
  as criterion for evaluation, 139, 182
  as desirable goal, 170, 171
  experimentation stage, 218–219
  as hopeful sign, 165
  immediate, 174
  increasing, 200
  motivation for, 8–9
  physiological stage, 220
  potential, tolerance for, 202, 218–220
  problems of, 172
  psychological and social components, 217
  rates of, of dischargees, 25
  tolerance of, 33–34, 202, 218–220
  total, 162, 202
  as goal of rehabilitation, 111
  movement toward, 218
  as ultimate goal in rehabilitation, 173
  transition to, 187, 216–218
  "working toward," 133, 134, 170
  as program goal, 172
Ackerman, N. W., family dynamics study, 193
Acting-out behavior, 59, 104
  personality of addict, 56
  restrictions on, 71
Adaptation stage of drug use, 208–210
Addiction. *See also* Opiate addiction
  character of, questionnaire on, 232–233
  as chronic illness, 19, 35, 140
  criterion of, at Lexington Hospital, 128

Addiction—*Continued*
  developmental stages of, 200
  and familial factors, 193–194, 204, 205
  life cycle of, 162
    conceptual model of, 201–204
    series of stages within, 203
  physiochemical components of, 187
  physiological aspects of, 3, 58, 192
  potential, tolerance for, 202–203, 206–211, 215
  psychological factors, 204–205
  and social components, 204–205, 217
  as a "sickness," 191
  states of, 34
  as symptom or way of life, 193
  tolerance of, 217
Addiction area, location of rehabilitation center in, 36
Addiction-prone individual, 207
Addiction set, pre-drug condition, 204–206
Addiction system, 119, 193, 198
  avoidance of identification with, 213
  and criminality, 207–208, 215
  "failures" in, 144, 200
  flattening influence of, 193
  intensity of involvement with, 221
  necessary skills associated with, 209
  and socialization process, 211, 214–215
  stages of, 202
  tolerance of, 202, 214–216
  transition to, Phase I, 211–214
  varying patterns of drug use in, 190
Addict population
  selected characteristics of, during intake period, 291–302
  in urban areas, 145
Addicts
  classification of, 20–21, 200
  "competent," 213
  criminality in, 134
  cure of, 188
  differences in individuals, 189–190
  friendships detrimental to achieving goals, 157
  "hidden," 210, 221
  making of, 198–199, 204
  medically supervised, 210
  negative feelings of, 105
  number of convictions, 144
  and psychological factors, 191–192
  reasons for drug use, 178
  status as probationer, 13
  "street junkie" type, and cyclazocine, 9
  as treatment personnel, 4
  willingness to cooperate with program, 142
Addict sub-culture. *See* Addiction system
Admission requirements for rehabilitation program, 118–119
Adolescents, 204
  and anxiety–producing situations, 208
  sniffing during experimental stage, 207
Age
  of experimental groups, 121–122, 292
  of first drug use, 127–128, 299
  median age, 127
Agencies, hard-to-reach, 102
Agency help, revision of philosophy of, 92
Aggressiveness
  of children in problem families, 97
  worker's need for, 92
Albert Einstein College of Medicine, 10, 11, 19, 200, 223
  study on cyclazocine, 8–9
Alcoholics Anonymous, 6
Alcohol use, 177, 297
  and drugs, 300
  questionnaire on, 254–255
    follow-up, 272
Alienation, 196
Amphetamines, 141, 177, 206
Anomie, 196
  Merton's concept of, 206
Antagonist, narcotic, 7
Anxieties, basic, relief of, 7
Anxiety, 56
Arrests, 255–256
  experimental group, 301
  for first twelve months of probationers, 183
  follow-up questionnaire, 272–273
  number of, preceding drug use, 129
  rates, comparison of rational authority and Riverside Hospital, 184
  recidivist, 182–185
Attitudes, community, 6
Attitudinal indicators, 148
Augustus, John, as originator of probation system, 53
Ausubel, D., classification system of, 194
Authority
  borrowed, in case management of offenders, 82

charismatic, 50
concept of, 49–50
legal, 50
main forms of, 58–60
personal, 59–60
  of rehabilitation worker, 16–17
  by probation officers alone, 188. *See also* Probation officer, authority of
problems in relating to, 18
professional, 60
as prosecuting and persecuting institution, 183
"rational," 13–22, 27, 49–79, 175, 178
  cases compared with Riverside Hospital cases, 175
  components in use of, 13–16
  and crisis-intervention, 33
  in probation officer–probationer relationships, 189
  and research work, 35
  as structuring device, 46
  use of, 133, 223
  use of term, 13
  vs. voluntary programs, 44
rejection vs. acceptance of, 50
structural, 58–59
traditional, as a transitory phenomenon, 50
use of, 14, 17, 45
  case histories on, 63–66, 71–78
  development of techniques for, 66–71
  evaluation of process, 112–115
  historical perspective, 83
  as holding function, 56, 71–72
  in joint management, 88–89
  to prevent backsliding, 19
  by social workers and nurses, 40
  resistance of workers to, 68
  stages and dynamics in, 60–62
  in sustaining patient contact, 30–33

Baptists, 124
Barbiturates, 128, 141, 177, 206
Becker, H.
  study of drug abusers, 214
  study of marijuana use, 192
Beecher, H. R., study in opiates, 192
Behavior
  conventional, 105
  criminal or retreatist, 196

drug-seeking, 8, 199
  extinguished in use of cyclazocine, 8
  reinforcement of, 7
normative, 4
pathological, of family members, 29
Behavioral changes in addicts, 111–112, 115
  before or independent of abstinence, 187
Behavioral criteria, 148
Behavioral indicators
  developing, 134–136
  differing in patients, 134
  psychological, 135
Behavioral reaching-out, defined, 91
Birthplace of experimental groups, 122, 292
Bonime's depressives, 32
Boredom, 154
Bowen, Murray, family dynamics study, 193
Brill, Leon, and reaching-out, 101
Bruch, Hilda, and obesity cases, 194
Buell, Bradley, social pathology study, 93

California Department of Correction, 99
California Rehabilitation Center, Civil Narcotics Program *Five Year Progress Report,* 176
Caplan, G., and crisis intervention, 31
"Career Development Program," 99
Case activity analysis form, 114, 117
  sample of, 234–235
Case planning in joint management, 85
Caseworker, control of negative reactions to addict, 104
Casework relationship, ongoing, 103
Catholicism, Caribbean, 124
Cattell, Raymond, and therapeutic change, 171
Central nervous system, 190
Chein, I., and addict life styles, 191, 193, 195
Chemotherapy, 7–13, 200, 219–220, 223
Children, support of, 294
Child Welfare, Bureau of, 94
"Chippies," 192
"Chipping," 9, 168, 178, 182, 191, 208
Choices, constructive, of probationer, 70
Churches, work with addicts, 125
Civic Center Clinic, Brooklyn, 8
Class differences between patient and therapist, 57

Clausen, John, narcotics addiction defined, 197
"Clean man" days, 172
"Clean man" months, number of, 181–182
Clients, unwilling, and reaching-out, 97–98
Clinics, emergency, in crisis-intervention, 31
Cloward, R., studies of alienation, 196, 205
Cocaine, 207
Coercion, use in enforcing regimen, 86, 89. *See also* Authority, use of
Combined Movement Index, 166–167
　matched variables of age and race, 168
Communal approach to treatment, 3–5, 26
Communication
　problems of client, 105
　"rational authority" as, 16
　isolation of addict from, 21
　local, focus on, 27
Community agency
　and probation department, barriers between, 83–84
　services of, 26, 27, 82
Community-based approach to treatment, 5–6, 27, 28
Community Chest and Councils of the Greater Vancouver, British Columbia, area, 95
Community mental health center, concept of, 28, 31
Community Orientation and Day-Night Care Centers, 99
Community Research Associates, three-city study of, 93
Community resources
　mobilization of, 107
　use of by family, 283–284
Compulsion, term distinguished from coercion, 68–69
Conditioning, 197, 198. *See also* Wikler's operant conditioning
　in compulsive narcotics use, 8
　Pavlovian, 199
　and tendency to relapse, 7
　theories of, 58
Conference
　cornerstone, 61–62
　initial structuring, 61–62, 85, 116
　　case histories, 63–66

　joint-management, 75
　preliminary social assessment, 60–61
Confidentiality, problems of, 84, 89
Conformists, 196
Conformity demanded of addicts, 57
Contact, therapeutic, sustained, 4
Contract, "psychiatric," 62
Control
　legal, as basis of probation, 52–53
　loss of, and use of coercive acts, 70–71, 75–76, 86
　movement of, and matched variables of age and race, 166–168
Control group
　compared to experimental group, 161–185
　　lost cases included as failures, 169
　　matched on race and age, 167
Conventional activities, 154–155
　checklist of, 156
Conventionality, 164
　index of, and lower-class, 157
Conventionality Movement, index of, 165
Conviction. *See* Criminal conviction
Cooperative projects in use of authority, 81–89
Copping syndrome, 211
Cornerstone conference. *See under* Conference
Counterphobic mechanism, 209
Court agency, cooperation with health department, 81
Courts
　attitude to probation, 117–118
　New York City, 81, 144
　　cooperation with Center program, 44
Craving, 195
　as difference between "chippies" and addicts, 192–193
Cressy, D. R., and conditioning, 198
Criminal activities
　and narcotics habit, 250, 255–256, 301–302
　follow-up questionnaire, 269
　types of, 145, 146
　unrelated to habit, 145, 147
Criminal convictions
　and narcotics, 119, 121, 128–129
　as criteria for sample group, 121
　first twelve months, 84

INDEX

rates, 134
    recidivist, 182–185
Criminal involvement
    index of, 141–148, 163
        criteria for, 148
            arrests and convictions as, 144
            illegal methods used, 145
        at intake, 147
        number of times arrested, 143
        number of times convicted, 144
        scores for, 147–148
Criminality, 2, 162, 163
    as area of greatest improvement, 165
    as means for affluent living, 57
    reduction in, 141
Criminality Movement, index of, 153
Criminals
    failures, 144
    successful, 144
Crises
    acute, 101, 103
    "graded," concept of, 32
    intervention in, 107–108
    perpetual state of, 93–94
    term as applied to addicts, 31–33
Crisis-intervention as treatment approach, 30–33
Criteria
    absolute, 171
    and difficulty of comparing drug rates, 176
    for evaluating program, 133–134
Criterion, unidimensional evaluative, 165
Cummings, J., and Cummings, E., concept of ego growth through crisis-resolution, 32
Curfew hours in probation, 64
Cyclazocine, 7, 223
Cyclical pattern of addiction, detoxification, and relapse, 28

Daily drug use form, 114, 117
    sample of, 232–233
Damascus Church, 6, 223
Daytop Village, 4, 188, 192, 216, 219, 223
Death by overdose, 216
Decision-making, joint, 81
Defense mechanism, addiction as, 19
Delinquent orientation, 191
Dependence as basic problem, 108
Deprived areas, fostering addiction, 28, 56, 126–127

Destructive activities, 105
Detoxification, 3, 33, 82, 107, 116, 119, 154, 174, 188, 215
    avoidance, 212–213
    defined, 212
    cyclical pattern of, 218
    follow-up questionnaire, 269–271
    of hidden addict, 210
    maintenance, 213–214
    defined, 213
    motivation for, 212
    questionnaire on, 251
    rehabilitative type, 217
    stages of, 34
Diagnosis
    and classification, previous efforts, 194
    problems in, 190–194
    and treatment, framework for approaching, 197
    "rational" approach to, 222–223
Dianetics, 72
Differences, individual
    of case workers, 68
    importance in treatment, 20–22
Differential association theory, 198
    Sutherland's, 208
Dischargees, hospital, follow-up studies, 25–28
Disease due to heroin use, 216
Diskind, Meyer H., study of parolees, 176
Doctor, medical, function in Center program, 42–43
Dole-Nyswander approach to addicts, 191
Double-bind symbiosis, 193
Dropouts. *See under* Drug use
Drug abusers, "hidden," 9
Drug activity, 252
Drug addiction. *See* Addiction
Drug culture. *See* Addiction system
Drug-maintenance programs, 175
Drug movement scale, 182
Drug-prone personality, 191
Drugs. *See also* Opiates
    choice of, 118, 141, 199
    classified as "dangerous," 2
    and crime, 119, 121, 128–129. *See also* Arrests; Criminal activities; Criminal convictions; Criminal involvement
    experiment with, 191
    "hard," 206

Drugs—*Continued*
  knowledge of one's dependence upon, 198
  legal, substituted for heroin, 10
  as legitimate pharmaceutical products, 206
  physical dependence on, 199
  "soft," 206
  using and acquiring, 215
Drug substitution. *See* Chemotherapy
Drug use, 162. *See also* Addiction
  amount and frequency of, 136, 139
  causation of use of heroin, 206–207
  changing patterns in, 190
  daily pattern of, 136–137
  of dropouts, 125, 208
  early, of experimental groups, 127–128
  by family, 296
    questionnaire on, 262–264
  first, of experimental group, 299
  follow-up questionnaire, 264–267
  illicit, monthly return to, 177
  index of, 145
  irregular. *See* Experimental stage
  patterns of, 170–171
  questionnaire on, 248–250
  rating scale, 277–278
  regular. *See* Adaptational stage
  total, index of, 141
Dyadic therapeutic relationship, 29

East Harlem Protestant Parish Narcotics Center, 26
Economic problems of addicts' families, 127
Eddy, Rev. Norman, 26–27
Education of experimental groups, 125, 309
Efron, Hy, 120
Ego growth, through crisis resolution, 32
Ego, weak, of addict, 56
Elmira Reformatory in New York, first parole system, 51
Emotional needs, in addiction, 3
Employer contact, use of, for reinforcement (case history), 75
Employment
  assistance, request for, 129–130
  continuous, 149
  questionnaire on, 238–239, 240–241, 257–259
Employment record of experimental group, 297–298

Escalona, S. K., study on children, 193
Ethnicity. *See also* Race of experimental groups
  of probationers, 230
  in questionnaire, 238
Etiology, 194, 197, 206
  diagnostic approach to, 195
  problems in, 190–194
  genetic approach to, 195
  psychodynamic approach to, 195
Euphoria, 199
  negative, 195
  positive, 195
Evaluation
  indices for, 133–159
  initial, Washington Heights Rehabilitation Center, 275–276
  monthly, Washington Heights Rehabilitation Center, 277–278
  phasing of, 117–118
  physical, 116
  psychiatric, 114, 116
  by worker
    bimonthly, 114
    final, 114
Evaluation program
  follow-up questionnaire, 257–273
  intake questionnaire, 237–256
Ex-addicts
  professional, 5
  and use of drugs in therapy, 11
  as workers, 99
Ex-criminals as workers, 99
Experience, shared, vital importance of, 4
Experimental groups
  compared to control group, 161–185
    lost cases included as failures, 169
    matched on race and age, 167
  Groups I and II, 188
  profile of, 119–121
Experimentation stage (irregular drug use), 206–209

"Failures," 168, 178
  "double," 196
Families
  multi-problem, 93–94
  studies of, 95
Family
  behavioral and adjustment problems, 285–286

disorganized, considered "untreatable," 97
drug-use in, questions on, 244, 246
economic situation of, rating form, 282
establishing rapport with, 62
extended, 4
health conditions, rating of, 283
influence on drug use, rating for, 287
involvement in use of authority (case history), 73–75
leisure-time activities, 284
psychosocial assessment of, 117
questionnaire on, 242–245
reaching-out to, 95–98
    case histories, 108–109
relationship to center worker, 288–289
worker's help with (case history), 107–108
Family-centered approach
  to rehabilitation, 29–30
  to treatment, 5, 41
Family dynamics and drug addiction, 193
Family evaluation form, 281
Family life, four basic areas of, 93
Family members, 29, 30
Family process, approaches to understanding, 30
Family relations
  follow-up questionnaire on, 261–263
  rating form, 286–287
Family situation of experimental groups, 126–127
Family structure, matriarchal, 56
Father
  as authority figure, 50
  education of, 237–238, 295
  influence of, 193
  occupation of, 127, 237, 296
Federal Bureau of Narcotics, 173
  traditional orientation of, 33
Federal Narcotic Addiction Rehabilitation Administration, 89
Federal prisons, first use of parole, 51
Finestone, H., study of deviant groups, 214
First-aid station, neighborhood center as, 100
Five Families, 93
Follow-up, one-year, 139, 145
Follow-up period, 161
Follow-up questionnaires, 113, 146

Follow-up studies, 3, 176
"Follow-up Study of Narcotic Drug Addicts after Hospitalization," 176
Ford, Abraham, 119
Forms
  in evaluation, 113–114
  samples of, 228–289
Freud, Sigmund
  attitude to family relationships, 29
  contribution to intrapsychic processes, 29, 30
Frustration tolerance, low, of addict, 56

Gerard, D., study on addict families, 193
Glue, 128
Goals
  family, 288
  individual, 134
  middle-class, as problem in working with addicts, 57
  for reduction of drug use, 134
  of rehabilitation, 216
  socially defined, 205
  of treatment, 222–223
Grant, Douglas, career development program of, 99
Group "encounters," 99

Habit, financial support of, 207
Hallowitz, Emanuel, and Neighborhood Service Center, 99–100
Hard-core groups, reaching-out techniques used with, 102
Harlem, service center in, 99
HARYOU (Harlem Youth Opportunities Unlimited), 63, 64
Help
  balanced with compulsion, 104
  requested by center patients, 129
Heroin, 178, 207
  as drug of choice, 128
  as first drug used, 127
  first shot, monthly return to, 173
  percentage of patients using each patient month, 178, 180
  return to, in first four months of treatment, 174
Heroin Movement Index, 136–138
Heroin use
  measurement of progress, 161–162
  reduction of, 165
Heroin Use Index, at intake, 138

Heroin Use Movement
  index of, 148, 153, 162
  Scale, 139–140, 163
Heroin users and methadone, 10
Holding device, concept of authority as, 15
Hollingshead Index of Social Position, 127
  scale rating, 296
Home visits
  indiscriminate, 98
  as reaching-out technique, 98
Homosexuality
  questions on, 242
    follow-up, 261
Hospitalization, 116, 212
  "brief-service" concept, 31
  follow-up questionnaire, 269–272
  forced (case history), 75–76
  questionnaire on, 252–254
Hospitals, 27
  federal, 2–3
  general, narcotics wards in, 27
Household
  expenses, contribution of addict to, 155, 157
  physical characteristics of, 281
How They Were Reached, 96
Hubbard, L. Ron, and dianetics, 72
Hunt, G. Halsey, follow-up study, 176
Hustler, 196
"Hustling syndrome," 19, 190, 211

Illness, chronic, addiction as, 19, 35, 140
Image
  parental, "bad" vs. "good," 83
  self. *See* Self-image of addict
Imprisonment, used as sanction, 59, 189
"Improved" group, 162, 163
"Impulse-ridden" character disorders, 93
Indenture, English system of, and modern parole system, 51
Individualization in reaching-out, 92
Inebriate personality, 194
Information sharing, 41, 81–84, 87, 105
  court and community agencies, 46
  worker and probation officer, 16
Initial Evaluation Form, 117
Initial evaluation by worker, 113
Initial Screening Form, 113, 115
  sample of, 228–230
Intake
  data, 161

interviews, 136
  questionnaire, 113, 145, 146, 291–302
  sample of, 237–256
Interagency activity, coordinating, 105
Intervention, implications for, 221–223
Interview. *See* specific types of interviews, as Intake interview; Joint interview
Involvement, therapeutic, 59
"Irish System." *See* Maconochie, Alexander, system of prisoner release

Jewish patients, 125
Job stability, 149
  assignment of weights for, 150–152
  length of time and number of jobs, 151
JOIN, 65
Joint interview, 86
Joint management, 16, 81–89, 116
  concept of, 65–66
Joint-Management Groups. *See also* Experimental groups
  Group I, 118, 120, 188
    description at intake, 121–127
  Group II, 188
    description at intake, 121–127
Joint-management relationships, structuring of, 85–86
Joint-management techniques, 41
Junkies, 191, 202, 207, 210, 211, 212, 214, 215

Kicking. *See* Detoxification
Klonsky, George, study on parolees, 176

Lasagna, L., study of opiates, 192
Laws
  and drug use, 2
  and authority problems of addicts, 18
  civil commitment of addicts, 13, 83
Learning theory, 197
Legislation. *See* Laws
Leisure-time activities, 154
  questions on, 246–247
Lewis, Oscar, and "culture of poverty," 93
Lexington Hospital. *See under* United States
"Life Cycle of Addiction," 34
Life-cycle concept, implications of, 222

INDEX

Life styles of addicts
  of Chein, I., 195–196
  of Cloward, R., 196
  description of, 21
  formulation of, 195–197
  New York Medical College, 196
Lincoln Hospital Mental Health Services Division, 99–100
Lindemann, Eric, "grief work," 31
Lindesmith, A. R., learning theory, 198, 199
Lost cases, 168–169

Maconochie, Alexander, system of prisoner release, 51
Manhattan General Hospital, 3, 27, 76, 119
  methadone study, 10
Manhattan State Hospital, 3, 8, 27
Man-month concept, 181
Man and society, 50
Marginal human beings, 93
Marijuana, 177, 181, 206, 207, 210
  as beginning of drug use, 127
Marital counseling, 108
Marital relations, 285
  questionnaire on, 245
    follow-up 263–264
Marital status
  of experimental group, 293
  questionnaire on, 240
    follow-up, 259
Massachusetts, and first statewide probation law, 53
"Maturing out," 200
Mead, George Herbert, and socialization process, 211
Medical-psychiatric approach to treatment, 2–3, 27
Medical reports, 114
Meeting, joint, of Probation and Center staffs, 87
Menninger, C., "psychiatric contract" of, 62
Mental health program, effective, 99–100
Mental health team, neighborhood, 100
Merton, R. K., concept of anomie, 205
Methadone, 33, 220
  maintenance on, 9–13, 175
  tolerance to, 10
Metropolitan Hospital, 3, 27, 119
Middle-class value system, 205
Missionary zeal in rehabilitation, 6

Money, as overriding symbol, 57
Moral constraints, concept of, 49
Moralistic attitude toward drug use, 11
Morphine-like drugs, physical dependency upon, 7
Mother, influence of, 193
Motivation of client, 96
  lack of, 14
Multifaceted approach, 12

Nalorphine, 7
NARA. *See* Federal Narcotic Addiction Rehabilitation Administration
"Narcissistic" supplies of addict, 32
Narcotic drugs. *See under* Drugs
Narcotics addiction. *See* Addiction
Narcotics addicts. *See* Addicts
National Institute of Mental Health, 36, 38, 44
  Clinical Center of, 193
Negroes and addiction, 123
Neighborhood Service Centers, 99–102
Neophyte, 205, 206
  and mainlining, 207
New York City
  Community Mental Health Board, 37
  Criminal Courts, 81, 144
  Department of Health, 67, 81
    Adult Maintenance Clinic, 43
    narcotics coordinator, 37
    nursing services, 37
  methadone programs, 12
  Narcotics Register Project, 123
  Office of Probation, 145
    cooperation with Center, 44, 45, 70, 81, 142
    evaluation of processes, 113
    questionnaire, 228–230
    Special Narcotics Unit, 45, 115, 118–120
  Youth Board Program, 94, 95–97
    studies of, 96–97
New York Demonstration Center, 37, 101–104
  follow-up study, 26–28
  recommendations, 103–104
New York Medical College, 196
New York State
  Division of Parole, 27, 176
    goals for cooperation with, 39
    referral of patients, 37
  Employment Training Program, 78
  Narcotics Control Commission, 89

NIMH. *See* National Institute of Mental Health
Nonaddict friends, 155, 157–158
Norms, group, conformity to, in communal approach, 4

O'Donnell, J., and classification of addicts, 171
Odoroff, Maurice E., follow-up study of, 176
Office of Probation. *See under* New York City
Ohlin, L., and "retreatist behavior," 205
Only children, percentage of addiction, 126
"On-off" drugs as criterion for evaluation of program, 170
Opiate addiction, three basic categories of, 194
Opiates, 172, 174, 178, 192, 207
  permanent changes from prolonged use of, 188
Opiate use, defined, 182
Opiate users, physiologically addicted, 57–58

Parad, A. J., study of crisis, 31
Parents
  absence of, 126
  effects of early experiences with, 18
  of experimental group, 295
  manipulation of, 83
  questionnaire on, 242
  reaching-out to, 95
  role of worker as, 70
Parole
  concept of, 51–52
  eligibility for, 52
  termination from, 52
Parole officers. *See also* Probation officers
  and Center program, 43
  use of authority, 14
Pathology, social, 93, 96, 99
  beginning stages of, 96
Patients, steps in treatment and evaluation of, 115–117
Pawning to support habit
  questionnaire on, 250
  follow-up, 268
Peer group associations, 57
Permissiveness of probation officer, 87
Personality disorders, 200

Personality studies, general problems in, 199–201
Personality traits of addicts, 191. *See also* Acting-out behavior; Addiction-prone individual; Drug-prone personality
Pharmacological investigations, 190
Pharmacothymia, 195
Philanthropic organizations and aftercare of released prisoners, 51
"Phoenix Houses," 4, 223
Physician-addict, 202
Physiological level of treatment, 57–59
Physiological stage, 210–211
Population characteristics and probation groups, 120
Population, minority group, and identified addicts, 56
Poverty, "culture of," concept of Oscar Lewis, 93
Presidential Commission's Report on Mental Illness and Health, 28
Preventive work and family approach, 5
Prison vs. probation or parole, expense of, 189
Private agency, and borrowed authority, 17
Probation, 52–58
  as alternative to imprisonment, 53
  benefits derived from, 53
  conditions of, 44, 61–64, 82, 116
  criteria required by Center, 44
  eligibility for, 53, 115
  mechanisms, effective use of, 189
  methods of selection for, 35
  minimal criteria for, questionnaire on, 232–233
  termination of, 113, 117
  vs. voluntary treatment, 35
Probationary controls, coercive use of, 107
Probationary supervision, 133
Probationers
  and consequences of choices, 70
  education level of, 125
  negative feelings of, 86, 88
  race of, 123
  religion of, 124
  requirements for, 118–119
  resistance to treatment (case histories), 76–77
  responsive to use of authority (case history), 77–78

Probationer status of addict, 58
Probation officers, 116, 143
  authority of, 14, 61, 70
    case histories, 63–66, 71–73
      holding patient in treatment (case history), 71
      and psychiatric patient (case history), 72–73
    reservations about using, 87
  case records, 114
  and Center program, 43
  vs. community agencies, 84
  on joint-management teams, 188
Problems, immobilizing, 31
Process evaluation, 112–115
Program
  effectiveness of, 178
    measured by ability to apply brakes, 162
Program drug use indicators, 178–181
Program goals, 165, 166
  areas of rehabilitation, in criminality, 135, 141
    in drug use, 135
    in social conventionality, 135
    in work, 135
  criteria, middle-class bias of, 135
"Progressive State System." See Maconochie, Alexander, system of prisoner release
Progress of patient, criteria for evaluation, 38
Protestants, 124
Psychiatrist, function in Center program, 42
Psychiatry, "community," concept of, 31
Psychodynamic factors in learning process, 197
Psychodynamic formulations, 194–195
Psychological level of treatment, 56
Psychopathic diathesis, 194
Psychopathic personality, 194
Psychopathology
  of addict, 56
  shared, 29
Psychotherapy, attitude of addicts to, 130
Public Health Service Hospital at Lexington, Kentucky. See under United States
Puerto Ricans, 123, 124
  and religious approach, 6
  white and Negro, 124
Punitive approach to treatment, 2, 27, 46

Questionnaires
  in evaluation, 113–114
  samples of, 227–289

Race of experimental groups, 122–124, 292
Rado, S., adaptational approach of, 194, 195
Ramirez, E., model programs of, 99
Rapport between worker and addict, 59, 142
Reaching-out, 18, 40–41, 67, 91–110
  by addict, for help, 103
  attitudinal, defined, 91
  case histories on, 106–109
  as casework technique, 14–15, 27
  evaluation of process, 112–113
  expansion of services, 98
  importance in use of authority, 69
  two main dimensions of, 91
Reaching the Unreached, 94
Readdiction, follow-up questionnaire, 269–270
Reality, ability to cope with, 32
Reality testing, 105
"Recent Developments in the Treatment of Paroled Offenders Addicted to Narcotic Drugs," 176
Recidivism, 58, 130, 218–219
  criteria as value judgments, 169
  criterion for, return to alcohol as, 177
  defined, 172
Recidivist rates, 20, 133, 169–172, 175
  arrest or conviction, 134
  criterion for evaluation of program, 170
  for all drugs, 176–177
  heroin, 172–178
Redistribution, illicit, 11
Referrals, 105, 117
  difficulty in, 41
Regular use. See Adaptation stage of drug use
Rehabilitation
  complete, 216
  environment as effect on, 189
  evaluation techniques, 112
  forms of, needed in chemotherapy program, 11
  involuntary basis for, 13
  length of time of, 117
  necessity for, 12
  in prison, 189

Rehabilitation—*Continued*
  program, as brake on continuance, 140
    development of Washington Heights program, 25–46
    readiness for, 129–130
    resistance of patient, 71–72
    ultimate goal of, 202
Relapse, 171, 199
  allowance for, 40
  high rate among dischargees, 25–26
  likelihood of, 34, 58
  sanctions invoked, 82
Relationships. *See also* Family relations; Marital relations
  as factors in addiction, 28
  psychodynamic, between worker and addict, 59
Religion
  of experimental groups, 124–125, 292
  questionnaire on, 238
Religious approach to treatment, 6, 27, 223
Research interviewer, 113
Research, need for, 35–36
"Research Problems in Follow-up Studies of Addicts," 171
Research staff, 117
  of Center program, 43, 44
Research worker and probationer, 64
Residence
  of experimental group, 293
  and probation, 118, 120
  questionnaire on, 240
Residential patterns of addicts, 126
  questionnaire on, 257
Resocialization efforts in isolated setting, 189
Retreatist behavior, 196, 205
Riverside Hospital, 3, 27, 175
  follow-up, 184
Rockefeller University, methadone study, 10
Role models, ex-addicts as, 4–5
Route, defined, 230

St. Paul Family Unit Report Study, 93
Salvation of addicts, 6
Sample groups. *See* Experimental groups
Sample, problem of obtaining, 45
"Scapegoat," 29
Scientology, 72
Self-administration, drugs prescribed for, 11

Self-image
  of addict, 183, 198, 199, 207, 211, 213, 214, 215, 216–217
  negative, 19, 209, 210
  reinforcement of, 12
    prison subculture as negative reinforcing agent, 189
  tolerance for, 34, 212
  professional, of caseworker, 60
Sentence, suspension of, as element of probation system, 53
Sex of experimental groups, 121
Sexual activity
  of experimental group, 294
  questionnaire on, 240–241
    follow-up, 259–261
Siblings of addicts
  number of, 126
  questionnaire on, 242
Sin, addiction viewed as, 6
Sniffing, 200, 207
Social adjustment, and methadone maintenance, 10–13
Social conventionality
  criteria for, related to leisure-time activities, 154, 155
  index of, 154
    intake questionnaire, 158
    Part I, 155–156
    Part II, 157
    Part III, 157–158
    total score of, 158
Social factors, chronic, and multi-problem families, 95, 97
Socialization process, 4–5
  in addict's world, 34
Social pathology. *See under* Pathology
Social position of addicts' families, 127
Social Service Exchange clearance, 116
Sociological level of treatment, 56–57
Sodium pentothal, in "ventilation" of anxiety, 31
Spare-time activities. *See* Leisure-time activities
"Specialized Probation" Group (Group II), 118, 120
Sperling, Melitta, and obesity cases, 194
Status system in concept of "community," 4
Stay-well as category of patients, 139, 162, 163
Stealing, 145

INDEX

Stereotyping of addicts, dangers of, 20–21
Stigma, of addiction, 6
Structure
  of cooperation, established by conference, 61–62, 63–66
  firm, and probation, 70
  need for, in evaluating treatment programs, 26
  and use of graded crises, 33
  use of, for self-discipline, 72–73
Structured household, 108
Structuring device, rational authority as, 15–16
Success
  evaluating rates of, 181
  goals of, 196
"Successes," 168
"Superego lacunae," 56
Supervision, as element of probation system, 14, 53
Supportive role of worker, 108
  techniques for, 102
Synanon, 4, 26, 33, 168, 175, 182, 188, 198, 216, 219, 223

Target population, of experimental program, 130
Task Force, 200
Teen Challenge, 6, 21, 27, 223
Termination
  questionnaire, 113
  status form, 114
Therapist, middle-class, 57
Time periods, 178–179
  as criteria for classifying addicts, 135–139
  in measuring drug involvement, 143, 149
TLC. *See* Urinalysis, thin-layer chromatography
Tolerance
  for abstinence, 19, 202, 203
  concept of, 202–203
  for physiological effects of drugs, 19
  secondary, 204
Tracks, defined, 230
Tranquilizers as substitutes, 219–220
"Transactional dynamics," 29
Transitional Phase I. *See* Addiction system, transition to

Transitional Phase II. *See* Abstinence, transition to
Transitional population and narcotics addiction, 123
Treatment
  milieu, holding addict in, 112
  modalities, wide range of, 221
  survey of approaches to, 1–24
  viewed as total process, 5
Trigueño (term), 124
Twelve-month period in drug use, 145
  chart for, 137, 149
Two-worlders, 196

Uninvolved, 196
United States
  available drugs in, 206
  Public Health Hospital at Lexington, 2, 7, 27, 126, 175, 176
  Follow-Up Study, 25
  racial distribution of patients, 123
Urinalysis
  thin-layer chromatography (TLC), 11, 17, 44, 63, 65, 75, 78, 82, 117, 173
  records of, 114–115
  spot-checks, 85

Veteran status of experimental group, 298
Volkman, C., and differential association, 198

Washington Heights Rehabilitation Center, 13, 14, 15, 16, 104, 179
  early planning of, 36–46
  program, development of, 25–46
  evaluation of, 111–131
    criteria for, 134
  goals of, 81
  results of, 18–22
  prospectus for the future, 187–225
Wedging tactics, 16, 62, 83, 84, 87
Whites and addiction, 122–123
Wikler's operant conditioning, 198–199
Withdrawal symptoms, 192, 199, 210, 211, 213
  conditioned, 8
  and cyclazocine, 7
  defined, 230
  as eligibility requirement, 119
Withdrawal syndrome. *See* Withdrawal symptoms

Work
  amount of, 148
  index of, 148–154, 164
    criteria for, 148
      and job stability, 149
      and one-year follow-up, 152
      at time of intake, 152
        construction of, 153
        questionnaire, 153
  measurement of progress, 163–164
  variables in the area of, 149
Workers
  case records, 114
  Center, role relationship to probation officer, 61
  indigenous, 99
  rehabilitation, role of, 16–17
  "street-gang," 94
World Health Organization, 2
World War II, impact on psychiatric services, 30–31

Youth Board, 99